P9-CRC-270

ABOUT THE EDITORS

MARK BOWDEN is the author of the international bestsellers *Killing Pablo: The Hunt for the World's Greatest Outlaw* and *Black Hawk Down: A Story of Modern War,* a finalist for the National Book Award. Bowden worked on the screenplay for the film adaptation of *Black Hawk Down,* directed by Ridley Scott. *Killing Pablo* is being adapted for film with Bowden again working on the screenplay. Bowden teaches creative writing and journalism at Loyola College, Maryland, and he is a frequent contributor to many major American magazines. His most recent book is *Guests of the Ayatollah: The First Battle in America's War with Militant Islam.* He lives in Pennsylvania.

OTTO PENZLER is the proprietor of the Mysterious Bookshop in New York City, the founder of the Mysterious Press, and creator of the publishing firm Otto Penzler Books. He is the editor of many books and anthologies, and has been the recipient of the Edgar Award, the Ellery Queen Award, and the Raven Award from Mystery Writers of America for his many contributions to the mystery genre. He lives with his wife, Lisa Atkinson, in New York City and in Kent, Connecticut.

THOMAS H. COOK is the author of nineteen books, including two works of true crime. His novels have been nominated for the Edgar Award, the Macavity Award, and the Dashiell Hammett Prize. He lives in New York City.

The Best American CRIME WRITING

2006

The Best American CRIME WRITING

Editors

2002: NICHOLAS PILEGGI

2003: JOHN BERENDT

2004: JOSEPH WAMBAUGH

2005: JAMES ELLROY

The Best American
CRIME WRITING
2006

Edited by
MARK BOWDEN

Series Editors
OTTO PENZLER AND
THOMAS H. COOK

AN ECCO BOOK

HARPER PERENNIAL

NEW YORK • LONDON • TORONTO • SYDNEY

HARPER ● PERENNIAL

THE BEST AMERICAN CRIME WRITING 2006. Copyright © 2006 by Otto Penzler and Thomas H. Cook. Introduction copyright © 2006 by Mark Bowden. All rights reserved. Printed in the United States of America. No part of this book may be used or reproduced in any manner whatsoever without written permission except in the case of brief quotations embodied in critical articles and reviews. For information address HarperCollins Publishers, 10 East 53rd Street, New York, NY 10022.

HarperCollins books may be purchased for educational, business, or sales promotional use. For information please write: Special Markets Department, HarperCollins Publishers, 10 East 53rd Street, New York, NY 10022.

FIRST EDITION

Designed by Lovedog Studio

Library of Congress Cataloging-in-Publication Data is available upon request.

ISBN-10: 0-06-081552-3
ISBN-13: 978-0-06-081552-3

06 07 08 09 10 BVG/RRD 10 9 8 7 6 5 4 3 2 1

Contents

Preface

IN THE LATE DARCY O'BRIEN's brilliant study of the Hillside Stranglers, Angelo Buono and Kenneth Bianchi revel in the grim fantasy of a girl reared from birth exclusively for their pleasure. They watch and wait until the moment of flowering is reached, then rape and murder her. She is not a human being, but a plant grown for one dark harvest, then cut down.

Nothing in the history of crime writing more deeply illustrated the banal and commonplace source of criminal acts, that they are rooted in simple selfishness.

This year's edition of *The Best American Crime Writing* amply demonstrates the irreducible and uncomplicated truth so powerfully rendered by Darcy O'Brien. From the comic to the macabre, bumbling criminals to cunning ones, it is selfishness that rules the day. The continuum runs from narcissism to solipsism, the antisocial to the sociopathic, the Me who must go first to the Me besides whom there is no other.

This is not to say that things never get complicated, for as with

Medusa's head, odd and coiling things may spring from a single source.

ONE OF THEM IS MONEY. It is Saddam Hussein's money that provides the irresistible temptation in Devin Friedman's story of G.I. Joe corruption, while in Skip Hollandsworth's tale, it is the mere proximity of banks, along with an unlikely disguise, that beckons Cowboy Bob to "her" last ride. Howard Blum and John Connolly's "Hit Men in Blue?" suggests how wickedly money can be gained. Paige Williams's "How to Lose $100,000,000" demonstrates just how quickly it can be lost. Money is also the issue in Mary Battiata's riveting study of how little of it, when in dispute, can generate a murder.

Sex is predictably the issue at hand in other tales. How much it sometimes costs is the cautionary lesson learned in Mark Jacobson's "$2,000-an-Hour Woman." But, again, it is selfishness that provides the dark core of sexual crime. Escaping the consequences of that selfishness is the central focus of Denise Grollmus's "Sex Thief," and Robert Nelson's "Altar Ego." The failure to escape it forms the narrative thrust of John Heilemann's "The Choirboy," a heartrending tale of justice delayed . . . but not forever.

Escape also provides the thematic center of Richard Rubin's "Ghosts of Emmett Till," an escape that is offered, in this case, by society itself, time and conscience the only arbiters of how effective it will be. In S. C. Gwynne's "Dr. Evil," it is an honored profession's ineffective self-regulation that opens the escape hatch to a criminally incompetent doctor, horrendously botched surgery evidently still no reason to snatch the scalpel from his hand. In Chuck Hustmyre's "Blue on Blue," it is, at least briefly, the blind flash of a badge that provides a hiding place for a murderous cop, while in Deanne Stillman's riveting "The Great Mojave Manhunt," it is the desert waste that offers up concealment—nature, as always, indifferent to the kind of man it hides.

AND, OF COURSE, there are always those who don't escape at all, as Jimmy Breslin illustrates to such comic effect in "The End of the Mob."

These then are the stories in this year's edition of *The Best American Crime Writing*, tales by turns harrowing and hilarious, a feast of human malfeasance chosen to satisfy the connoisseur's taste for what Browning called the "fine Felicity . . . of wickedness" that is the just reward of reading fine true crime.

In terms of the nature and scope of this collection, we defined the subject matter as any factual story involving crime or the threat of a crime written by an American or Canadian that was first published in the calendar year 2005. Although we examined a huge array of publications, inevitably the preeminent ones attracted many of the best pieces. All national and large regional magazines were searched for appropriate material, as well as nearly two hundred so-called little magazines, reviews, and journals.

WE WELCOME SUBMISSIONS by any writer, editor, publisher, agent, or other interested party for *The Best American Crime Writing 2007*. Please send the publication or a tear sheet with the name of the publication, the date on which the article appeared, and, if possible, the name and contact information for the author or representative. If the first publication was in electronic format, a hard copy must be submitted. Only material with a 2006 publication date is eligible. All submissions must be received no later than December 31, 2006; anything received after that date will not be read. This is neither arrogant nor capricious. The timely nature of the book forces very tight deadlines that cannot be met if we receive material later than that. The sooner we receive articles, the more favorable will be the light in which they are perused.

Please send submissions to Otto Penzler, The Mysterious

Bookshop, 58 Warren Street, New York, NY 10007. Regretfully, no submissions can be returned. If you wish verification that material was received, please enclose a self-addressed stamped postcard.

Thank you,
Otto Penzler and
Thomas H. Cook
New York, March 2006

Introduction

THE MOST TYPICAL WAY for a crime story to begin is with a date. S. C. Gwynne starts, "On June 8, 2003. . . ." Paige Williams's begins, "On Christmas Day 2002. . . ." Sometimes the date comes with an hour and a minute: "Saturday, March 4, 1995. 1:55 A.M.," opens Chuck Hustmyre's.

Precision, because when you are describing someone committing a crime, you want to make sure you've got your facts straight; because most crime stories are based at least in part on trials and police files, and reflect the preoccupation of the criminal justice system with proof: This specific transgression of the law was committed in exactly this way at precisely this time against the herein named victim, and warrants precisely this verdict and punishment; but ultimately because the crime story is about something more than assigning blame and retribution. What fascinates us is the moment when things slipped . . . off . . . the . . . rails. It's the same thing that prompts filmmakers to slow down the camera at the moment of impact, or breakdown. It's the point where there was a tear in the social fabric, a clear crossing of the line that defines ordinary life, decency, civil discourse, honest commerce, or acceptable behavior. When exactly—"Now, on the last Monday of November 2004," writes John Heilemann—grounds the transgression in reality, which is itself thrilling, because what scares us about crime is not its strangeness, but its familiarity. The consequences, the things that concern the judges, juries, and police, are about putting things right, restoring the fractured social order or contract, but we know that in a deeper sense things can rarely be put right, and that the real world, as opposed to the imaginary order of laws and contracts, is much much messier and more interesting. So we settle in to read on. Because the story isn't about blame and punishment, it's about who, what, when, where, how, and, most importantly, why.

In that greatest of true crime stories, *In Cold Blood*, enjoying a revival this year, Truman Capote built suspense toward the terrible murder of the Clutter family by walking us through the final day of each doomed family member, interrupting the ambling narrative with the steady drumbeat of their murderers' approach. When Perry Smith and Dick Hickock pull into the driveway of the Clutter home in darkness, Capote abruptly skips over the critical hours of the crime to the following morning, when neighbors discover the Clutters' bloody remains. He does this to maintain suspense—we all want to know exactly what happened inside that house—and keep us reading but also because he doesn't want to describe the crime until he has laid the groundwork for us to understand why it was committed. *In Cold Blood* isn't a whodunit, it's a why-dunit.

Most crime stories are ultimately about the doer. Donald Kueck, John Shallenberger, Matt Novak, Antoinette Frank and Rogers LaCaze, John Ames, Louis Eppolito and Stephen Caracappa, Eric Scheffey, Mohammed Bouyeri, Jason Itzler, Peggy Jo Tallas . . . these are the characters who animate these stories and make us want to keep reading. We are fascinated by the exact details of their crimes, but what we hope those details finally add up to is an understanding of why they did what they did.

In that sense, the crime story has long been at odds with the tendency to explain all criminal and antisocial behavior as mental illness. How boring would the world be if evil were just a malfunction? If all we needed to live law-abiding, respectable lives was a level head? For all but a few genuinely afflicted souls, crime is a deliberate choice. Crime writers have always known that their best subjects were completely sane. Their stories show how and why perfectly sane people do supposedly insane things.

There is a bit of larceny and murder in all of our souls, although most of us choose to restrain it, out of virtue but also out of timidity. I once wrote a story about a criminal who believed he was, in fact, the most honest man in the world. He admitted that he enthusiastically cheated on his wife and took breathtakingly ambitious leaps into illegality, not because he was mentally ill or evil, but because he recognized the truth about all men. "All men cheat on their wives when they can get away with it"—he told me—"and they all break the law when it's to their benefit." He believed he was more honest than other men because he admitted these things about himself, and embraced them. The fact that he was telling me these things from a federal prison cell was just conclusive proof of the hypocrisy of man.

So maybe that's the heart of it. Maybe the criminal chooses his or her path because it is, for them, the truest one, or the more courageous one. Trapped in an unhappy relationship, why not kill our spouse? Can't make ends meet and need a little excitement in your life? Why not cross-dress and knock off a few banks? Crave sex with small boys? Why not manage a boys' choir or an orphanage?

The precision in these stories fixes crime to real people, real places, real dates and times, and in doing so shows how frightfully ordinary it is. The perpetrators are not mentally ill, they are greedy, covetous, selfish, and amoral. Thankfully, few of us make these choices, but crime stories remind us that we are, nevertheless, constantly faced with them. Virtue and lawfulness are choices we make every day—when we are lucky, in the absence of severe temptation. These stories coldly examine the alternatives, and by illustrating the painful and usually self-destructive consequences, comfort us on our way.

—Mark Bowden

The Best American CRIME WRITING

2006

John Heilemann

THE CHOIRBOY

FROM *New York* MAGAZINE

THE E-MAIL ARRIVED UNBIDDEN four years ago, bearing the stamp of a sender whose name he didn't recognize. All the message said was, "Are you the Lawrence Lessig who went to the Boychoir School?"

It had been a long time since anyone had identified the Stanford Law School professor that way. But it was true: From 1972 to 1976, Lessig had spent his sixth-through-ninth-grade years at the American Boychoir School in Princeton.

So Lessig wrote back, "Yeah, I'm the guy who went to the Boychoir School. What's up?" And with that, he opened up a closed doorway to his past—and found himself swept right through it.

Now, on the last Monday of November 2004, Lessig has just arrived at the Richard J. Hughes Justice Complex in Trenton, New Jersey. He is here to make an argument before the Supreme Court of New Jersey. His client, the plaintiff, is his e-mail correspondent. The defendant is their alma mater.

Since its founding in 1937, the nonsectarian Boychoir School has gained worldwide renown for producing a choir rivaled only by the more famous one in Vienna; its kids have sung for presidents, popes, and behind Beyoncé at this year's Academy Awards. But now Lessig's client, John Hardwicke, is claiming that in the seventies, the school was a ghoulish sanctuary for the sexual abuse of children. In his two years there, Hardwicke says he was repeatedly molested and raped—induced, as the brief on his behalf to the state supreme court puts it, to "perform virtually every sexual act that could conceivably have been accomplished between two males"—by the music director, the headmaster, the proctor, and the cook.

This is not the sort of case for which Larry Lessig is famous. At forty-three, Lessig has built a reputation as the king of Internet law and as the most important next-wave thinker on intellectual property. The author of three influential books on the intersection of law, politics, and digital technology, he's the founder of Creative Commons, an ambitious attempt to forge an alternative to the current copyright regime. According to his mentor, the federal appellate judge Richard Posner, Lessig is "the most distinguished law professor of his generation." He's also a celebrity. On a *West Wing* episode this winter, he was featured as a character. "The Elvis of cyberlaw" is how *Wired* has described him.

I have known Lessig well, professionally and socially, for nearly five years. I've never seen him look as nervous as he does this morning. Dressed in a dark suit, his hair slicked back, tiny wirerims perched on his nose, he moves slowly, ponderously, as if the weight of the stakes in the case is resting literally on his shoulders. The school (known until 1980 as the Columbus Boychoir School) has argued that, under New Jersey's Charitable Immunity Act, a statute designed to shield nonprofits from negligence lawsuits, it can't be held financially liable no matter how heinous Hardwicke's abuse. If the supreme court agrees, Hardwicke's case will be dismissed before even being heard by a jury. And scores of sex-abuse suits against New Jersey Catholic churches and schools will be rendered void as well. The church, not surprisingly, has weighed in on the side of the school.

During his work on the case, Lessig has been asked more than once by the press if he had experiences at the school similar to Hardwicke's. And Lessig has replied, "My experiences aren't what's at issue here. What's at issue is what happened to John Hardwicke."

The answer is appropriate, politic—but it's not entirely true. For Lessig has told me that he too was abused at the Boychoir School, and by the same music director that Hardwicke claims was one of his abusers. Lessig is by nature a shy, intensely private person. The fact of his abuse is known to almost no one: not the reporters covering the case, not the supreme-court justices. The fact of his abuse isn't even known to Larry Lessig's parents.

In taking this case, however, Lessig has cast aside his caution about a secret that haunts him still. And while his passion about his client's cause is real and visceral, Hardwicke isn't the only plaintiff here. Lessig is also litigating on behalf of the child he once was.

THE BOYCHOIR SCHOOL sits on seventeen acres not far from the Princeton campus, surrounded by stands of evergreens and a scattering of suburban houses. You approach the grounds up a narrow drive, past a PRIVATE PROPERTY sign, until you come to a big grass oval in front of a handsome brick Georgian mansion. Three stories high, with fifty-odd rooms, the mansion is known as Albemarle and was once the home of Gerard Lambert, the founder of the chemical company that morphed into Warner-Lambert.

In the late sixties, there were several dozen fifth-to-ninth-grade boys living in Albemarle. Every morning, a bell would ring to signal the start to their day, in which classes were interspersed with three one-hour rehearsals, along with private voice tutoring and piano lessons. "Music was in the walls of the school; it was everywhere," a former student recalls. Decked out in uniforms of navy-

blue pants and button-down shirts or turtlenecks, the boys sang
Bach, Handel, Mahler, Copland, Bernstein, and American spirituals.
All through the school year, they toured the United States, driving
around in a big bus kitted out with desks and a lunch counter. In
the summer, the best of the choristers were taken on tours of
Europe; on one occasion, they performed for Pope Paul VI—who
placed his hands on the head of a soloist, Bobby Byrens, and
declared, "He has the voice of an angel."

In 1968 the choir director, Donald Bryant, was fired over "a love
affair with a little boy," one of the school's former board members
later told the *New York Times*. (A number of such accusations would
ultimately be leveled against him.) But Bryant's departure failed to
set things right. Instead, the Boychoir School hired his replacement, along with a new headmaster, on the recommendation of
John Shallenberger, the wealthy scion of a Pennsylvania coal-
mining family and a patron of boys' choirs. Shallenberger also happened to be a chronic pedophile: Convicted over four decades on
multiple charges related to child molestation, he eventually fled the
country to avoid prosecution in his home state. (He died this
February, at eighty-seven, in Mexico, where he was overseeing an
orphanage.)

The following year, John Hardwicke arrived at the school as a
twelve-year-old seventh-grader. The son of a prominent Maryland
lawyer, Hardwicke had no special love for choral singing; he
enrolled in the school because his father encouraged him to do so.
"What turned my dad on was that beautiful mansion, the idea of
me associating with good families and touring around the world,"
Hardwicke says. "A stupid decision, in retrospect, but he had my
best interests at heart."

One night in his first year, Hardwicke was visited in his room by
a man he recognizes from pictures today as having been John
Shallenberger, who was following the Vienna Boys' Choir on a
tour of America at the time. It was bedtime, Hardwicke recalls, and
although Shallenberger did nothing untoward, he offered a piece

of advice: "He told me that I really oughtta not sleep with underwear on."

In the fall of 1970, the music director Shallenberger recommended, a Canadian named Donald Hanson, took up residence at Albemarle. In his late twenties, terrific-looking, with a thick shock of dark hair, he was just about the coolest adult the boys had ever encountered. He was a brilliant pianist, he drove a Jaguar, and the women who worked at the school all seemed to have a crush on him. "He was very charismatic, like a teen idol, a rock star," says Hardwicke. "He was an incredibly charming master manipulator."

About a week after Hanson's arrival, the music director asked Hardwicke to lend him a hand washing his Jaguar. As Hardwicke remembers it, Hanson touched him suggestively on the shoulder—and from there the contact escalated into a horror show.

Over the next several months, Hardwicke says, he and Hanson had sex "two, three, maybe even four or five times a day." Sometimes Hanson would masturbate on Hardwicke's body. Sometimes he would urinate on the boy in the shower. Hardwicke says that Hanson read to him from pornographic books and showed him child pornography. Also that Hanson once had sex with him inside his parents' house.

Nor was Hanson the only perpetrator, Hardwicke says. He claims he was fondled once by the headmaster and twice by a proctor. He claims to have been masturbated on by one of Hanson's friends. And he claims that, during a spell the next summer when he was visiting Hanson at Albemarle, the school's cook came upstairs and raped him in his sleep.

The morning Hardwicke awoke with his underwear off and the cook still in his room, Hanson drove him back to his family's home in Maryland. Because Hardwicke's voice had started to change, he wouldn't be returning to the Boychoir School that fall. He said good-bye to Hanson, walked into the house, and thought, *Nothing will ever be the same.*

THAT SAME SUMMER, Larry Lessig first came to Albemarle. He had just turned ten, a sweet-voiced kid who sung at his church at home in Williamsport, Pennsylvania. He'd come to attend a summer camp that the school conducted for choirboys. And after auditioning, he was invited to stay and enroll as a fifth-grader.

Lessig's father, who ran a steel-fabricating firm, was adamantly opposed. "There's no way I'm going to send you away to school!" he thundered on hearing the suggestion. But Lessig was seduced by what the school promised, and the next summer, he asked again. His father was torn, but finally relented for the sake of his son's future. "It was a kind of *Billy Elliot* moment," Lessig says. "You could see him making this sacrifice—just hating the idea of losing me."

Lessig's first hint of Hanson's proclivities came one day when another boy scaled a wall outside the mansion. Climbing down, the boy told Lessig he'd seen Hanson in bed with a student. Lessig's response was total disbelief. "I remember thinking I could no longer trust this kid," he says. "It was obviously so ridiculous."

In the fall of his eighth-grade year, Lessig learned otherwise. On a Friday night, after Hanson had taken the boys shopping at the mall in Princeton, they all came back, as they often did, and gathered in his quarters to watch TV. As Lessig sat beside Hanson on the couch, the music director covered their laps with a blanket and proceeded to fondle him. Forever after, Lessig would remember the movie that was playing on TV: *Run Silent, Run Deep*.

The following June, on Lessig's fourteenth birthday, after the choir had returned from touring in California, Lessig was preparing to head home for the summer when Hanson pulled him into his room—"to give me a 'birthday present,'" Lessig says. "I remember feeling totally overwhelmed by him. It wasn't forcing in the sense of violence . . . It's not like I was afraid. But there was this recognition of, wow, there's nothing I can do. Here I am. Bam. It's over."

And yet, of course, it wasn't.

Lessig had been a bright light at the school since his first year there. With a perfect-pitch soprano voice, he'd been a soloist next in line behind Bobby Byrens ("My idol," Lessig says). And with a sharp and probing mind already in evidence, he soon emerged as an academic star and student leader, a striver, intensely driven. Now, in his ninth-grade year, Lessig was named head boy, which made him "in charge of taking care of the kids," he says. "There was no proctor when I was head boy; *I* was discipline. And there were kids who were real shits—it was a *Lord of the Flies*–like experience."

Being head boy also signified something else: He was Hanson's favorite. And accordingly he was assigned a room next door to the music director's, at the far end of a hallway on the third floor. By midway through the year, the two of them were essentially living together. "We put up a door in front of our rooms, blocking off the hallway, blocking out the rest of the world. We created a suite. And there was a classroom right next to it. So every day the teacher comes up, watches me come out of that door—which is also Hanson's door—and walk into class. There's no way anybody doesn't know what the hell is going on. But nobody says anything."

Lessig may have been head boy, but he wasn't Hanson's only prey. All along, Lessig says, he knew that Hanson was sleeping with "at least ten" other boys. "The weird thing about the sexuality was that there was no jealousy attached to it at all," he explains. "It was totally recreational. It was just like playing squash. *He's playing squash with me, he's playing squash with him. Who cares? What does it matter?*"

Among the boys, Hanson's promiscuity was well known, Lessig says. He would call students out of class to satisfy his cravings. The private voice and piano lessons he administered were especially notorious: "It was five or ten minutes of music, then it would turn into other things," Hardwicke recalls. And while none of this was ever spoken of explicitly among the boys, there was ribbing, teasing, nodding, winking—constant signals of in-the-knowness. As for the teachers, Lessig says, "Hanson was the boss. What was going to be said?"

Sometimes on trips home, Lessig felt faint stirrings of unease. But it never occurred to him to tell his parents. His relationship to Hanson, unlike Hardwicke's, was tender, sustaining; his parents would never understand. "Like all pedophiles, Hanson was really good at connecting with kids," Lessig says. "You just felt you were together; there was no ambiguity about it. He was a friend. A deep, close friend. We talked about everything. He told me about music. He told me about the world. . . . For a kid cut off from everyone else in this weird universe, to have the most important person in the world give you love and approval is the greatest thing you can imagine. What else is there?"

On some level, Lessig realized that the relationship was "fucked up and shouldn't happen," he says. But he also had a precocious fourteen-year-old's exaggerated sense of his own maturity. "I felt that I could handle it," he says. "That everything was under control."

There were moments, however, when reality came crashing through. In Lessig's final year, he found himself gripped by "an insane depression," he says, over "the insanity of what was happening." In his closet he'd found a hatch in the ceiling that led to a crawl space above. He climbed up there and crouched alone for hours in the dark.

One evening near the end of Lessig's final year at the school, he went with Hanson for a walk around the grounds. As darkness descended on Albemarle, Lessig finally, tentatively, gave voice to his gathering misgivings about Hanson's behavior.

"Is this really right? Should you really be doing this?" Lessig asked.

"You have to understand," Hanson replied, "this is essential to producing a great boychoir." By sexualizing the students, he explained, he was transforming them from innocents into more complicated creatures, enabling them to render choral music in all its sublime passion. "It's what all great boychoirs do," Hanson said.

AFTER LESSIG MOVED BACK to Williamsport for high school, he brooded on what had happened in Princeton. Two years later, he contacted the boychoir's headmaster, Stephen Howard, and persuaded Howard to appoint him as the alumni representative to the board of directors. Then Lessig went and told Don Hanson that what he was doing was wrong—wrong for the kids, wrong for the school, even wrong for Hanson.

"It's harmful, it's destructive, you'll get caught, you'll get hanged," Lessig said. "It's really got to stop."

Hanson didn't argue. Instead, he told Lessig that he had a boyfriend now, a former student who'd left the school with whom he was carrying on. All of his needs were being met.

Lessig wasn't satisfied. "You should recognize that I'm now on the board," he said. "If it doesn't stop, I'm going to out you."

"You're right," Hanson said. "Absolutely, I promise, it will never happen again."

Lessig believed Hanson utterly. He had yet to learn that pedophilia is an illness, an all-consuming compulsion. At seventeen, he was flush with the sense of his power to defuse such a delicate situation. "I knew all these things that nobody else did," he recalls. "I was keeping the institution together. I really wanted it to succeed. And the picture of the institution succeeding with Hanson continuing as choir director was really what I thought should happen."

But in the fall of 1981 Lessig got a call from Stephen Howard: Hanson had been accused of molesting two students. Lessig by then was an undergrad at the University of Pennsylvania, studying economics and management with an eye to following his father's path and going into business. Lessig drove up to Princeton for an emergency board meeting, where he learned that Hanson had tried to kill himself by putting his head inside a gas oven. Lessig thereupon told Howard everything he knew about Hanson's history of abuse.

In March 1982 Howard sent a letter to the school's parents, informing them that Hanson had resigned "for reasons of personal health." Without mentioning the scandal, the letter lauded Hanson for his service: "He alone held the school together in the early seventies . . . hiring and firing staff, running the admissions and concert offices, from time to time driving the bus and even washing the dishes . . . His story at the Boychoir School is one of total devotion to the boys and dedication to the best interests of the School."

After his dismissal, Hanson retreated to Canada, while Lessig gave up his seat on the board and got on with his life. His academic brilliance now unfurling in earnest, he went to Trinity College, Cambridge, where he studied philosophy for three years before entering law school. For a time, his attitude to what Hanson had done, he says, was, "No harm, no foul."

Then, at Yale Law School, Lessig took a course taught by archfeminist Catharine MacKinnon and began to ponder his relationship with Hanson in a different, more sophisticated light. "There was this moment when I realized that I had been, in the traditional way, a woman in all relevant respects—totally passive, an object of sexual aggression," he says. "I'd adopted this supportive, protective role with respect to him." Among his many other afflictions, Hanson was an alcoholic. "There was this one time I literally saved his life," Lessig recalls. "I came into his bedroom and he was passed out, vomiting, and I had to flip him over to stop him from suffocating. And this, I felt, was my role. I was his wife."

Lessig had been involved with a number of women in college and graduate school. And he began to see self-destructive patterns in his relationships. "I remember throwing tantrums," he says, "as I recognized how this thing had intruded in my life."

After landing a plum professorship at the University of Chicago Law School, Lessig entered therapy. "The therapist was really great," he observes with an ironic chuckle. "He said, 'This is very significant, but you're lucky—at least you didn't become a homosexual.' "

What happened next is something Lessig refuses to discuss. But according to Hardwicke's lead attorney, Keith Smith, Lessig sued the Boychoir School and received a settlement. Both the suit and the settlement are officially under seal, with a confidentiality agreement that bars either side from disclosing their existence, let alone any of the details. What Lessig can say, however, is that the school and its lawyers are aware of his abuse by Hanson. And that, in his interactions with them before the Hardwicke case, he thinks that "they behaved well."

In the next decade, Lessig had almost zero contact with the school, as his legal career went supernova and his personal life settled happily. From Chicago, he moved on first to Harvard Law School and then to Stanford. He married, had a son, and set up digs in a rambling Spanish house not far from the ocean in San Francisco. Soaking in the hot tub on his balcony at night, watching the fog creep in, Lessig believed, with good reason, that he had put the Boychoir School behind him.

And then one day in 2001 came the e-mail from John Hardwicke.

THE DISTANCE FROM LESSIG'S to Hardwicke's house is vast in every sense. In deepest rural Maryland, not far from the Pennsylvania line, it's a small Cape Codder with rickety shutters and a mudslick for a driveway. On the day I visit, in February, the front walk is covered with snow; horses graze in a pasture next door. Inside, John and his wife, Terri, pad around in stocking feet, smoking Marlboro Medium 100s one after another. There are stuffed toys strewn around the house—Terri's creations. In the living room, a court jester sits amid a metric ton of brick-a-brac, next to a full-size harp.

After a while, the Hardwickes' fifteen-year-old daughter bounces through the door in a pair of pink Chuck Taylor hightops. Her father worries about her taste in music—the Velvet Underground—and the fact that she has a steady boyfriend. "When I hear her listening to 'Heroin,' well, I don't know," Hardwicke says. "There's only two things that can ruin your life: drugs and sex."

Hardwicke pours a cup of coffee and sits with his legs tucked underneath him on the floor of the TV room. At forty-seven, he is tall and thin, with pale-pink skin, a snow-white beard, and watery blue eyes. He begins by telling me about the first time he discussed his abuse with a reporter. "I felt this incredible evil hovering around me that I just knew was going to kill me," he says. "And then this evil communicated, 'No, it's not you, it's your wife. We're going to start with her.' "

If the effects of Lessig's abuse were subtle and slow to emerge, for Hardwicke they're glaring and have plagued him relentlessly throughout his life. After he met Terri at Catholic University, they were married and started a business together doing freelance PR, graphic design, brochures, and such. But Hardwicke, who was told repeatedly by Hanson that he was gay, has struggled for many years with confusion over his sexual orientation. Well into his marriage, he found himself engaging in anonymous trysts with men.

"It made me feel awful," he says, pulling his knees up to his chest. "It became sort of this thing that I couldn't control, and I'd literally want to throw up afterward . . . I was pretty convinced that it was some kind of demonic possession, almost. I mean, I can remember several times after the event where I'd get gas for the car and it would be, like, sixteen dollars and sixty-six cents."

At one point, Hardwicke concluded he was gay and announced he was leaving Terri. But a friend who knew of his experiences suggested he seek therapy instead. Because he felt complicit in the acts, he didn't think of them as molestation. But his therapist, Dr. Emily Samuelson, a trauma specialist, disagreed with that assessment.

Within twenty-four hours after Hardwicke told Samuelson about being raped by the school's cook, Hardwicke's mother was killed in a car accident, propelling his paranoia to imponderable heights. His daughter was in the car, too, but she "walked out unscathed," he says. "And I got to thinking later it was a metaphor for molestation. Some are killed, some are scarred, some are crippled. Others walk out untouched. It all depends where you were sitting in the car."

After a few months of seeing Samuelson, in 1999, Hardwicke decided to approach the school and asked his father to help him do it. Hardwicke's father, who by then had become Maryland's chief administrative law judge, is a faculty member at Johns Hopkins. So they arranged to meet the school's then-president, John Ellis, at the Hopkins Faculty Club. Ellis arrived with the school's attorney. Up to that point, Hardwicke had never contemplated suing the school. "My intention was to have them apologize," he explains. "I was trying to have somebody say, 'It's not your fault.' "

Hardwicke takes a long, deep drag on his cigarette. After several months of back-and-forth, he realized that no apology would be forthcoming and decided to explore a lawsuit. His father contacted some friends of his at Piper Rudnick, the largest law firm in Maryland, where he had briefly been an associate in the fifties.

Assigned to handle the litigation was an earnest, thirty-three-year-old, chubby-cheeked associate, Keith Smith, who was startled by the depths of Hardwicke's depression when they first met in late 2000. "I've never seen anyone as black as John was," Smith tells me. "He couldn't work, couldn't get out of bed most days."

Not long after the firm signed on, the school made a settlement offer of two hundred thousand dollars. Hardwicke considered the sum "insulting."

I ask him if he can quantify the damages he's suffered. His back stiffens, face reddens, voice rises an octave or two.

This is what bothered me so much about filing a lawsuit. The first thing Piper Rudnick wanted to do was create a list of ways that I'd been damaged. And I'm just, like, fucking unwilling to do this. What do you mean create a list? I'm not going to give you a list . . . because I can't. I know I've been changed, hurt unbelievably. There's not a moment that goes by that I haven't been affected by this. Mr. Hanson used to masturbate the stick shift in the car, so I get in my car and immediately that memory comes to mind. Mr. Hanson shaved my face one of the first times it was ever shaved. So I put on shaving cream and he's there. Mr. Hanson drank brandy, so I can't stand brandy. Beer tastes like his urine. I kiss my wife and Mr. Hanson's tongue is in my mouth. How do you count damage like that?

Obviously, I say, the damage is very real to you.

"It is real," Hardwicke says. "There's a snake that was put inside me, and it coils through my intestines and has become mixed up in my whole being. It's alive and it talks and I can't get it fucking out."

Piper Rudnick filed Hardwicke's lawsuit in January 2001. And around that time, Hardwicke started calling and e-mailing alumni from the school. He wanted to tell his story to people who might understand. He also wondered if there were others who had suffered similarly. It didn't take long for him to discover that there were many others—several dozen by his current count. There was his classmate Robert Staab, for one. There was also Bobby Byrens. There were Chuck Clinton, Mark Goebel, and Doug Palmatier. And, of course, there was Larry Lessig, the famous lawyer in California.

WHEN HARDWICKE FIRST telephoned Lessig, the call did not
go smoothly. Hardwicke asked about Lessig's experiences with
Hanson, promising he would keep the information confidential.
But Hardwicke had already mentioned the names of some former
students he'd spoken to. Lessig, agitated and deeply wary, told
Hardwicke, "You've already revealed other people's secrets to me. I
don't know why I'd trust you to keep my secrets confidential."

Lessig, however, did agree to talk to Hardwicke's lawyers. But
when Keith Smith called, Lessig said, "I'd love to talk to you, but I
can't." The implications of Lessig's phrasing were plain to Smith: "It
tells me right away there's a contract, a settlement agreement, that
says he can't talk." Smith was interested in deposing Lessig as a
potential witness. Now he knew that he would have to subpoena
him—overriding any past confidentiality agreement.

Lessig had few doubts about the merits of Hardwicke's suit.
"Sometimes he described the sexual acts in sadistic terms that were
hard for me to credit," Lessig says. "But there were certain signposts
that were totally credible to me," ranging from Hardwicke's
description of Hanson's brazenness to the special handshake he
used—a little tickle on your palm with his middle finger—to signal
his desire for sex.

Lessig wished the plaintiff well, hoped he'd win, would be com-
pensated. But Lessig didn't want to be deposed. He worried about
having the seal broken on his past, about having these furtive scenes
from his boyhood recounted in a court proceeding. Besides, his
mind was elsewhere: on an epic copyright case, *Eldred v. Ashcroft,*
that had become his abiding obsession. But Hardwicke continued
badgering Lessig with a stream of calls and e-mails. Finally the lawyer told Hardwicke, "John, I'm in the middle of an extremely
important battle—and this is not it."

In January 2003, three months after arguing *Eldred v. Ashcroft*
before the U.S. Supreme Court, Lessig read a story in the *New York*

Times about Hardwicke's case. Earlier, the school's lawyers had moved to have the case thrown out on the grounds that the Charitable Immunity Act provided the school blanket protection from such a lawsuit. Now the trial-court judge, Jack Sabatino, had sided with the school. "The Act insulates charitable organizations from liability for any degree of tortious conduct, no matter how flagrant," Sabatino opined. "Accordingly, plaintiff's contentions that employees and agents of the American Boychoir School acted willfully, wantonly, recklessly, indifferently—even criminally—do not eviscerate the School's legal protection."

Lessig was floored. Enacted in 1958, amended in 1995, the Charitable Immunity Act, as he understood it, was designed to shield nonprofits from being sued for negligence. But Hardwicke's suit had nothing to do with negligence—his injuries had been inflicted intentionally. Thus Sabatino's ruling was "flagrantly wrong," Lessig says. "Here was this innocent who was being doubly screwed—first literally by the Boychoir and now by the legal system."

Angry as Lessig was at the opinion, he was angrier at the school. "It's like, what the fuck?" he says. "You *know* this happened. You *know* this was pervasive. Why do you force people to hire lawyers to fight all these bullshit claims when you *know* you're guilty? You ought to be figuring out ways to make people whole again. It's this failure to take responsibility for what they did that just began to make me furious."

Six days after reading the story in the *Times,* Lessig received the news that he'd lost the Eldred case. Crushed, despondent, and perhaps in need of a new obsession, he called Keith Smith and volunteered to argue Hardwicke's appeal. Hardwicke was thrilled; Smith, conflicted. He had devoted thousands of hours to the case, but now Lessig was going to get the glory of making the argument in the higher courts. Smith was aware that Lessig's track record as an appellate lawyer was limited to two arguments in the Eldred case, both of them unsuccessful. But Smith was swayed by Lessig's legal stature and his biography. "I felt Larry could approach the argument from a standpoint that I can't," Smith says. "He experienced this."

For the past two decades, Lessig had kept the story of his abuse a closely guarded secret—especially from his parents. By plunging into the Hardwicke case, Lessig says, he understood that it was likely he would "be forced to confront this with my family; people are going to look at me differently."

The argument before the New Jersey appellate court took place in November 2003. Its essence was straightforward. To Lessig's knowledge, there was no prior case in the history of New Jersey in which the courts had ruled that charitable immunity applied to intentional wrongful acts. And the acts at the school in the seventies, he said, were not merely intentional: The sexual abuse that occurred was "pervasive and institutionalized." If the supreme court granted total immunity in such cases, Lessig concluded, New Jersey could become "a haven for sex abuse by charitable institutions."

When the argument was over, the school's litigator, Jay Greenblatt, told Lessig the performance was "one of the best oral arguments I've heard in my career." Four months later, the three-judge panel sided 2 to 1 with Lessig and Hardwicke, prompting the school to appeal to the state supreme court.

Lessig was in Washington when he learned the news, about to board a train for New York. Ten minutes later, his first victory as a litigator notched in his belt, he was in the bar car, beaming, babbling, buying drinks for everyone.

AFTER HEARING SO MANY awful things about the Boychoir School, I drove down to Princeton to hear what its officials had to say in its defense. The school's current president, Donald Edwards, gave me a tour of the grounds. We stopped at the rooms that once made up the Hanson-Lessig suite. "He lived *here*? You know more than I do about that," Edwards said in a tone of mild shock.

Bearded and bespectacled at sixty-three, Edwards feels beleaguered by the case. "This is the only litigation I've ever gone through, and it's the only one I will ever go through," he said in his genial, soft-spoken way. "It's an adversarial process, and I've built a forty-year career on being nonadversarial."

Edwards joined the school's staff as head of fund-raising and publicity in 1999, then was elevated to president in 2002. In the spring of 2000, a few months after Hardwicke surfaced with his allegations, the school sent out a letter informing the parents and alumni for the first time about the reasons behind Hanson's firing (though it didn't name him). The school encouraged former students to come forward with information about past incidents of sexual abuse (though it didn't disclose that it had, in fact, settled several other lawsuits in the eighties and nineties). And it hired an expert for advice on its child-protection policies.

In April 2002, the *New York Times* and *Nightline,* fed leads by Hardwicke, broke the story in tandem. Hardwicke then set up a Web site that further spread the details. The fallout for the school was harsh. Concert bookings evaporated; recruiting students became an uphill slog.

Edwards's frustration with all of this isn't hard to comprehend. The abuse took place long ago; today, the school is safe and ever-vigilant, he says. "The irony is, probably the one person who will never bear any burden if there is a judgment against the school is Donald Hanson," Edwards notes. "The people who are bearing the burden now are our students, faculty, parents, and trustees, none of whom were around in 1970 and 1971."

All of that is true, of course. But one of the legal system's central functions is to allocate responsibility for harms that occurred even decades ago—thus creating incentives for sound behavior in the future.

In any event, it would be easier to sympathize with the school had its fight against Hardwicke not been so vicious—and, at times, so ham-handed. When, for example, the lawsuit was filed, the school's lawyers submitted an official reply that argued that Hardwicke had no case because he consented to the sex with Hanson—and that by not revealing it sooner, he was more negligent than the school. (To be precise, the term the document used was "fraudulent concealment.") Both statements were leaped upon by the *Times* and *Nightline*.

"That was very unfortunate," Jay Greenblatt, the school's litigator, tells me one afternoon in his office in Vineland, New Jersey. Greenblatt was appointed to the case by the school's insurance company, which also pays his fees. He came aboard after the reply was written. "It was a boilerplate-type pleading," he limply explains. "I don't even know if it was reviewed."

Greenblatt is a past president of the New Jersey State Bar Association. At sixty-eight, he's got a rumbling voice, close-cropped gray hair, and wears a big gold signet ring. He tells me the school would have preferred to settle with Hardwicke, if only to avoid the flood of adverse publicity. But, Greenblatt goes on, "this isn't just a matter of money. His goal is to close the school. I think that he along with his id wants to do it. He's looking to punish someone for what unfortunately occurred to him at the hands of a man thirty-five years ago."

In the absence of the prospect of a settlement, Greenblatt says, the school turned to charitable immunity, which, he maintains flatly, "doesn't apply only to negligence." Besides, he argues, the school can't be held liable for Hanson's private behavior—which he equates with an employee's stopping in a bar after work and slugging someone in the mouth. "Is the company responsible?" he asks. "No. Why not? Because they're not acting within the scope of employment."

If the case does go to trial, Greenblatt clearly intends to wage an assault on Hardwicke's credibility. "I don't know where fact ends and fantasy begins with John," he says. "I believe he was molested. I believe that molestation took place in private and that no one knew about it or reasonably should have known about it. However, of course, if he was being molested fifteen times a day in half of the rooms of the institution, it could create the implication that somebody should have known . . . So the more notorious it was, the better for his case."

Yet despite Greenblatt's assertions to the contrary, what shines through all the school's dealings with Hardwicke is a stark unwillingness to countenance that the plaintiff might be telling the truth. "I don't know a lot about what the school was like in 1970 and 1971," Edwards says. "I do know that the kind of schedule we live with today doesn't leave enough time for what John Hardwicke describes happened multiple times a day. That sort of thing—I just find it very hard to believe."

THE NIGHT BEFORE THE State Supreme-Court argument, over dinner in Philadelphia, Lessig tells me he intends to describe obliquely, before the justices, the years-ago conversation in which Hanson said he needed to sexualize the boys for the sake of the choir's splendor. "It shows, however ridiculous it is, that Hanson believes he's doing this for the benefit of his employer," Lessig explains. "So it makes the abuse within the scope of employment.

"Now, we don't yet have that conversation in the record," Lessig goes on, "and I'm in this weird position of knowing it. So we're just going to simply say, look, we will establish at trial that fact. And they could say, how do you know you're going to establish it at trial? And then I'm in this very awkward position of having to say why."

And how do you intend to resolve that awkwardness? I ask.

Lessig says, "I don't know."

THE NEXT MORNING, at the supreme court, a windowless modern space with walls of marble and frosted glass, Greenblatt argues first. He is peppered with questions and seems at times unfamiliar with his own brief. After thirty-five minutes, Lessig rises to take his turn. At the podium, he reaches down for a paper cup; his hand quivers so violently that water spills en route to his lips.

Lessig speaks for only twenty minutes. He is rarely interrupted. The judges' eyes widen when Lessig says that "between thirty and fifty percent of the boys at this school were sexually abused or harassed." And they squirm in their chairs when Lessig—emboldened by the fact that a Piper Rudnick associate has found something in the record to support the Hanson revelation—announces, "It was the perversion of this music director . . . to believe that sexual abuse was part of producing a wonderful boychoir."

When Lessig is done, Greenblatt, clearly irritated, stands up and offers his rebuttal. Of the Hanson revelation, he says, "How convenient . . . I know of no such fact." And of the 30 to 50 percent figures, he continues, "[T]hat might be *personal knowledge* of Mr. Lessig, but it hasn't been in the record of this case."

Sitting in a high-backed chair, Lessig cringes as if he's been stabbed in the stomach, glares at Greenblatt, and shakes his head. He's just been outed in open court.

Afterward, Lessig, the Hardwickes, and the legal team drive to Princeton for lunch. While everyone believes that the argument went well, they are stunned by Greenblatt's indiscretion. Walking into the lobby of the restaurant, a French place off Nassau Street, Lessig turns to his companions and says softly, "Hanson took me here for dinner."

Later that afternoon, Lessig flies home to California, where he receives a barrage of vituperative faxes from Greenblatt—which the school's lawyer has helpfully cc'd to the press. Greenblatt insists there's nothing in the record to support Lessig's surprise assertions. He makes repeated insinuations about Lessig's "firsthand knowledge." And, hurling charges of "mendacity," he says that "Hanson surely would have been fired years earlier" had Lessig spoken out during his stint on the board.

A few weeks later, Greenblatt elaborates to me. "He had a

responsibility not only to the children but to the school," he says. "And if he had that knowledge, didn't divulge it, and any child was injured thereafter by Hanson, then he bears that responsibility—and perhaps, just perhaps, that plays some part in his role in this matter."

Lessig's reaction to Greenblatt's gambit is disgust mixed with shock and rage. In faxes of his own, Lessig calls his outing a "breach of a basic sense of decency" and professes to be "astonished" by Greenblatt's "ignorance of the facts in this case."

I ask Lessig about Greenblatt's charge that by failing to expose Hanson earlier, he bears a measure of guilt.

"I do feel that," Lessig says. "But I don't suffer that feeling, because very quickly I recognize what it is to be a teenager."

To Lessig, Greenblatt's charge is a tawdry attempt to score points at the expense of his reputation. "Before this case, I never would've had a desire that the Boychoir School close," Lessig says. "It's an interesting place, it's a great experience, it teaches kids to work hard. But the way I feel about it now is, fuck it. If they have to shut down because of this case, I don't care."

EVERYONE CONNECTED to *Hardwicke v. American Boychoir School* assumed that the supreme court would have ruled long before now. Every morning, they check the Web to see if the opinion has been posted.

For Don Edwards, victory would mean the school could bury its lurid past, at least legally speaking. A loss would open the door to suits from other boys whose alleged abuse Hardwicke has dredged up. Edwards says, "It's not like I wake up thinking the case will destroy the school—but it's not impossible that it could."

For John Hardwicke—and for all the potential child-sex-abuse litigants against the Catholic Church in New Jersey—a negative ruling by the supreme court would be a devastating blow, if not a mortal one. He is currently among a group of campaigners working on a parallel track to persuade the state Legislature to amend the Charitable Immunity Act so that it clearly exempts cases of child sexual abuse. At the same time, a ruling in his favor would mean that Hardwicke is only one step closer to putting his case before a jury. "I'll actually be in the position where I thought I was four years ago," he says. "I think I'll be ninety-five years old going, *I think we're just about done.*"

Yet even if Hardwicke does collect a monumental payout, it's far from clear that money will make him whole again. As he sits in his living room, talking about his high-achieving siblings—one brother a partner at a large law firm, one sister an executive at Ernst and Young—his ravaged expectations for himself are never far from the surface. If not for what took place at the school, he says, "I think that I actually could have been a leader of my fellow people. I could've gone on to be a lawyer or politician or something really helpful to society."

Lessig, of course, is exactly that, and the disparity between his and Hardwicke's lives suggests that the metaphor coined by the latter may in fact be true: When it comes to consequences of child sex abuse, it really does depend on where you were sitting in the car. It affects different people in profoundly different ways.

"This thing happened to me," Lessig says, "and I can see how it changed me. But to be too angry about it would require me to kind of hate myself. Now, there are certain things I did hate about what it did to me: the way I would destroy relationships and the pain I would inflict on people when I did. But there are other parts—the weirdness of me and my relationship to the world. Being deeply reflective about institutions, responsibilities, and my role. Spinning deeply from the age of fourteen about issues. And it's like, well, if this hadn't happened to me, who would I have been? Maybe I would have gone to work with my dad and run the steel plant and become a Republican congressman from Williamsport. I would have been a totally different person."

Lessig's sense that the effects of his abuse have been less than cataclysmic is among the reasons Donald Hanson has never been his bête 'noire. A few years after being fired by the school, Hanson decamped for England, where Lessig ran across him one day in Cambridge—and went punting with him on the Cam. (Since then, Hanson has been hiding out in France, or in Switzerland, or in Canada; no one is certain where.)

"I've never felt angry, or really angry, at Hanson," Lessig says. "Hanson's sick. He's got a disease. The real evil isn't the Hitler. The evil is the good German. The evil is all those people who could've just picked up the goddamn telephone and stopped it."

For Lessig, the Hardwicke case is a chance to battle the good Germans he sees as still inhabiting the Boychoir School and other, similar institutions: "I'm not trying to punish them," he says. "All I'm trying to do is get them to pick up the phone."

But Lessig's participation in the case (and in this story) is about something more, I think. All along, Lessig has gone to great lengths to keep his parents from learning that he was working on the Hardwicke litigation—and thus confronting his abuse with them. The question, though, is how far in the dark Lessig's parents actually are.

Lessig once told me a story about the summer after he left the Boychoir School. Hanson invited him to take a trip to the Hanson family compound in Canada. Lessig badly wanted to go. But his mother said no, and when Lessig asked why, she said, "I don't know, there's something weird about this." Lessig threw a titanic fit. "I screamed, slammed the door, walked out of the house," he said. "I came back three hours later, and we never said anything about it ever again." Lessig paused. "They knew."

So if they knew—that is, they know—isn't keeping it from them a charade?

"You underestimate the power of the human mind to ignore things that aren't placed right in front of you," he said. "It doesn't have to be such a successful charade to succeed in not forcing them into this deeply depressing, painful recognition of not taking steps to protect your kid."

What has brought all this into focus for Lessig is the birth twenty months ago of his son, Willem. Lessig recalls his father's tirade when he asked to go to the Boychoir School. "It wasn't until I became a father that I understood," he says. "I can't imagine sending my son away to school. I can't imagine how they could do it."

Willem has also afforded Lessig an insight into his deliberations over whether to reveal his abuse to his parents: "I think to myself, *My God, I would never want my child not to tell me something like that.*"

But Lessig and his parents remained locked in a silent impasse: the parents too fearful, and perhaps too guilty, to press him about what happened; the son too angry with them to volunteer the information. When Lessig saw his mother and father at Christmas, at their home in Hilton Head, they told him they'd received a card from a friend that mentioned his latest legal adventure: *We saw Larry's name in the paper,* the card reported. *We see he's fighting a lawsuit with that boychoir in Princeton.*

His parents inquired, What lawsuit? Lessig refused to tell them. Now he doesn't have to—and they don't have to ask. For better or worse, the impasse has finally been broken.

JOHN HEILEMANN *is a contributing editor at* New York *magazine, where he writes the "Power Grid" column, and also a columnist at* Business 2.0. *He was a finalist for the National Magazine Award in reporting in 2001, and he is the author of* Pride Before the Fall: The Trials of Bill Gates and the End of the Microsoft Era, *and has been a staff writer for* The New Yorker, The Economist, *and* Wired. *He lives in Brooklyn.*

Coda

In the days following the story's publication, Lessig's e-mail inbox was flooded with hundreds of messages. Most expressed support and sympathy; others shared stories that echoed his, and sought advice about counseling or therapy. On various Web sites, Boychoir School alumni came forward with stories of their own, few of them as dark as Hardwicke's, but many troubling all the same. Meanwhile, Donald Edwards, in a letter to the Boychoir School's faculty, staff, parents, and trustees, offered for the first time a public apology to the victims of Hanson's abuse—an apology, however, that was marred by the letter's blithe conclusion. "There is little any of us can do outside the legal process to address the past," Edwards wrote, as if the school's conduct in the Hardwicke case was a good-faith attempt to confront the past, as opposed to evading it.

Among the responses to the story, one was especially shocking. In an article in the *Toronto Star,* Don Hanson emerged from hiding (though without revealing his whereabouts) to denounce the accusations against him. "This is an awful lot of slander, this whole thing," he said, adding that Lessig's involvement in the case "just pisses me off, just destroys me. He was the best head boy that I ever had in the choir." Regarding Hardwicke, Hanson was harsher: "He has an axe to grind. I threw him out of the school down there . . . [He] was a known predator of kids his own age. He approached me. He wanted to come to my room." (Hardwicke replied: "To place the blame on the victim is an age-old game; I was a child.")

For Hardwicke, Hanson's taunts were infuriating, but they were nothing compared to the sustained silence of the New Jersey Supreme Court—which continued, inexplicably, for months. While awaiting the ruling, Hardwicke redoubled his efforts to amend the Charitable Immunity Act. Although the amendment had the support of many members of the New Jersey legislature, its progress was stalled by the determined opposition of the Catholic Church. But in the fall of 2005, owing largely to the publicity surrounding Hardwicke's case, the amendment acquired irresistible momentum, passing both the state assembly and the state senate. On January 5, 2006, Acting Governor Richard Codey signed it into law: No longer would charitable institutions be immune from being sued for negligence in cases of child sexual abuse.

A few days later, the state supreme court requested briefs from both sides in *Hardwicke v. American Boychoir School* on the implications of the amendment for the case at hand. In their brief, Lessig and Keith Smith made the logical argument: that if charities were not immune from negligence claims in child sex-abuse cases, "it would be bizarre," as Lessig put it elsewhere, "to imagine them immune from liability for intentional torts." The school's brief, predictably if contortedly, argued just the opposite: that because the legislature referred specifically only to negligence, then charities were still immunized from other types of claims, including the type being made by Hardwicke.

For Lessig, the interminable wait for a decision was nearly as excruciating as it was for Hardwicke. Yet no matter how the court ultimately ruled, Lessig had no doubt that the case was a turning point for him. No longer was this aspect of his past a secret from his family. Indeed, he was planning to write a book in which his experiences at the school would be a fulcrum on which a broader legal and moral meditation would pivot. To many denizens of the Web, Lessig was now even more of an icon than he'd been before; in countless posts, he was hailed for his "heroism" and "bravery" in revealing his abuse and taking up Hardwicke's cause.

His response was perfectly in character. "[F]irst, a plea: that we drop the H-word and B-word from commentary about this," Lessig wrote on his blog. "This is an important social issue because of how ordinary it is in fact; and we need it to be understood to be ordinary, so as to respond in ways that can check and prevent it."

Jimmy Breslin

THE END OF THE MOB

The Mafia's Worst Enemy Was Part of the Family

FROM *Playboy*

LATE AT NIGHT I am watching Bobby De Niro in some *Analyze* movie, and I feel sorry for him because these Mafia parts, at which he is so superb and which he could do for the next thirty years, soon will no longer exist. Simultaneously he could be forced into new subjects. Al Pacino, too. Which is marvelous because both are American treasures and should be remembered for great roles, not for playing cheap punks who are unworthy of getting their autographs. I would much prefer De Niro or Pacino to Sir Laurence Olivier in anything.

Now, watching the late movie, I am remembering where I saw it start for De Niro. It was on a hot summer afternoon when the producer of a movie being made from a book I wrote, *The Gang That Couldn't Shoot Straight,* asked me to meet De Niro because he was replacing Pacino in a big part. Pacino was going into some movie called *The Godfather.* De Niro was looking for his first major movie role.

We talked briefly in a bar, the old Johnny Joyce's on Second Avenue. De Niro looked like he was homeless. It was a Friday. On Sunday morning my wife came upstairs in our home in Queens and said one of the actors from the movie was downstairs. I flinched. Freak them. Downstairs, however, was De Niro. He was going to Italy on his own to catch the speech nuances of people in towns mentioned in the script. He was earning seven hundred and fifty dollars a week for the movie. I remember saying when he left, "Do not stand between this guy and whatever he wants."

What he wanted first was to play Italians who were in the Mafia. The crime actors had been mostly Jewish: Edward G. Robinson, Alan King, Rod Steiger, Eli Wallach, Paul Muni, Jerry Orbach. De Niro and Pacino took it over. They were the stars of an American industry of writers, editors, cameramen, directors, gofers, lighting men, soundmen, location men, and casting agents who were all on the job and on the payroll because of the Mafia.

Now the whole Mafia industry is slipping on a large patch of black ice. Soon it will be totally gone.

"We had one wiseguy in the first season," Bill Clark, former executive producer of the now departed *NYPD Blue,* told me the other day. "That was all, because they just couldn't make it as characters for us. Their day was gone."

Both of us remember when it wasn't. There was a hot late afternoon in July 1979 when Carmine Galante, the boss of the Bonanno Mob at the time, was shot dead at a picnic lunch in the backyard of Joe and Mary's Restaurant on Knickerbocker Avenue in Brooklyn. Bill Clark, then a homicide detective, was the first detective on the scene. He looked at Galante and grabbed the phone and called my office at the New York *Daily News.*

The great A.M., secretary, took the call. She was a Catholic schoolgirl who was a true daughter of the Mafia in the Bronx.

"Tell Jimmy that Galante is down on Knickerbocker Avenue," Clark said. Then he hung up. Inspectors were barging in to grab the phone and have it for themselves the rest of the day. There was no such thing as a cell phone.

Secretary A.M. sat on the call for one hour.

"People shouldn't know about a thing like this," she said.

Today, aside from grieving showmen, the only ones rooting for the mobsters to survive—or at least for keeping some of them around—are FBI agents assigned to the squads that chase Mafia gangsters across the hard streets of the city. Each family has a squad assigned to it. The squads are numbered, such as C-16 for the Colombo squad. Each agent is assigned to watch three soldiers and one capo in the family. The work is surveillance and interviews. Agents will interview a cabdriver or a mobster's sister. It doesn't matter. Just do the interview. Then they get to their desk and fill out FD-302 forms that get piled up in the office. They must do it in order to keep the FBI way of life in New York. They earn seventy thousand dollars or so a year, live in white suburbs, and do no real heavy lifting on the job. After a five-hour day they go to a health club, then perhaps stop for a drink with other agents, and they always talk about what jobs they want when they retire. If, after interviewing, surveilling, and paying stool pigeons, they do not come in with some Mafia dimwit whose arrest makes the news, they face doing true work for their country: antiterrorism detail in a wet alley in Amman, Jordan, or tent living in Afghanistan.

"What do you want?" Red Hot said. He is on First Avenue, in front of the great De Robertis espresso shop.

"We just want to talk to you," one of the two FBI agents said.

"You'll have to wait here until I get a lawyer to stop by," Red Hot said.

"We just wanted you to take a ride with us down to the office."

"The answer is no," Red Hot said.

"We just want to get fresh fingerprints. We haven't taken yours in a while."

"That's because I was in jail. And nothing happened to the prints you have. What are you trying to say, that they faded? They wore out?"

His friend Frankie "Biff" LoBritto cut in, "Red Hot, if you go with them, you won't come back. They'll make up a case in the car."

When the agents left, Red Hot said in a tired voice, "They'll be back. They're going to make up something and lock me up. Don't even worry about it."

Some nights later Red Hot was walking into De Robertis when he dropped dead on the sidewalk.

"He ruined the agents' schedules," Frankie Biff said. "They were going to put him away for sure without a case."

I will now take you into intensive care to observe the last of the Mafia.

The floor under them didn't even give a warning creak before opening up and causing everybody to tumble into the basement. This happened in March of this year when the United States Attorney in Brooklyn announced that, in the 1990s, two detectives, Louis Eppolito and Stephen Caracappa, had killed at least eight people for money paid by Anthony "Gaspipe" Casso, a demented killer and a boss of the Luchese Mob.

From out of the basement climbed Tony Café. Immediately the FBI visited him for the second time. It needed some help. If there were any shooters roaming around Brooklyn, Tony Café had to stop them. For if any bodies appeared on the streets or in the gutters of Brooklyn, perhaps the FBI agents, in absolutely desperate trouble for having Eppolito and Caracappa accused of shooting people practically in front of them, would be thrown like miscellaneous cargo onto transport planes bound for Kabul and Baghdad.

Politicians and the news media claimed the two detectives had committed the most treacherous and treasonous acts in the history of the police department. Would that it were true. Police officers serve wonderfully well and in these times do not even take a free cup of coffee. But there are isolated madmen who still pass the test and who have guns and could use money, and over the years the belief has been that many Mob shootings in Brooklyn have been done by cops.

Tony's favor to the FBI consisted of finding the only two Mob gunmen left in Brooklyn and ordering them to keep their fingers still.

There were other issues for the Mob. As ordered by the mandates of Christmas for Mafia captains, collections were taken up late in 2004 for traditional presents for the bosses of the five New York City Mafia families. The bosses now mainly were worried defendants and long-term prisoners. There was only one recognized boss, Joe Massino of the crime family named for the late big old mobster Joe Bonanno. I don't know what the other families did about Christmas collection money, for there was nobody worth a gift certificate.

The men in the Bonanno crime family raised two hundred thousand dollars for Massino, the last boss. His liberty, however, was as shaky as a three-legged chair. He was in jail under the Gowanus Expressway in Brooklyn, held without bail while standing trial in federal court some blocks away. There were three murders and seven or eight prosecution witnesses of the type known as rats, including his wife's brother, "Good-Looking Sal" Vitale. Seated in the first row of the courtroom one afternoon was the wife, Josephine Massino. On the witness stand her brother was telling the court how Joe Massino's people came busting out of a closet and began firing away at three Bonanno mobsters he felt were dangerous dissidents.

Joe Massino sat at the defense table with a computer. He was good and overweight. He had a round, bland face and short white hair. The heritage of great suits ended at his plain blue suit and open-collar white shirt. Glasses were perched on his nose as his pudgy fingers touched the computer keyboard. I don't know what he was looking for. What he needed was an old movie of the battle of Dien Bien Phu, where he could identify closely with the French, who lost; the brother-in-law, Good-Looking Sal, would be shooting at him from the hillside. When Massino stopped typing, his hand went to the top of his head and, with thumb and forefinger, moved the glasses. This was the style of removing eyeglasses for all those in the underworld in Queens County.

On this day he noticed a reporter who had just had a death in the family. Massino mouthed, "I'm sorry." This was probably the last time we'd see someone in the Mafia showing the old-world class it was always reputed to have but rarely did.

Watching her brother destroy her husband, Mrs. Massino wailed softly, "This is the same as a death in my family. You don't know what I am going through."

"How could Sal do this? Joe taught him how to swim," Tony Rabito, from Massino's restaurant, the Casa Blanca, complained. Sal Vitale is on his way to prison for a whole lot of years.

Joe Massino always was a very good swimmer. He could swim from Coney Island all the way across a wide inlet to Breezy Point, on the ocean. He taught his wife's brother, Good-Looking Sal, how to swim. This is a very big thing; you teach a kid to swim so he never drowns. Joe Massino could do that. He taught all the strokes to Good-Looking Sal. A lot of good that did.

During the trial, from out of the past, from Jimmy Weston's on Fifty-fourth Street and P. J. Clarke's on Fifty-fifth, from Pep McGuire's on Queens Boulevard, from his scungilli restaurant on Second Avenue, came Tony Café, who is called that because he was always in saloons. He arrived at my building one night with a handwritten open letter from Joe Massino's daughter. She pointed out that Massino had been in prison and Good-Looking Sal Vitale had been running the Bonanno family when many of the murders were committed. While this was true, she was not able to cover all the murders. But she did try.

"I don't know why the government is so mad at Joe," Tony Café said. "He's a nice fat guy, likes food."

AT THIS TIME TONY WAS A BLESSED UNKNOWN, but that would change.

Tony Café's previous experience was to make the mistake of rolling through the nights twenty-five years ago with the whole Mob and its new big hitter, Donnie Brasco.

"He is Joe DiMaggio!" everybody said one night at the old Pep McGuire's on Queens Boulevard.

When next seen, Brasco took the witness stand in room 103, federal court, Manhattan. Tony Café (his courtroom name Anthony Rabito) sat listening with his lawyer, Paul Rao.

> Q: What is your name?
> A: Joseph Pistone.
> Q: What is your occupation?
> A: I am a special agent for the Federal Bureau of Investigation.

Tony was sentenced to eight years. Rao told the judge that Tony had served two years in the artillery in Korea, that both his brothers had served and that he deserved something for this.

> THE COURT: Mr. Rabito, is there anything you would like to add to what Mr. Rao has told us on your behalf?
> DEFENDANT RABITO: Judge, I think I got a fair trial. There are a couple of things I don't like. I fought for that flag. I was in the Army. I believe in the press. I believe in you. You open up somebody's head, you find love in my head, but in some people you find the little Italian flag.

The judge took two years off the sentence, one for each year Tony spent in the service. He did six years at Otisville federal prison in upstate New York. I didn't see him when he came out and never heard about him, so I figured he wasn't up to much, which I thought was good because a second sentence would run a thousand years. In court for one thing or another over several years,

I would take a look at the government's Mafia three-deep charts.
The pictures of the Bonanno varsity players were mounted on
cardboard. I never saw Tony's picture nor found his name in a news
story, even if it was about guys at the bottom.

Bad things now happened in the courtroom. Joe Massino was
convicted and faced sentences of more years than he had to give
for his country.

Right away, in Washington, Attorney General John Ashcroft
directed prosecutors in Brooklyn to start a capital punishment case
against Massino for another murder. They find you guilty in federal
court on any charge, from stealing a postage stamp to murder. If
the federals said they wanted an execution case, Massino was going
to die.

No, he wasn't. He called for a prosecutor and said he wanted to
cooperate. He knows everybody and everything about the waning
days of the Mafia. He is a traditional mobster. He eats until he can't
fit at the table. He had a restaurant with the best pork braciola for
miles. He flicks a thumb down and somebody dies. He has a wife
and daughters and several girlfriends. He lives in Howard Beach,
Queens, which had an overcrowding of big gangsters. His house
was a few blocks from that of John Gotti and also Vic Amuso,
another boss. The first sounds of anger about Massino's turning
came from Vito from Metropolitan Avenue. He had put up fifteen
hundred dollars for Massino's Christmas present.

"Joe is a rat. I don't give my money to rats," he said. "I want my
money back."

"How are you going to get it from him? He's in jail," he was
told.

"From his wife," he said.

"You go ask his wife."

When mobsters are reduced to fighting under the mistletoe,
there is no reason for them to exist.

And now, in this court building at the same time, you saw the
reason the Mafia must die. Four members of Local 15 of the

Operating Engineers Union were in court to plead guilty to selling out workingmen. They work cranes, backhoes, bulldozers, and hoists. They are proud and physical and, along with Local 40 of the Iron Workers, were about the first to walk up to the fiery mountains of the old World Trade Center, fierce, powerful, unafraid, and did all the gruesome heavy lifting for the next year. They were Irish, and their union heads admitted to being controlled by Mafia gangsters. Tom Robbins of the *Village Voice,* who seems to be the only reporter in the city who thinks labor is important, called the union the Mob's Engineers.

The government indicted twenty-four Mob guys in Brooklyn, including one Jackie DeRoss, who was listed as a union member but was recognized on the street as an underboss in the shrinking Colombo family. His sons, John and Jamie, had union books and were placed on jobs where attendance might have been taken. In Manhattan another eighteen mobsters in the union were indicted; one was Ernie Muscarella, a reputed boss in the Mob.

The one that bothered the most was Tom McGuire Jr., the business agent for the local. Everybody in labor knew his father, who had been business agent before him. Junior, out of Manhattan College, was unable to wail that he had to steal in order to make it in life. He was in the son game, as in "son of. . . ." If America is weaker at this time, blame the son game, the nepotism, as much as, in this case, the Mafia.

As Massino told agents stories that would end the Mafia, McGuire was in the same court building pleading guilty to a charge of selling union books. There were many other charges, including extorting fifty thousand dollars a year from a paving company and then giving an eighty-thousand-dollar bribe to the president of the International Union of Operating Engineers in order to become a vice president of the international. But selling the union books was the hideous crime. People beg, plead, and implore for a union book. If your son can get a book, you can sleep all through the night; union jobs pay up to forty-five dollars an hour, and your son has a fine living for life. Tom McGuire Jr., now sixty, pudgy, and arrogant, sold union books for twelve thousand dollars. He had a man running things for him, purportedly a Local 15 member, Anthony Polito. He took care of anything to do with organized crime. There were no-show jobs to be given to wiseguys or allowing work rules for health and safety to be ignored on any job where contractors had come up with money. Polito is in prison.

Reading through the government's indictment, I found that one of its legal standards for introducing evidence was based on *United States v. Brennan,* the defendant being "a former New York State Supreme Court justice who was charged with fixing four criminal cases," the indictment reads. "The government's witness, Anthony Bruno, served as a middleman."

I used to see Justice Brennan on Queens Boulevard, and we'd have a beer once in a while. He would walk across the street to the courthouse and fix narcotics cases and, I believe, a homicide for the Mafia. He was another one of those who come without a shred of shame. His was a complete character collapse that turned him into a cheap errand boy. Reading on, I found a page of testimony about the labor men pleading guilty in Brooklyn federal court to robbing their own.

Simultaneously Joe Massino sat in the jailhouse and bargained for his life, his ten million dollars in plunder, and his two houses, one for his mother and the second, larger one for his wife and daughters. For life and possessions he would give up the entire underworld he had sworn to keep secret.

There are murders all over the place, and he must solve so many of them for the FBI. This is catastrophic for the guys on the street. Any mobsters nearing the end of their sentence will be hit with new charges and never see civilization again.

The publicity stool pigeons, "Sammy the Bull" Gravano being the latest, are illusions. Massino will end the Mafia. All the murders

THE END OF THE MOB 39

and dialogue that have been a large part of this nation's culture will disappear. All Mafia books and shows, *The Sopranos* foremost, will be based on nothing and therefore too unrealistic to make.

Massino put himself into a small room with desperation with the murder of one Gerlando Sciascia, who was known as George from Canada because he was from Canada. According to testimony, Sciascia and Massino killed three Bonanno family dissidents in 1984. Sciascia then thought he was as good as Massino. They found Sciascia and his ambitions in a lot in the Bronx. Entire flights of stool pigeons immediately went to the grand jury to put a gun into Massino's hand in premeditated murder. And now he talks.

Bosses must go first. There are five families, and they are supposed to have bosses, but most of them change every forty-eight hours. The Gambino family had John Gotti. The old man of the Gambino crew, Joe N. Gallo, told Gotti, "It took one hundred years to put this together, and you're ruining it in six months."

This appears to be right. This old crime organization—which started in the narrow, wet alleys of Palermo and Lercara Friddi and other towns in Sicily, then rose out of the packed streets of the old downtown east side of New York, with names like Joe the Boss and Lucky Luciano, then with Al Capone coming out of Brooklyn and putting the Mafia into Chicago—had a murderous, larcenous hand everywhere. It weakened with time and the convictions of commission members in New York, but nothing matched the magnitude of what Gotti did to the Mafia. He had Paul Castellano hit in the midst of rush hour on the east side of Manhattan. It was brazen, and Gotti loved it. He failed to hear the sound of tank treads on Mulberry Street. They were bringing in an armored division to get him. They did.

He proudly put his son, Junior Gotti, in charge, and agents fell from the skies on him. He did six years and now is up for attempted murder, and he may not be seen for decades. The new head of the Gambino family was Nick Corozzo. He said he was exhausted from not working and needed a vacation. He flew to Miami and was on the beach for about half an hour when two men in subdued business suits walked along the beach toward him.

"So what's up, fellas?" Nick said.

"You are," they said. They displayed FBI cards. Nick the Boss went off the beach in handcuffs and then to court, where nobody wins. He is back on the street now but is a loud target.

The family named after Joe Profaci, an old-time Mafia boss, was shot up by an insurgency group, the Gallos, in the 1960s. Crazy Joe Gallo was shot dead at Umberto's Clam House on Mulberry Street. The news business loved the story. Joe Colombo took over. He believed he was a legitimate citizen. He invented the Italian American Civil Rights League and ran a rally at Madison Square Garden during which his crowd shouted *"Uno, uno, uno,"* the old Roman cheer for Benito Mussolini. *New York Post* columnist Murray Kempton observed, "The entertainment was provided by Diahann Carroll and Sammy Davis Jr., two striking illustrations of pre–Norman Sicilians."

Colombo then ran an outdoor rally at Columbus Circle during which he was shot, later dying from his injuries. The killing gave the Mafia a bad name. The next boss was Carmine Persico Jr., known as Junior. He is in federal prison in Lompoc, California, for about the rest of his life. During a succession disagreement, one Vic Orena, pronounced "Vicarena," was convicted of mayhem and sentenced to two lifetimes and one eighty-year sentence.

"Which one should I do first?" he asked Judge Jack Weinstein, who nodded to his clerk. "You name it," the clerk said.

"Put me down for the eighty years first," Orena said.

He went to Atlanta, and his lawyers entered a motion to throw everything out and let him come home. He was certain his motion would prevail over the whole government. He called Gina, his girl on Long Island, and told her, "Get my suits and have the tailor take them in. I've lost weight down here. Then go and get me some new shirts. I'm going to win this motion and make bail. We're going to Europe on the first day."

Orena was brought up by prison bus from Atlanta. His motion, a foot-high stack of paper, was on Weinstein's desk. The judge had studied it for some days.

Gina was in the courtroom with a suit for her now-slim love. The clerk called out "All rise," and Weinstein entered the courtroom. The door to the detention pens opened and a slim Vic Orena came in, his eyes glistening with hope.

"What is he doing here?" Weinstein asked. "He belongs in prison."

"He is here on his motion," the lawyer said.

"Motion denied," Weinstein said. "Marshal, take this man back to prison."

Vic Orena, his one and a half minutes of hope over, went through the door and onto a prison bus that would stop five or six times at dingy county jails on the way to Atlanta.

His love, Gina, with his suit folded neatly over her arms, went back to Long Island.

Vic Orena is still doing the eighty-years part of his sentence; then all that remains for him to do is the two lifetimes.

There is now no real Colombo family boss whose name is worth typing.

THE LARGEST, FIERCEST, AND BUSIEST FAMILY, the Genovese, had Vincent "the Chin" Gigante as boss—the boss in a bathrobe. Babbling in pajamas, robe, and truck driver's cap, he staggered through the night on Sullivan Street in Greenwich Village and entered the black-painted private club at number 206, where the guys played cards all night. The Chin, suddenly alert, sat down at the game. The cards were dealt. He picked up his hand and without looking at it called "Gin!" Money was pushed to him. Next he tired of picking up the cards. While they were being dealt, he called "Gin!" Always he got paid.

When in front of Judge Jack Weinstein in Brooklyn, he flopped around in his chair and mumbled for hours without stopping. My guess, and it is well educated, is that he was saying the Hail Mary, a lovely prayer that is short and can be repeated without end. Lawyers presented results of new tests they said showed the Chin had Alzheimer's. Weinstein, who reads science periodicals every morning, was greatly interested in the new test, the PET scan. "Congratulations. You are on the cutting edge of science," he told the lawyers. "But you omitted one important part of your test. In order to show that it is Alzheimer's, you need an autopsy."

Gigante shook and went to prison. The outfit was left with nothing.

Now there were five families in name and no bosses. At the start of 2005, in the midst of all the squalling over the Christmas money that went to Joe Massino's wife, federal agents came through Brooklyn like armed locusts and arrested twenty-seven members of the Bonanno family.

It followed that one morning when Tony Café was at home in Brooklyn, where he lives with his eighty-year-old sister, the last of four sisters, the first three dead of cancer, he heard knocking on the door downstairs. He looked out. He could see two agents, each holding up identification.

Tony Café sighed. "I'll be right down," he called. He threw his wallet to his sister.

When he got downstairs there were three agents, one of them a little Irish woman who did the talking.

"Are you going to lock me up?" Tony asked.

"No, but you're number one."

She made it official. A week before, an article by Jerry Capeci appeared in *New York* magazine and was first to mention that Tony Café—proper name Anthony Rabito—was suddenly an important figure. Capeci, whose *Gangland News* is on the Internet, is the authority on the Mafia to the extent that all those left in crime know that on Thursday, when Capeci's work comes out on the Net and in the afternoon's *New York Sun,* they will find out where they stand, if anybody is left to stand. Now on Tony's stoop, the FBI confirmed that Tony was number one in the Bonanno family. He was in shock as the agent, Kim something, told him, "We don't want any bodies in the street, we don't want witnesses bothered, and we don't want agents threatened."

"I live upstairs with my sister. I don't have any money or guns in the house," he said.

The agents sniffed and left.

And now Tony Café, who is allegedly the boss replacing the last boss of the Bonanno family, was sitting alone at the bar of Bamonte's Restaurant on Withers Street in Greenpoint, Brooklyn, his hair short and turning white, his voice like gravel pouring from a truck, and his build entirely too wide.

Bamonte's appears to be an out-of-the-way place, but it is on Broadway in the world of New York people who know what they eat. It is a short drive across the Williamsburg Bridge. At lunchtime half the city seems to walk past the bar and into the dining room.

Here was police commissioner Ray Kelly coming in and shaking hands with everybody. At the bar Tony Café held out his hand, and Kelly grabbed it and then moved on. Later, in the gloaming, Tony Café sat in the empty restaurant and said, "The police commissioner shook my hand. How do you like it? He didn't know who I was. Nobody knows who I am. I don't know anybody else. They're all in jail. Once the top of the family turns like Joe did, nobody from the other families will talk to you."

"What was the worst thing to happen to the outfit?" he was asked.

"Gotti," he said slowly, "when he had the case against him with a woman prosecutor and he fixed the jury. That got the government mad. Nobody was safe after that. They got Gotti and then they came after everybody else. Because of him, all of a sudden I'm standing out here alone."

JIMMY BRESLIN *was awarded the Pulitzer Prize for Distinguished Commentary in 1986. His nationally syndicated columns have appeared in* Newsday *and various other New York City newspapers. He is the author of numerous works of nonfiction, including* The Short Sweet Dream of Eduardo Gutierrez *and, most recently,* The Church That Forgot Christ. *He lives in New York City.*

Mark Jacobson

THE $2,000-AN-HOUR WOMAN

FROM *New York* MAGAZINE

JASON ITZLER, THE SELF-ANOINTED world's greatest escort-agency owner, prepared to get down on his knees. When a man was about to ask for the hand of a woman in holy matrimony, especially the hand of the fabulous Natalia, America's No. 1 escort, he should get down on his knees.

This was how Jason, who has always considered himself nothing if not "ultraromantic," saw it. However, as he slid from his grade school–style red plastic seat in preparation to kneel, the harsh voice of a female Corrections officer broke the mood, ringing throughout the dank visitors' room.

"Sit back down," said the large uniformed woman. "You know the rules."

Such are the obstacles to true love when one is incarcerated at Rikers Island, where Jason Itzler, thirty-eight and still boyishly handsome in his gray Department of Corrections jumpsuit, has resided since the cops shut down his megaposh NY Confidential agency in January.

There was also the matter of the ring. During the glorious summer and fall of 2004, when NY Confidential was grossing an average of $25,000 a night at its five-thousand-square-foot loft at Seventy-nine Worth Street, spitting distance from the municipal courts and Bloomberg's priggish City Hall, Jason would have purchased a diamond with enough carats to blow the eye loupe off a Forty-seventh Street Hasid.

That was when Itzler filled his days with errands like stopping by Soho Gem on West Broadway to drop $6,500 on little trinkets for Natalia and his other top escorts. This might be followed by a visit to Manolo Blahnik to buy a dozen pairs of $500 footwear. By evening, Itzler could be found at Cipriani, washing down plates of crushed lobster with yet another bottle of Johnnie Walker Blue label and making sure everyone got one of his signature titanium business cards engraved with NY Confidential's singular motto: ROCKET FUEL FOR WINNERS.

But now Jason was charged with various counts of criminal possession of a controlled substance, money laundering, and promoting prostitution. His arrest was part of a large effort by the NYPD and the D.A.'s office against New York's burgeoning Internet-based escort agencies. In three months, police had shut down American Beauties, Julie's, and the far-flung New York Elites, a concern the cops said was flying porn stars all over the country for dates. Reeling, pros were declaring the business "holocausted" as girls took down their Web sites and worried johns stayed home.

Many blamed Itzler for the heat. In a business where discretion is supposed to be key, Jason was more than a loose cannon. Loose A-bomb was more like it. He took out giant NY Confidential ads in mainstream magazines (the one you're holding included). In restaurants, he'd get loud and identify himself, Howard Stern–style, as "the King of All Pimps." Probably most fatally, Itzler was quoted in the *Post* as bragging that he didn't worry about the police because "I have cops on my side." After that, one vice guy said, "it was like he was daring us."

Only days before, Itzler, attired in a $5,700 full-length fox coat from Jeffrey, bought himself a Mercedes S600. Now the car, along with much of the furniture at Jason's lair, including the $50,000 sound system on which he blared, 24/7, the music of his Rat Pack idol, Frank Sinatra, had been confiscated by the cops. His assets frozen, unable to make his $250,000 bail, Jason couldn't even buy a phone card, much less get Natalia a ring.

"Where am I going to get a ring in here?" Jason said to Natalia on the phone the other night. He suggested perhaps Natalia might get the ring herself and then slip it to him when she came to visit.

"That's good, Jason," returned Natalia. "I buy the ring, give it to you, you kiss it, give it back to me, and I pretend to be surprised."

"Something like that," Jason replied, sheepishly. "You know I love you."

That much seemed true. As Jason doesn't mind telling you, he has known many women since he lost his virginity not too long after his bar mitzvah at the Fort Lee Community Jewish Center, doing the deed with the captain of the Tenafly High School cheerleader squad. Since then, Jason, slight and five foot nine, says he's slept with "over seven hundred women," a figure he admits pales before the twenty thousand women basketball star Wilt "the Stilt" Chamberlain claimed to have bedded. But, as Jason says, "you could say I am a little pickier than him."

Of these seven hundred women, Jason has been engaged to nine, two of whom he married. "It was really only one and a half," Itzler reports, saying that while living in Miami's South Beach he married "this hot Greek girl. She was gorgeous. The first thing I did was buy her this great boob job, which immediately transformed her from a tremendous A/B look to an out-of-sight C/D look. But her parents totally freaked out. So I got the marriage annulled."

This aside, not counting his sainted late mother, Jason says Natalia, twenty-five, about five foot three and perhaps one hundred pounds soaking wet, reigns as the love of his life.

Without Natalia, she of the smoldering brown eyes that have excited who knows how many hedge-fund managers, billionaire trust-fund babies, and NFL quarterbacks, Jason would never have been able to build NY Confidential into the sub rosa superhotness it became. It was Natalia who got top dollar, as much as $2,000 an hour, with a two-hour minimum. In the history of Internet escorting, no one ever matched Natalia's ratings on TheEroticReview. com, the Zagat's of the escort-for-hire industry. On TER, "hobbyists," as those with the "hobby" of frequenting escorts are called— men with screen names like Clint Dickwood, Smelly Smegma, and William Jefferson Clinton—can write reviews of the "providers" they see, rating them on a scale of 1 to 10 for both "appearance" and "performance."

In 2004 Natalia recorded an unprecedented seventeen straight 10/10s. On the TER ratings scale, a 10 was defined as "one in a lifetime." Natalia was the Perfect 10, the queen of the escort world.

"Yo! *Pimp Juice!* . . . that her?"

It was Psycho, a large tattooed Dominican (PSYCHO was stenciled on his neck in Gothic lettering) who was referring to Jason by his jailhouse nickname. Itzler nodded. There was no need to gloat. Moments before, Jason scanned the grim visiting room. "Just making sure I've got the hottest chick in the room." Like it was any contest, Natalia sitting there, in her little calfskin jacket and leather miniskirt, thick auburn hair flowing over her narrow shoulders.

Besides, half of Rikers already knew about Jason and NY Confidential. They'd read, or heard about, the articles Itzler had piped to his pulp enablers at "Page Six," including how he could get "$250,000 an hour for Paris Hilton with a four-hour minimum."

But you couldn't believe everything you read in the *New York Post,* even at Rikers. Natalia's presence was proof. Proof that Jason, a little Jewish guy who still sported a nasty black eye from being beaten silly in his sleep by some skell inmate, wasn't full of shit when he told the homeys that he was the biggest pimp in the city, that he got all the best girls. How many other Rikers fools could get the Perfect 10 to visit them, at nine o'clock in the morning, too?

"Psycho . . . Natalia," Jason said. "Natalia . . . Psycho."

"Hey," Natalia said with an easy smile. She was, after all, a girl you could take anywhere. One minute she could be the slinkiest cat on the hot tin roof, wrapping her dancer's body (she was the tap-dance champion of Canada in 1996) around a client's body in a hotel elevator. Then, when the door slid open, she'd look classic, like a wife even, on the arm of a Wall Street CEO or Asian electronics magnate. She was an actress, had played Shakespeare and Off Broadway both. Ever the ingénue, she'd been Juliet half a dozen times. Playing opposite Jason's however-out-of-luck Romeo was no sweat, even here, in jail.

Not that Natalia had exactly been looking forward to coming to Rikers this raw late-spring morning. Riding in the bus over the bridge from East Elmhurst, freezing in her lace stockings as she sat beside a stocky black man in a Jerome Bettis jersey, she looked out the window at the looming prison and said, "Wal-Mart must have had a two-for-one on barbed wire."

It wasn't that she didn't miss Jason, or the heyday of when they lived together at Seventy-nine Worth Street, the harem stylings of which came to Jason while getting his hair cut at the Casbah-themed Warren Tricomi Salon on Fifty-seventh Street. It was just that this marriage thing was flipping her out, especially after Jason called the tabs to announce the ceremony would be held inside Rikers.

"Every little girl's dream, to get married at Rikers Island," Natalia said to Jason. "What are they going to get us, adjoining cells?"

But now, holding hands in the visiting room, surrounded by low-level convicts, just the sort of people who rarely appeared in either of their well-to-do childhoods or in the fantasy life of Seventy-nine Worth Street—neither of them, pimp or escort, could keep from crying.

"Are those happy tears or sad tears?" Jason asked.

"Just tears," answered Natalia.

"Crying because your boy is in jail?"

"That and . . . everything else."

It was a tender moment. Except then, as he always does, Jason began talking.

"Don't worry about this Rikers marriage," he said, back in schemer-boy genius mode. "This isn't the real marriage . . . When I'm out we'll have the princess marriage . . . the white dress, everything. Your mom will be there. My dad . . . This is just the publicity marriage. You know: getting married at Rikers—it's so . . . rock star!"

Natalia looked up at Jason, makeup streaming from her face.

"It's great, isn't it?" Jason enthused. "A brilliant idea."

"Yeah," Natalia said wearily. "Great, *in theory.*" Almost everything Jason Itzler said was great, in theory.

THEY CALL IT THE OLDEST PROFESSION, and maybe it is. The prostitute has always been part of the New York underworld. According to Timothy J. Gilfoyle's *City of Eros,* in 1776, Lieutenant Isaac Bangs of the Continental Army complained that half his troops were spending more time in lower-Manhattan houses of ill repute than fighting the British. In the nineteenth century, lower Broadway had become, in the words of Walt Whitman, a "noctivagous strumpetocracy," filled with "tawdry, foul-tongued and harsh-voiced harlots."

By the eighties, the image of the New York prostitute encompassed both the call-girl minions of Sydney Biddle Barrows, the famous Mayflower Madam, and the hot-pants-clad hooker trying to keep warm beside a burning fifty-five-gallon drum outside the Bronx's Hunts Point Market. On Eighth Avenue's so-called Minnesota Strip were the runaways in the wan-eyed Jodie Foster–in–*Taxi Driver* mode. The nineties brought the "Natasha Trade," an influx of immigrant Russian girls and their ex-Soviet handlers who locked the women up in Brighton Beach apartments and drove them, fifteen at a time, in Ford Econoline vans to strip joints on Queens Boulevard.

The Internet would reconfigure all that. Today, with highly ad hoc estimates of the New York "sex worker" population hovering, depending on whom you ask, anywhere from five thousand to twenty-five thousand, horny men looking for a more convivial lunch hour don't have to cruise Midtown bars or call a number scribbled on a piece of paper. All that's needed is a high-speed connection to any of the many "escort malls," such as the highly clickable CityVibe or Eros.

The typical site includes a photo or two, a sparse bio, a schedule of when the escort is available, and a price ("donation") list. There is also the standard disclaimer, detailing how any money exchanged "is simply for time only and companionship" and that anything else "is a matter of personal preference between two or more consenting adults." For, as everyone in the escort business is quick to say, selling "companionship" is not against the law.

The system is not without its bugs. The most common question: "Is she the girl in the picture?" Says a longtime booker, "About two-thirds of the time, when a guy calls up asking for a girl they've seen on the site, she doesn't work for us, quit six months ago, or we Photoshopped her picture from the Victoria's Secret catalogue.

"If they ask for Nicolette, I take out the three-by-five card with NICOLETTE written on top. It lists the contacts of girls who kind of look like the fake Nicolette. What blows my mind is the stupid bastards spend hours searching the sites looking for their super-fantasy, are willing to shell out seven hundred dollars an hour, and then when someone else knocks on the hotel-room door, they go, 'Oh, whatever.' They can still go back to Indianapolis, show the girl in the picture to their buddies, and say, 'See her? Like, *awesome, dude!*' "

It was this kind of slipshod, postmodern fakery that Jason Itzler says he started NY Confidential to wipe out. At NY Confidential, you always got the girl in the picture.

"That's because we were the best," says Itzler. "At NY Confidential, I told my girls that the pressure is on them because we have to provide the clients with the greatest single experience ever, a Kodak moment to treasure for the rest of their lives. Spreading happiness, positive energy, and love, that's what being the best means to me. Call me a dreamer, but that's the NY Confidential credo."

Such commentary is typical of Jason, who, in the spirit of all great salesmen, actually believes much of it.

Not yet forty, Jason Itzler has a story that is already a mini-epic of Jewish-American class longing, a psychosocio-sexual drama crammed with equal parts genius (occasionally vicious) boychik hustle, heartfelt neo-hippie idealism, and dead-set will to self-destruction. Born Jason Sylk, only son of the short-lived marriage between his revered mother, Ronnie Lubell, and his "sperm dad," Leonard Sylk, heir to the Sun Ray drugstore fortune built up by Harry Sylk, who once owned a piece of the Philadelphia Eagles, Jason spent his early years as one of very few Jewish kids on Philly's Waspy Main Line. If he'd stayed a Sylk, says Jason, "I would have been the greatest Richie Rich, because Lenny Sylk is the biggest thing in the Jewish community. He's got a trust that gives money to stuff like the ballet, a house with an eighteen-car garage, and a helicopter landing pad. Golda Meir used to stay with us when she was in town."

After his parents' divorce, Itzler moved to New York with his mother, whom Jason describes as "the hottest mom in the world. She had this Mafia princess–Holly Golightly thing about her. Her vanity license plate was TIFF. My mother being beautiful made me into who I am today, because when you grow up around a beautiful woman, you always want to be surrounded by beautiful women."

Also a big influence was his mom's father, the semi-legendary Nathan Lubell, "the biggest bookmaker in the garment industry, a gangster wizard," says Jason. "He owned a lot of hat stores, a bunch of the amusement park in Coney Island, and was hooked up with Meyer Lansky in Las Vegas hotels. I used to love it when he took me to the Friars Club, where he was a king. Even as a kid, I could feel the action."

With his mom remarried, to Ron Itzler, then a lawyer in the firm of Fischbein, Badillo (as in Herman), Wagner, and Itzler, the family lived in the Jersey suburbs. Displaying his compulsive intelligence by setting the all-time record on the early-generation video game Scramble, Jason, "pretty much obsessed with sex from the start," wrote letters to *Mad* magazine suggesting it put out a flexi-record of "teenage girls having orgasms." Summers were spent in the Catskills, where as a cabana boy at the Concord Hotel he befriended people like Jason Binn, now the playboy publisher of the *Hamptons* and *Los Angeles Confidential* magazines, a name Itzler paid homage to with his NY Confidential.

Itzler remembers, "At the Concord, when Jason Binn said he was the son of a billionaire, and my stepfather told me, yeah, he was, I got light-headed."

In the late eighties, after getting through George Washington University, even though he was "mostly running wet-T-shirt contests," Itzler entered Nova Southeastern University, a bottom-tier law school in Fort Lauderdale, Florida, where he embarked on what he calls "my first great chapter" as "the twenty-two-year-old phone-sex king of South Beach." Advertising a "Free Live Call" (after which a $4.98-a-minute charge set in), Itzler's company was doing $600,000 a month, hitting a million and a half within a year.

"I had so much money," Jason recalls. "I bought an Aston Martin Virage, three hundred feet of oceanfront property. Like a moron, I spent half a million decorating a one-bedroom apartment."

Alas, it would all soon come tumbling down, owing to what Jason now calls a "kind of oversight," which left him owing $4.5

million at 36 percent interest. Forced to declare bankruptcy in 1997, he lost everything, including his visionary acquisition of one of the fledgling Internet's most valuable URLs: pussy.com.

The demise of Itzler's phone-sex company set a pattern that would be repeated in 2000 with his next big act, the SoHo Models fiasco. With typical overreach, Jason rented an eight-thousand-square-foot space at the corner of Canal and Broadway and declared himself the new Johnny Casablancas. Unfortunately for the young models hoping to find their faces on the cover of *Vogue,* the true business of SoHo Models was to supply Webcam porn. For a fee, the voyeur would type in "take off blouse . . . insert dildo." Squabbling among gray-market partners soon ensued. Within months, Jason found himself dangling over the side of the Canal Street building, held by the ankles by a guy named Mikey P.

Jason says he would have gotten through these setbacks more easily if his mother were still alive, but Ronnie Itzler died of cancer in 1994, "after which I went kind of a little nuts." Following the collapse of the phone-sex firm, he twice attempted suicide, once running himself through with a steak knife and on another occasion drinking "a milk shake" he claims contained "75 Valium, 75 Klonopin, and a couple bottles of Scotch." Much to his surprise, he survived both times.

Desperate for money after the SoHo Models disaster, Itzler decided his best option was to go to Amsterdam to buy four thousand tabs of Ecstasy. "In retrospect, it was a totally retarded idea," says Jason, who would leave Newark airport in handcuffs. He was sentenced to five years in the Jersey pen. The fact that his grandfather, whom he'd idolized as a gangster, stopped talking to him when he got locked up "was hard to take."

"Jail is terrible, really boring," says Jason. "But it does give you plenty of time to plan your next move."

———————

ON PAROLE AFTER SERVING seventeen months of his smuggling sentence, living in a funky third-floor walk-up in Hoboken per the terms of his release, Jason started NY Confidential (he would remain on parole his entire pimp career) in late 2003. Business was spotty at first but picked up dramatically in early 2004, when Natalia walked into the company's place at Fifty-fourth Street and Sixth Avenue, an office previously occupied by the magician David Blaine.

"It was my birthday," Natalia remembers. "I'd just been cast as Ingrid Superstar in this play, *Andy & Edie.* I wanted to be Edie, but Misha Sedgwick, Edie's niece, also wanted it, so forget that. I was eating in a restaurant with Peter Beard, the photographer. I was a kind of party girl for a while. I met Peter one night, and we hit it off. He said I should meet this guy Jason."

Beard, a nocturnal bon vivant known for his "discovery" of exotic models like Iman, and who had been associated with Jason during the SoHo Models episode, warned Natalia off Itzler's new venture. Eventually, however, Natalia decided to give Jason a call. "Being an escort never crossed my mind. It wasn't something girls like me did. I was an actress. From a very nice home. But I was involved in an abusive relationship, with this Wall Street guy," she says. "In the beginning, all I wanted was enough money to move out."

Jason says, "When Natalia came over with Peter, I said, *Wow, she's so hot. She has one of the all-time great tushes.* But there was this other girl there, too. Samantha. When she took off her shirt, she had these amazing breasts. So it was Natalia's butt against Samantha's boobies. I went with the tits. But when Natalia came back from making a movie, she moved in with us. Samantha could tell I was kind of more into Natalia. So we become boyfriend and girlfriend."

At the time, Jason's top girl was Cheryl, a striking blonde ballroom dancer from Seattle who says she got into the business to buy her own horse. "I did NY Confidential's first date," Cheryl recalls. "I had on my little black dress and was shaking like a leaf. Jason was nervous, too. He said, 'Just go up there and take your clothes off.' I told him, 'No, you've got to make it romantic. Special.' "

It was Cheryl who came up with the mantra Jason would later instruct all the NY Confidential girls to repeat, "three times," before entering a hotel room to see a client: *"This is my boyfriend of six months, the man I love, I haven't seen him for three weeks . . . This is my boyfriend of six months, the man I love . . ."*

"That's the essence of the true GFE, the Girlfriend Experience," says Jason. As opposed to the traditional "no kissing on the mouth" style, the GFE offers a warmer, fuzzier time. For Jason, who says he never hired anyone who'd worked as an escort before, the GFE concept was an epiphany. "Men see escorts because they want to feel happier. Yet most walk away feeling worse than they did before. They feel dirty, full of self-hatred. Buyer's remorse big-time. GFE is about true passion, something genuine. A facsimile of love. I told guys this was a quick vacation, an investment in the future. When they got back to their desks, they'd tear the market a new asshole, make back the money they spent at NY Confidential in an hour.

"What we're selling is rocket fuel, rocket fuel for winners."

Jason decided Natalia would become his great creation, the Ultimate GFE. It mattered little that Natalia, for all her French Scottish sultriness, might strike some as a tad on the skinny side. Brown-eyed, dark-haired, olive-skinned, not to mention lactose-intolerant, she didn't fit the usual description of a big ticket in an industry filled with PSE (Porn-Star Experience) babes with store-bought bazangas out to here. Jason took this as a challenge. If he was into Natalia, he'd make sure everyone else was, too. It was a simple matter of harnessing the available technology.

The main vehicle was the aforementioned TheEroticReview. com, "the *Consumer Reports* of the escort industry," according to the site's founder and owner, the L.A.-based Dave Elms, a.k.a. Dave@TER. "The most important thing was to break Natalia out big," Jason says. "To get the ball rolling with a number of fabulous reviews, I sent her to some friends, to sort of grease the wheel. I knew those 10/10s would keep coming, because no man wants to admit he got less. They're brainwashed that way."

If any hobbyist had the temerity to hand out a paltry 8/8, or even a 9/10, he would be contacted. "Don't break my girl's streak, this is history in the making," Jason cajoled, offering to throw in a couple hours of free time to get the customer to do a little recalculating. If that didn't work, good reviews could be ensured by the $5,000 everyone working at NY Confidential (except Jason) swears was FedExed to Dave@TER on the fifteenth of every month. Dave, who says he "would not argue with that" when asked if he is the single most important person in the escort business, vehemently denies any payoffs, from NY Confidential or anyone else.

With her 10/10s piling up, Natalia's hourly rate jumped from $800 to $1,200 with a two-hour minimum. (The split: 45 percent for the escort, 45 percent for the agency, 10 percent for the booker.) If clients haggled, they would be told to call back when they were "more successful." Jason says, "I always ask prospective clients to give me strong points about themselves, where they went to school, if they're good-looking. It established rapport but also put them on the defensive, let them know that *I was interviewing them,* to see if they were good enough to go out with our girls."

Jason's hyping sometimes was faintly embarrassing. "Jason would be saying, 'Natalia is the greatest escort in the history of the world, as good as Cleopatra or Joan of Arc,'" says Natalia, "and I'd be like, *'Jason!* Joan of Arc was not an escort, she was a religious martyr.' Then he'd be saying I was the greatest escort since Mary Magdalene."

But all the hype in the world (an Asian toy manufacturer wanted to mass-produce Barbie-style Natalia dolls, complete with tiny lingerie) wouldn't have helped if Natalia, who never imagined she'd wind up staying in "every expensive hotel in New York," hadn't turned out to be a natural.

"I'm a little moneymaking machine, that's what I am," she says as she takes a languorous drag of her Marlboro while stretching out on her apartment couch in a shiny pink satin corset, Marlene Dietrich–style. Then she cracks up, because "you know, the whole thing is so ridiculous sometimes."

People wonder what it is about Natalia that made her the Perfect 10. "From the start, you know this is going to be fun," says one client. "It is like having sex in a tree house." Says another, "Nat isn't this all-knowing geisha thing. But in a way, it's deeper, because she gets to a place inside where you used to be free." And another: "With her, there's none of that shit like this is costing enough for a first-class ticket to London and the girl's in the bathroom for, like, half an hour. Natalia's this one, total this-is-all-about-you."

Suffice it to say, it's in the pheromones. According to Natalia, she's always gotten along with men. "Jason understood who I was," she says. "Yes, he sold the shit out of me, but he sold me as myself, someone anyone can be comfortable with, someone who really likes sex. Because the truth is, I do. I loved my job, totally."

It is another old story, along with the heart of gold, that many "providers" actually like what they do. But even if she professes to be "horrified" by stories about sexual trafficking and "sickened" by nightmarish exploitation of the street prostitute, Natalia says, "At the level NY Confidential was at, the guys I was meeting, I would have gone out with 80 percent of them anyway. People have so many misconceptions, preconceptions, about my life. Last year, I got a call to play an escort in a Broadway play. But the part was so dark, so icky. I said no. It didn't fit my experience at all."

You never knew who might be behind the hotel door. Once, she was summoned to a guy's room, told only that he was a famous, championship athlete. "I'm not a big sports fan, but I recognized him, the quarterback. He turned out to be very laid-back. He mostly wanted to make me happy. In the middle, he looks up and says, 'Well, you know me, I'm more of a giver than a receiver.' "

What no one could have predicted, least of all Natalia, was how driven she would be. "I knew she was talented," Jason says. "But once she started going, she was unstoppable, like the Terminator."

A glance at Natalia's booking sheets raises an eyebrow. Annotated with Jason's exhortatory commentary ("Awesome guy!—$5200, wants to be a regular!" "Big Wall Street guy!" "Software king." "Hedge fund heavy! Says he will give investment lessons!"), the records of Natalia's bookings through June and July of 2004 reveal a workload exceeding 250 hours, or nearly a normal nine-to-five, at an average of $1,000 per hour, not counting little presents like fancy $350 underwear from La Perla.

"Victoria's Secret is all right," Natalia says. "But you know you have a good client when you get La Perla."

Some weeks were particularly frenetic. From July 29 to August 1, she had a four-day date in the Florida Keys for which Itzler charged $29,000. The very next day was a four-hour appointment. August 3 was filled with a ten-hour appointment and another two-hour job. August 4, three hours. August 5, a three-hour followed by another four-hour. August 6, two hours. August 7, one four-hour job and a two-hour. August 8, she was off. But August 9 was another ten-hour day, followed by a pair of two-hour jobs on August 10.

"It was like a dream," Natalia says. "I never got tired."

Asked if the work affected her relationship with Itzler, Natalia says, "Sometimes he'd say, 'Everyone gets a chance to spend time with you except me.' I'd say, 'You're the one booking me.' " As for Jason, he says, "If she ever did it with anyone for free, it would have broken my heart."

Moving from Fifty-fourth Street following a nasty fallout with partner Bruce Glasser (each party claimed the other had taken out a contract on his life), Itzler ran NY Confidential out of his parolee apartment in Hoboken. One visitor describes the scene: "The place was full of naked women and underwear. It was a rain forest of underwear. In the middle on the couch is Jason with all these telephones, one in either ear, the other one ringing on the coffee table."

Seventy-nine Worth Street, with its twenty-foot ceilings and mezzanine balconies, where Jason and Natalia would move to in the summer of 2004, was a whole other thing. "Right away, we knew this was it," says Natalia. "The loft felt like home." As per usual, Jason would take much of the cost of the lease from Natalia's bookings—money she would never receive. But money was never an issue with Natalia. If Cheryl, Jason's first superstar, experienced "a rush of power when the guy handed me the envelope," for Natalia, collecting the "donation," while essential, had a faintly unseemly feel.

"Maybe it sounds crazy," she says, "but I never felt I was in it for the money."

For Jason, the loft was an opportunity to make real his most cherished theories of existence. "To me, the higher percentage of your life you are happy, the more successful you are," says Jason, who came upon his philosophy while reading Ayn Rand. "I was really into the 'Who is John Galt?' *Atlas Shrugged* thing. I thought I could save the world if I could bring together the truly elite people, the most beautiful women with the most perfect bodies, best faces, and intelligence, and the elite men, the captains of industry, lawyers, and senators. This would bring about the most happiness, to the best people, who most deserved to be happy."

Years before, Jason wrote out the precepts of what he called "The Happiness Movement." Assuming his findings to be big news, Itzler packed up the manifesto, a copy of his half-finished autobiography, and a naked centerfold picture of Elisa Bridges, his girlfriend at the time, and mailed it to Bob Woodward. "I stuck it in this three-thousand-dollar Bottega Veneta briefcase so he'd notice it. He said I was a nut job and to leave him alone. I was so bummed I told him to keep the stupid briefcase."

On Worth Street, however, Jason (who says "the best thing about bipolarity is how much you accomplish in the manic phase") saw the chance to manifest his ideal. One of his first acts was to approach painter Hulbert Waldroup. Waldroup, a self-proclaimed "artist with attitude" who has been collected by Whoopi Goldberg and once appeared on the cover of *Newsday* along with his epic memorial to Amadou Diallo, was selling his work on the West Broadway sidewalk. "You're the greatest painter I've ever seen," Jason said. When Waldroup heard Itzler wanted to commission a ten-foot-by-ten-foot canvas of a "hot-looking" woman, he said the picture would never get in the door. No problem, Itzler said, Waldroup could do the painting inside the loft.

Waldroup soon had a job working the phones. "It was like I went in there and never came out," says Waldroup, now on Rikers Island, where he resides a couple of buildings away from Jason.

Seventy-nine Worth Street became a well-oiled machine, with various calendars posted on the wall to keep track of appointments. The current day's schedule was denoted on a separate chart called "the action board." But what mattered most to Jason was "the vibe . . . the vibe of the NY Confidential brand" (there was franchising talk about a Philadelphia Confidential and a Vegas Confidential). To describe what he was going for, Jason quotes from a favorite book, *The Art of Seduction,* a creepily fascinating tome of social Machiavellianism, by Robert Greene.

Discussing "seductive place and time," Greene notes that "certain kinds of visual stimuli signal that you are not in the real world. Avoid images that have depth, which might provoke thought, or guilt . . . The more artificial, the better . . . Luxury—the sense that money has been spent or even wasted—adds to the feeling that the real world of duty and morality has been banished. Call it the brothel effect."

Accentuated by the fog machine at Seventy-nine Worth Street, people seemed to come out of the shadows, float by, be gone again. "It was full of these familiar faces . . . like a soap-opera star, a politician you might have seen on NY1, a guy whose photo's in the *Times* financial pages," says one regular. In addition to Sinatra, music was supplied by the building's super, a concert pianist in his native Russia, who appeared in a tuxedo to play on a rented Baldwin grand piano.

"It was like having my own clubhouse," says Jason now, relishing the evenings he presided as esteemed host and pleasure master. He remembers discussing what he called a "crisis in Judaism" with a top official of a leading Jewish-American lobby group. Jewish women were often thought of as dowdy, Jason said. If the American Jew was ever going to rise above the prejudice of the *goyishe* main-stream, creativity would be needed. A start would be to get Madonna, the Kabbalist, to become the head of Hadassah. The official said he'd look into it.

Seventy-nine Worth Street was supposed to be Jason and Natalia's home, where they would live happily ever after. They had their own bedroom, off-limits to everyone else. "We were actually trying to live a semi-normal life, carry on a real relationship," says Natalia. "Jason felt abandoned after his mother died; my father left when I was very young. We sort of completed each other."

Natalia wrote her mom that she'd moved into a beautiful new place with a highly successful businessman. Her mom, a sweet cookie-baking lady leery of her daughter's life in New York, wrote back that she'd like to come down to visit. Natalia was going to put her off, but Jason insisted. Looking around the loft at the naked women, Natalia asked, "How am I going to have my mom come *here*?" Jason said he would close the place, and take the loss, for the time Natalia's mom was in town. Family was the most important thing, he said.

"Well," Natalia says, "Jason never closed the loft. My mom and I stayed in a little apartment uptown. Jason was supposed to come by to meet her, but it started getting late. Then the doorbell rings at 2:00 A.M. It's Jason, in his knee-length coat with these two nineteen-year-old girls. I'm totally flipping out: *Like, what the fuck are you doing?* He looked like the pimp from *Superfly*. My mom is saying, *'This is him?'* But then Jason sits down and starts telling my mom I'm a great young actress and my career is going to take off, how living in New York is so terrific for me. He charmed her, completely. She left saying, 'Well, your boyfriend is kind of weird. But he's very, very nice.'

"It was always like that."

FEW EXPECTED SEVENTY-NINE Worth Street to last very long. There were too many, as Natalia puts it, "variables."

For Jason, the main difficulty in running New York's hottest escort agency while on parole was the curfew. Even though his lawyer on the Jersey Ecstasy case, Paul Bergrin, was eventually able to extend Jason's lights-out time to 3:00 A.M., he still had to leave his Worth Street happiness house to sleep in his apartment in Hoboken.

"Everyone's partying, having the best time in the world, and the Town Car is outside to take me back to goddamn New Jersey."

"It was a big strain," says Natalia. "I finally get home from my appointments. All I want to do is sleep in my own bed, and Jason is screaming about how we've got to go back to Hoboken. He hated to be alone out there. We had horrible fights. One night, I jumped out of the car right at the mouth of the Holland Tunnel and ran away. Broke my heel on a cobblestone."

The parole situation led to other traumas. Court-mandated drug tests caused Jason to alter his intake. Always "on the Cheech-and-Chong side of things," Itzler couldn't smoke pot, which turned up on piss tests. Instead, Jason, who never touched coke and often launched into Jimmy Swaggart–like speeches about the evils of the drug, dipped into his personal stash of ketamine, or Special K, the slightly unpredictable anesthetic developed for use by veterinarians. "They didn't test for it," Jason says by way of explanation. He was also drinking a $200 bottle of Johnnie Walker Blue a day. Natalia's drug use cut into her Perfect 10 appearance. One night, she cracked her head into the six-foot-tall statue of an Indian fertility goddess Jason had purchased for their room. Knocked cold, she had to go to the emergency room.

Still, the business charged on. It takes a singular pimp to think it is a good idea to stage a reality-TV show at his place of business, but Jason Itzler is that kind of guy. "It was incredible," says independent producer Ron Sperling, who shot the film *Inside New York Confidential*. "Big-shot lawyers and Wall Street bankers flipped when they saw the cameras. Jason told them the movie was no problem. That it was *a good thing*. If they didn't want to be in it, they should just walk behind the camera. That's Jason. If he was a billionaire and no one knew about it, it wouldn't be anything to him."

Despite misgivings about legalities, VH1 expressed interest in *Inside New York Confidential*. Arriving late, Jason swept into the meeting with several girls. Along for the ride was a young Belgian tourist whom Itzler had encountered only moments before on West Broadway. "You're beautiful," Jason told the young woman. "But your clothes look like shit." Itzler bought her $2,500 worth of threads in about ten minutes, convincing her she would be great in his TV show.

"He asked for a million dollars an episode," says a VH1 exec. "We told him that was insane money, so he got mad and left."

Jason's manic spending increased. One afternoon, splashing on Creed Gold Bottle cologne ($175 per bottle) as "kind of a nervous tic," he bought twenty-six antique crystal chandeliers at $3,000 apiece. "We had so much furniture, there was nowhere to walk. I used to jump over the stuff for exercise," says Natalia. "We had this room upstairs we called the Peter Beard Room. Peter likes to sit on the floor, so we got these beautiful Moroccan pillows. One day, I come home, and there's a Playboy pinball machine there, with Hugh Hefner's face on it. Then I knew there was no point saying anything."

Jason's class insecurities also cropped up. One night, upstairs at Cipriani's, Itzler went over to where Lizzie Grubman was sitting with Paris Hilton. He asked Grubman about representing NY Confidential. Grubman, whom Jason regarded as just another Great Neck girl with a rich dad under the glitz, supposedly sneered, "I don't do pimps." Returning to his table, Jason said, "I hate that bitch. She runs over sixteen people and thinks she's better than me."

Jason's Utopian house of happiness turned into a stage for an ongoing paranoid soap opera. Feeling his grip slipping, Itzler begged his former fiancée Mona to help with the day-to-day running of the place. Mona, who had helped organize things in the earliest days of NY Confidential, ran a tight ship. But there were complications. It had been only eight months since Mona had been Jason's girlfriend, living with him in Hoboken. They broke up, leading to an enormous screaming match during which Mona called the police, claiming Itzler attacked her. Jason disputed this, allowing he "might have squeezed her hand too hard, trying to get my keys back." Mona would drop the charges, but not before Itzler spent some time under house arrest.

Jason says, "Maybe I'm just soft, because after Mona wrote the judge a tear-stained letter how I never beat her up and how she loved me, I forgave her." With Jason's parole problems increasingly keeping him in Hoboken, Mona soon filled the power vacuum at Seventy-nine Worth Street. Her key ally would be Clark Krimer, a.k.a. Clark Kent or Superman, a muscle-bound young banker hired by Itzler to manage credit-card accounts. This way, those wanting to disguise their use of NY Confidential services would appear to be spending their $1,200 or so at venues like the fictitious Gotham Steak. Clark and Mona soon became an item, consolidating their power.

The Clark-and-Mona regime upset "the vibe" of Seventy-nine Worth Street, turning it into, in the words of one working girl, "just another whorehouse." First to feel the fallout was Natalia. As queen of the castle, Natalia always dismissed the jealousies of the other escorts as "stupid girl stuff." This was different. She says, "Mona was a psycho-bitch. She hated me, and now she was running the place." When clients called, instead of Jason's rapturous invocations of Natalia's charms, Mona said, "I've got this girl, she's six-one, a rower on an Ivy League college scull team. She's cheaper than Natalia and way better." Natalia's bookings fell off.

One November afternoon, Natalia arrived at the loft to find Mona standing in front of the door to her room—*her room!*—demanding she turn over her keys to the loft. "This is where I live. My home," Natalia screamed. Eventually, however, Natalia decided to move out.

Through this, people began telling Jason he'd better cool things out, not keep bringing parties of vacationing second-grade school-teachers by the loft for fun. With guys in Con Edison vans watching the place from across the street, the least he could do was make sure the front door stayed locked.

"What do I have to hide?" Jason scoffed. "I'm not doing anything illegal."

Much of this self-deluding assessment was based on the contract Jason, utilizing his best Nova U. legalese, worked up between himself and the NY Confidential escorts. The document, signed by all the girls, stated they were "specifically forbidden" to have sex with the clients. Itzler showed the contract to Mel Sachs, the floridly attired defender of Sante Kimes, Mike Tyson, and, more recently, the pint-size exhibitionist-rapper Lil' Kim. Sachs made a couple of adjustments and said the contract passed muster, which was just what Jason wanted to hear.

"I'm bulletproof. Rich people don't go to jail," Jason proclaimed. He was certain that if anything came up, Sachs and Bergrin, a former Army major, could handle it. "Mel's my personal Winston Churchill, and Paul's the tough Marine general," Jason rhapsodized, either unaware or not caring that Bergrin is currently under federal investigation for his alleged part in the death of a police informer slated to testify against one of his drug-dealer clients.

"Mel became my best friend," says Jason, always impressed by a

man in a fancy suit. "He was always in my place. We all loved Mel."
Asked about these visits, Sachs, after some deliberation, said, "Well,
Jason is a personable guy. I liked talking to him. It was an interesting place, full of fascinating conversation. A lot of business people,
financial people, professional people."

Amid this gathering train wreck, one incident in November
2004 stands out as the beginning of the end. That evening, accom-
panied by a mutual friend, two mobsters, members of the
Genovese family, according to Jason, stopped by the loft.

"I never did any business with them. I just thought it might
open a new line of high-priced clients," says Jason, who bought
a $3,500 Dior suit for the occasion, with a matching one for his
bodyguard, a former Secret Service agent. The meeting had barely
begun when a girl named Genevieve burst through the door. A tall
blonde, she was returning from her first NY Confidential date,
reputedly stoned out of her mind, and was demanding to be paid
immediately. Told to wait, Genevieve started yelling, threatening to
call the police to adjudicate the matter.

"What's wrong with that girl?" one of the mobsters asked. Itzler
asked the bodyguard to quiet Genevieve down. But as the bodyguard approached, Genevieve pulled a can of pepper spray from her
handbag and blinded him. With the bodyguard writhing on the
floor, Genevieve locked herself in a room and called 911. A dozen
cops and an engine company of firemen arrived.

There was some debate about whether to open the door, but
the mobsters said, "It's the cops, you got to let them in."

"I'm looking at the security-camera monitors," remembers one
witness. "In one is the cops, another the gangsters, the third the
screaming girl, the fourth the Secret Service guy rubbing his eyes.
That's when I thought I'd take a vacation from this place."

The encounter would end relatively harmlessly. "It looked like
one of the cops recognized one of the gangsters," says the witness.
"They started talking, everyone exchanged business cards and left."

After that, the cops started coming to the loft almost every day.

"They'd knock on the door, come in, look around, and leave," remembers Hulbert Waldroup. Almost always, they took a stack of Jason's distinctive metal ROCKET FUEL FOR WINNERS business cards. The card had become something of a collector's item at headquarters, one cop says. "Everyone wanted one." Rumor has it that one ended up on Mayor Bloomberg's desk, to the mayor's amusement.

When the big bust inevitably came down on January 7, the loft was nearly empty. Krimer and Waldroup were at an art gallery when someone's cell phone rang. The caller said no one was picking up at NY Confidential. That was a bad sign, Waldroup said.

Frantically, Krimer and Waldroup attempted to connect to the Webcam security system Itzler had installed so he could watch the activities at Seventy-nine Worth Street from his Hoboken apartment. The cam was available from any wired-up computer. But no one could remember the password. "Fuck!" screamed Krimer. Eventually the connection was made.

"The place is being raided, and we're watching it on the Internet," says Waldroup. "The cops were like ants, over everything, taking all the files, ledgers, computers. On the couch were these people I'd worked with for months, in handcuffs. It was very weird."

Jason wouldn't find out about the bust until sometime later. "I was shopping for rugs with Ed Feldman, who is kind of a legend in the fashion business," Jason says. It was Feldman who, years before, had given the young Jason Itzler a copy of Budd Schulberg's all-time delineation of the Hebrew hustler, *What Makes Sammy Run?*

"Read it," Feldman said. "It's you."

Jason says, "I immediately checked into the Gansevoort Hotel and began partying. Had a couple of girls come over because I figured I wouldn't be doing that for a while. When the cops came, I thought, 'Well, at least I'm wearing my twenty-eight-hundred-dollar rabbit-fur-lined sweater from Jeffrey's, because who wants to look like a guy in a sweatshirt?' When they snapped on the handcuffs, all I remember thinking was how I thought NY Confidential would last for twenty-five years."

ALMOST SIX MONTHS LATER, Jason is still in jail. In the beginning, he was confident that his lawyers, Sachs and Bergrin, after all that money and all those free drinks, would bail him out. That did not happen. With none of his regulars, the trust-fund babies and famous artists Itzler considered his friends, rushing to his aid, Jason wound up in front of Judge Budd Goodman at the One Hundred Centre Street courthouse, penniless and lawyerless, tearfully asking to defend himself, a request that was denied.

"Ask me if I feel like a sap," Jason says.

Down deep, he always knew that when all was said and done, after everyone had had their fun, he'd be the one to pay for it. With the Bush administration coming down heavy on sexual trafficking—the religious right's top human-rights issue—Robert Morgenthau's office is not of a mind to offer deals to loudmouthed brothel owners, not this election year. As a "predicate" felon from his ill-considered Ecstasy importation, Itzler's facing a four-and-a-half-to-nine-year sentence. Even if he beats that, there is the matter of his busted parole in New Jersey. Sitting in Rikers, playing poker for commissary food, once again Jason has a lot of time on his hands.

One of the things to think about is what happened to all the money that was made at NY Confidential. A common theory, one Itzler advanced in a recent *Post* story, is that Clark Krimer, who may or may not be cooperating with the D.A., took it all.

"He stole four hundred thousand dollars," Jason says. "He should be in jail. If anyone laundered money, it's him." Asked if it was possible that he, Jason, had managed to spend a good portion of the missing money, Itzler scoffs, saying, "Who could spend all that?"

When it comes down to it, however, Jason says he doesn't want to think about Krimer or the fact that Waldroup remains in jail even if he only answered the phones. "I'm staying optimistic," Jason says, free of bitterness. "It is like I told the girls, if you smile a fake smile, keep smiling it because a fake smile can become a real smile."

"The problem with NY Confidential was it didn't go far enough," Jason says now. "If you really want to put together the elite people, the best-looking women and the coolest guys, you can't stop with a couple of hours. It has to be a lifetime commitment." Jason has consulted his prison rabbi, who presided over the recent Passover ceremony during which Itzler got to sit with recently arrested madam Julie Moya (of Julie's) during the asking of the Four Questions. The rabbi told Jason that as a Jewish pimp who sold women to Jewish men, he was liable for the crime of *kedesha.* The rabbi did not, however, think this transgression necessarily prevented Jason from becoming a *shadchan,* or a traditional matchmaker.

"I'm thinking about the future, the next generations," Jason says from his un–air-conditioned prison dorm. "I think I have a chance to do something good before I die. Who knows, the answer to the question 'Who is John Galt?' could be 'Jason.' "

As for Natalia, she is "keeping a low profile." Last week, she went to see Jason again. Thankfully he didn't talk too much about getting married inside the prison. Mostly they talked about the strange times they'd been through and how, even if it turned out the way it did, somehow it was worth it.

"I was a young actress who came to New York like a lot of young actresses, and I wound up with the role of a lifetime. I was the Perfect 10. I totally was. It wasn't the rabbit hole I expected to tumble down, but Jason and I . . . we were happy . . . for a time, really happy."

Since she received hardly any of her booking money and is pretty broke these days, people ask Natalia if she's planning on coming back to "work." The other night, a well-known provider, who said she used to hate Natalia when she was getting those 10/10s, offered to "pimp her out."

"That would be a feather in my cap," said the escort. "To be the one who brought back the famous Natalia."

"No, thanks," said Natalia, which is what she tells her old clients who call from time to time. "I say I'm retired, in repose. They say, 'Come on, let me buy you a drink. I'll be good.' I tell them, 'Look, we had fun and I love you. But that is over.' Mostly, they understand. Some are willing to stay friends, some can't wait to get off the phone. They've got other numbers in their book."

That doesn't mean a girl has to stay home at night. New York, after all, is a big place, full of opportunity. In a way, things have gone back to the way they were before she met Jason. "Wiser, but not necessarily sadder," Natalia says. Tonight she's going downtown. It is always good to look good, so Natalia goes through what was a familiar ritual back in the days when she was the Perfect 10—getting her nails done at the Koreans' on Twenty-ninth Street, combing out her wavy hair. For old times' sake, she's got on what she used to call her "money dress," a short satin pink number with gray jersey inserts, with the shoes to match. About ten, she's ready. She goes out into the street, lifts her arm, gets into a cab, and disappears into the night.

MARK JACOBSON *is the author of several books including the novels* Gojiro *and* Everyone and No One. *His nonfiction books include* 12,000 Miles in the Nick of Time: A Semi-Dysfunctional Family Circumnavigates the Globe, *and the recent* Teenage Hipster in the Modern World. *He has been a contributing editor at* Esquire, Rolling Stone, Natural History, *the* Village Voice, *and works for* New York *magazine. He was born and lives in New York City.*

Coda

The article that wound up getting called "The $2,000-an-Hour Woman" (my original title was "Rocket Fuel for Winners," after the rubric pimpmeister Jason Itzler had engraved on his metal business cards) wasn't easy to find. But once it got going it didn't let up. Partially this was due to the ever-fecund life story of Mr. Itzler, much of which actually appears to be true. Jason is one of those perfect journalistic subjects: a guy with a lot to say who can't wait to say it. In me he had a proper foil because, to reference Sydney Greenstreet in *The Maltese Falcon,* I like listening to a man who likes to talk. As long as that talk stays interesting. Itzler did, even if he did—and continues to—call me at least five or six times a day from his current residence at Rikers Island. That's the real torture for the Sammy Glicks of the world, getting locked up with a bunch of people who simply don't care what he has to say.

The piece's other leading figure, Natalia McLennan, would also wind up in Rikers sometime after the appearance of the story. This was too bad, since as the 1996 tap-dance champion of Canada and former Shakespearean actress (several productions as Juliet in *Romeo and Juliet,* also as Flute in *A Midsummer Night's Dream*) she is definitely not the Rikers type. Luckily, though, she was sprung after a month or so, although not before making the papers back in her Montreal hometown. Natalia, who does indeed have the proverbial heart of gold, did not hold me responsible for this unfortunate period of incarceration since, as she put it, "It wasn't exactly like I didn't expect something to happen after they put me on the cover of *New York* magazine without my clothes on." All told, I would say I met a better, more amusing, not to mention honest, class of people associated with New York Confidential than on my more usual beats, like state and national politics.

Skip Hollandsworth

THE LAST RIDE OF
COWBOY BOB

FROM *Texas Monthly*

PEGGY JO TALLAS WAS, BY ALL ACCOUNTS, the classic good-hearted Texas woman. For much of her adult life, she lived with her ailing mother in a small apartment in the Dallas suburbs. Every morning, after waking up and making her bed, always taking the time to smooth out all the wrinkles in the sheets with her hands, she'd walk into her mother's bedroom. She'd wrap a robe around her mother's shoulders, lead her to the kitchen, fix her cereal, and lay out her pills. For a few minutes, the two of them would sit at the table, making small talk. Peggy Jo, who didn't like to eat until later in the day, would often smoke a cigarette and drink Pepsi out of a coffee cup. Then, after her mother was finished eating, Peggy Jo would gently guide her back to her bedroom, prop a pillow behind her head, set a glass of tap water and her romance novel on the side table, and walk back into her own room to get dressed.

Usually, she liked wearing khaki pants, a simple blouse, and loafers. But on a lovely morning in May 1991, Peggy Jo, who was then forty-six years old, decided to wear something different. She walked over to her dresser, the top of which held a few small glass sculptures of dolphins with iridescent eyes that she had been collecting off and on for more than a decade. She opened one of the lower drawers and pulled out a pair of men's pants and a dark men's shirt. From her closet, she grabbed a men's brown leather jacket that she kept on a hanger. She then reached for a Styrofoam mannequin's head that was on a shelf in the closet. A fake beard was pinned to it and on top was a white cowboy hat.

She took off her nightshirt and put on the clothes along with some boots that were too big for her feet. She stuffed a towel under her shirt to make herself look heavier. She stepped into the bathroom, rubbed some adhesive across her face, pasted on the fake beard, and colored her hair with gray paint she had bought at a costume shop. She placed the cowboy hat on her head, put on a large pair of silver-rimmed sunglasses, and pulled on a pair of gloves. She then took a few minutes to write a note on a sheet of lined paper and put it in her pocket.

"Be back in a minute," Peggy Jo told her mother, tiptoeing past her room. She walked outside, got behind the wheel of her 1975 two-door Pontiac Grand Prix, drove to the American Federal Bank just off West Airport Freeway in Irving, pulled into the parking lot, stepped into the bank's lobby, and headed toward the counter, where a young female teller was smiling cheerfully.

"Hello, sir," the teller said. "How may I help you?"

Peggy Jo pulled out the note she had written. "This is a bank robbery," it read. "Give me your money. No marked bills or dye packs."

The stunned teller handed over a stack of cash from her drawer. Peggy Jo nodded, stuck the money into a satchel, and walked out of the bank. She then drove straight back to her apartment, where her mother was still in bed, getting hungry, hoping Peggy Jo would return soon to fix her lunch.

IN THE CRIMINOLOGY TEXTBOOKS, they are invariably described as products of a deprived socioeconomic background. Most of them are young male drug addicts who don't have the slightest idea what they are doing. When they burst into banks, their fingers twitch and their heads swivel back and forth as they look for security guards. They shout out threats and wave guns in the air. When they get their money, they run madly for the exits, bowling over anyone in their path, and they squeal away in their cars, leaving tire tracks on the road.

And then there was Peggy Jo Tallas. "I promise you, my Aunt Peggy was the last person on earth you would ever imagine robbing a bank," said her niece, Michelle. "Whenever I was in a car with her, she never drove above the speed limit. If anything, she drove below it. And she always came to a complete stop at stop signs."

But Peggy Jo didn't just rob a bank. Beginning with that May 1991 trip to American Federal, she robbed lots of banks. According to the FBI, she was one of the most unusual bank robbers of her generation, a modern-day Bonnie without a Clyde who always worked alone, never using a partner to operate as her lookout or drive her getaway car. She was also a master of disguise, her cross-dressing outfits so carefully designed that law enforcement officials, studying bank surveillance tapes, had no idea they were chasing a woman. What's more, she was so determined not to hurt anyone that she never carried a weapon into any bank she robbed. "I have to admit, I admired her style," said Steve Powell, a former FBI agent who spent most of his thirty-year career chasing bank robbers and who supervised bank robbery investigations for the Dallas office of the FBI in the early nineties. "She knew how to get in and out of a bank in sixty seconds. She was very skilled and very efficient, as good as any man I've ever come across."

Although female bank robbers are not unheard of—it is estimated that women commit less than 5 percent of the some 7,600

bank robberies that take place each year in the United States—
almost all of them are young women who, like most of the men,
rob banks for drug money. And only a few of those women rob
more than a bank or two before they quit or get caught.
Accordingly, when Powell and his team of FBI agents happened to
corner Peggy Jo near her apartment in 1992, they assumed they
would never be dealing with her again. She was one of those
women, they believed, who had succumbed to a strange bout of
middle-aged craziness. She wasn't poor. She wasn't an addict or an
alcoholic. And from what people who knew her said, she was
utterly harmless—"A sweet lady who once chatted with me about
the best way to grow plants on the front porch," one neighbor
noted. Seemingly repentant, Peggy Jo pleaded guilty to bank robbery and quietly went off to prison for almost three years. And that
seemed to be that.

But then, this past May, the story broke that a small bank in the
East Texas city of Tyler had been robbed by a sixty-year-old
woman. The woman was dressed in black, wearing a black wide-
brimmed hat and dark sunglasses that covered much of her face.
She was polite and did not use a gun when she confronted the
teller. She placed the money she received in a black satchel, nodded
"thank you," walked out the door, and climbed into a twenty-foot
Frontier RV with pretty purple shades around the windows. She
turned on the ignition, pushed on the gas pedal, and headed south
on Texas Highway 69, straight out of town.

After all those years, Peggy Jo Tallas had returned.

IF YOU WANT TO UNDERSTAND HER, her friends say, you've
got to go back to Dallas in the late fifties, when she was an irre-
pressibly free-spirited teenager, her hair brownish-blond and curly
and her green eyes as shiny as marbles. "She had a beautiful, wide
smile that made you want to smile back at her," said Karen Jones,
her closest childhood friend. "And what was most special about her

was that she loved doing things other kids didn't do. She once drove me around looking for stray dogs to adopt. And then she took me over to the Yellow Belly drag strip just to watch the cars race."

She was the youngest of three children. When she was four years old, her father died of cancer, and her mother, Helen, found a job as a nurse's aide to support the family. They lived in a tiny rent house in the suburb of Grand Prairie. Peggy Jo's sister, Nancy, was a high school majorette, and her older brother, Pete, played on the district's championship basketball team. Peggy Jo, however, dropped out of high school after the tenth grade. "She told me there was just too much else to do in life than spend so many days at school," Karen said. One day, in fact, Peggy Jo jumped in her car and drove to San Francisco because she wanted to see what life was like there. When she returned, she gave Karen a book of poems written by Lawrence Ferlinghetti, the co-founder of San Francisco's famous City Lights bookstore and an influential Beat poet whose work often decried the emptiness of modern life. (In one of his most famous poems, from *A Coney Island of the Mind,* he described America as a country of ". . . freeways fifty lanes wide/on a concrete continent/spaced with bland billboards/illustrating imbecile illusions of happiness.") "I laughed and thought, 'Of all people, Peggy Jo's been off reading poetry in San Francisco,' " Karen said. "But that was just who she was, always ready for an adventure."

When she was in her twenties, Peggy Jo got her own apartment in North Dallas and started working as a receptionist at a Marriott hotel near downtown. She and another receptionist, a cute blonde named Cherry Young, went out almost every night. Peggy Jo always drove in her little burgundy Fiat, gunning the engine, racing other cars from stoplight to stoplight. They hit all the great Dallas nightclubs: Soul City, the Fog, and the Filling Station, on Greenville Avenue, ordering Coors, playing pool, and flirting with men. They went to see the Doors and the Doobie Brothers and even the Rolling Stones, screaming at the top of their lungs as a young, wrinkle-free Mick Jagger gyrated madly across the stage. Peggy Jo took Cherry to a coffeehouse where amateur poets read out of their notebooks, and they also went to see movies. Peggy Jo's favorite, which she saw over and over, was *Butch Cassidy and the Sundance Kid*. Starring Paul Newman and Robert Redford, the movie tells the story of the famous bank- and train-robbing duo who lived in the last days of the Old West: two good-natured, Robin Hood–like outlaws who never believed that what they were doing was wrong because they never hurt innocent bystanders and they always robbed from institutions that took advantage of downtrodden citizens. Although Butch and Sundance knew they had little chance of survival, they refused to walk away from the life they loved, and they ended up in South America, still robbing banks, finally dying in a hail of gunfire.

According to Cherry, Peggy Jo didn't have any immediate plans to get married and have children, she didn't care about finding the right career, and she didn't worry about money. All she wanted was enough to get by, to pay her bills and have a little left over for a few drinks or a couple of meals each week at El Fenix. "She told me she was saving a little so that she could someday go to Mexico, just to live on the beach in a hacienda and wear bathing suits night and day," Cherry said. "She was beautiful and she was rambunctious. She always told me that deep down she was wild at heart."

But just how wild? One afternoon, when Peggy Jo and Cherry were driving around in the Fiat, they passed a Wells Fargo armored truck, and Peggy Jo made a rather odd comment: "You know, I could go rob that and not have to worry about anything for a while."

"You'd need a gun," Cherry said.

"Oh, heck, I'm smarter than that," Peggy Jo replied.

Cherry laughed. It never once occurred to her that Peggy Jo would ever work up the courage to commit an actual robbery. True, she could get a little feisty: When a police officer pulled her over one evening for speeding, she laughed and tore up the ticket in his face. And there was the night when she and Cherry had a spat at a restaurant in Fort Worth. To calm down, Cherry walked to another bar. A few minutes later, Peggy Jo walked outside and saw an unlocked pickup with the keys in the ignition. She jumped in and drove away. The police caught up with her, and she eventually pleaded guilty to a felony charge of unauthorized use of a motor vehicle, receiving a five-year probated sentence.

Still, it's one thing to go on a joyride in a stolen car after a night of drinking. It's another thing entirely to become an outlaw. "And what everyone needs to remember is that my aunt was a wonderful, loving woman," said Michelle (who asked that her last name not be used). "When she came over to babysit me and my brothers, she made up funny games for us to play, she cooked us popcorn, and then at the end of the night, she told us ghost stories, where the ghosts were always creaking up the stairs and doors were squeaking. She truly had a heart of gold."

HER LIFE WAS NOT WITHOUT disappointment, of course. In the mid-seventies, she told her friends she had fallen in love with a man who lived near Dallas. Then, several months later, she mentioned that the relationship was over. "She told me that she had gone to the town where the man lived and that she had seen his car parked in front of a business," Karen said. "She said she then saw a woman getting into the driver's seat. Peggy Jo walked up to the woman, asked her what she was doing, and the woman said, 'Well, ma'am, this is my husband's car.' Peggy Jo was completely devastated. She had no idea she had been dating a married man."

Not long after that, she moved into an apartment in Irving to live with her mother, who was battling a degenerative bone disease. Peggy Jo found a new job near the apartment at a computer factory, and then she worked in the office of a mobile-home construction company. She remained friends with Cherry, who by then was working as a cocktail waitress. "Every now and then, we'd have an old-fashioned night and hit all the old places and listen to rock and roll," Cherry said. "And one day she called and persuaded me to quit my job so that we could go to Florida and live for a couple of months on the beach."

But by 1980 Cherry had married and moved to Oklahoma City. Peggy Jo's childhood friend Karen had also married. Peggy Jo, who was still quite attractive, with a slender body and, in the words of Karen, "movie star long legs," certainly had plenty of chances to start another relationship, but she kept her distance from men. "I don't think she was ever able to get over the pain of the betrayal from the married man," Karen said. "I think she decided to be alone."

A year passed, then another, then another. And suddenly, just like that, it was 1984, and Peggy Jo was forty years old, with lines tracking out from the corners of her eyes and a touch of gray slipping into her hair. She found another job working for the Pony Express Courier Service, driving a van up and down Dallas's freeways, past a series of bland billboards, and delivering packages to businesses, and she also moved with Helen to a new apartment in another Dallas suburb—the Pecan Knoll Apartments, in Garland—to be closer to Michelle and her family. (Peggy Jo's sister, Nancy, was then living in East Texas; Peggy Jo and her brother, Pete, who had had disagreements in their younger years, were rarely speaking.)

Over the next couple of years, she endured her own medical problems. She injured her back and later underwent an emergency mastectomy, which kept her in bed for several weeks. She also began taking anti-anxiety medication, in large part because her income and her mother's Social Security checks barely covered the bills, especially as her mother's medical costs rose. "I think she was beginning to feel like she could never catch up," said Cherry, who occasionally came down from Oklahoma City to visit. "And she was too proud to ask anyone for help. She liked helping people. She didn't want people to help her."

Cherry paused. "And there's another thing that was going on with her," she finally said. "This is hard to explain, but I think Peg was starting to feel, well, like her life was slipping away. Do you know what I mean? It's the way women get sometimes. You get to a place in your life and you start looking back and you say to yourself that it's not working out the way you hoped. You think everything is slipping away and you feel—I don't know—crazy. You want to scream or something."

Cherry paused again. "I think Peg missed being wild at heart."

SHE HAD TO HAVE BEEN SCARED out of her wits when she walked into American Federal in Irving in May 1991. Although a note-job bank robbery does not involve the same kind of drama as an old-fashioned bank heist, in which the robber tunnels through the walls and blows apart the vault, it is still an incredibly daring act, a very public performance that is not only witnessed by employees and customers but is also always caught on tape.

Amazingly, however, Peggy Jo did not commit any of the amateur mistakes that many first-time bank robbers make. She kept her head down so the security cameras could not get a good shot of her face. She did not fidget as the teller read her note. During those long seconds that ticked away as the teller pulled the money out of her drawer, she remained absolutely silent, saying nothing. Then came that long walk out of the bank, when she had to be wondering if a security guard she had not seen was coming up behind her, a gun in his hand. But she did not break into a run. Nor did she squeal away in her car, running red lights and drawing more attention to herself.

In fact, after the FBI's Steve Powell interviewed bank employees and watched the surveillance tapes, he had no doubt that he was dealing with a professional bank robber. Powell, who grew up in the small Panhandle town of Tulia, eventually noticed that the robber had worn his cowboy hat backward. And he figured that the beard was fake. But it never occurred to him that the suspect wasn't a man.

In December 1991 Peggy Jo, dressed in the same outfit, stole $1,258 from the Savings of America, which was also located in Irving. This time, an eyewitness was able to write down the license plate number of the Grand Prix. But when Powell's agents tracked the license plate and converged on the owner's home not far from the bank, they found a lady sitting in her living room who said she had not been out of the house that day. She took them outside to show them her car, which was a red Chevrolet. That's when she noticed that the license plate was missing. Obviously, the FBI agents said, the bank robber had stolen the license plate earlier that day and put it on his own car to mislead them.

A month later, Peggy Jo struck again. This time, she moved to the other side of Dallas, hitting the Texas Heritage Bank in Garland for approximately $3,000. In May 1992 she robbed $5,317 from the Nations Bank in the adjoining suburb of Mesquite. During the robbery, she wisely handed back a stack of bills that contained a hidden dye pack, a small package that is triggered to explode a few seconds after it passes underneath an electronic eye positioned at a bank's exit, staining the money with permanent ink and sometimes staining the robber himself.

By then, Powell had named the robber Cowboy Bob. "And he was making me start to pull my hair out," he said. "How could this thin, little dried-up cowboy be whipping us this bad, time after time?"

In September 1992 Cowboy Bob robbed First Gibraltar Bank in Mesquite of $1,772. Police officers roared up in their squad cars, followed about ten minutes later by several vehicles filled with FBI agents. They tracked the license plate on Cowboy Bob's car to a Mesquite resident who, predictably, went outside to his driveway to find his license plate missing.

Then, while agents were wrapping up their investigation at First

Gibraltar, a call came in that Mesquite's First Interstate Bank, about a mile away, had just been robbed by a man in a beard, a cowboy hat, a leather coat, and gloves. And he had hit the jackpot, escaping with $13,706. He was so pleased, the teller said, that he gave her a kind of salute as he left, tipping his hat with his gloved hand.

"Cowboy Bob is at it again!" shouted Powell, jumping into his car and racing toward First Interstate. "Son of a bitch!"

This time the license plate that an eyewitness saw on Cowboy Bob's brown Pontiac Grand Prix was traced to a man named Pete Tallas. FBI agents found Tallas at work at a Ford auto parts factory in nearby Carrollton. "The agents asked me if I owned a Grand Prix with a certain license plate number, and I said, 'That's right,' " recalled Peggy Jo's brother. "I told them I had given it to my mother and Peggy Jo a year or so back because they couldn't afford a car. They said, 'It was just used in a bank robbery.' I said, 'Bullshit, that car can't go fast enough.' "

Pete gave the FBI the address of Helen and Peggy Jo's apartment. When Powell and the other agents arrived, they spotted the car in the parking lot. As they discussed the possibility of storming the apartment and catching Cowboy Bob red-handed, they saw a woman in shorts and a T-shirt walk toward the car.

Powell stared at her. "It must be Cowboy Bob's girlfriend," he murmured to the other agents. They allowed her to drive away from the apartment so that the assumed boyfriend wouldn't see them. When they finally stopped her around the corner, Powell introduced himself to the woman, who politely said hello and told him her name was Peggy Jo Tallas. She admitted that the car was hers, and she said she had driven it earlier that morning to a nursery to buy fertilizer. Powell opened the trunk of the car: There was, indeed, a bag of fertilizer. He asked her if he could look around her apartment. For a moment, just a brief moment, she paused. No one was in the apartment, she said, except for her sick mother.

Helen slowly eased herself out of her bed after she heard the doorbell ring and walked to the front door. She opened it and screamed as the FBI agents darted past her, their guns drawn. They moved into Peggy Jo's bedroom. Her bed was immaculately made, and all of her clothes were hanging neatly in her closet.

"What the hell?" said one agent.

Then, looking on the top shelf in her closet, another agent saw the Styrofoam mannequin's head with the beard pinned to it. He noticed the cowboy hat. When he looked under the bed, he saw a bag full of money.

"Come on, Peggy Jo, you're hiding a man from us," Powell said.

She gave him a look. "There isn't any man," she said. "I promise you that."

Powell kept studying her. That's when he noticed the spots of gray dye in her hair and the faint splotches of glue above her lip. "I'll be damned," he said as he pulled out his handcuffs. He read Peggy Jo her rights and drove her to the downtown FBI office, where other agents were waiting. "Gentlemen," Powell said, "Cowboy Bob is actually Cowboy Babette."

THE NEWSPAPERS, OF COURSE, had a field day, writing story after story about the cross-dressing bank robber who used her mother's apartment as a hideout. The reporters hunted down Peggy Jo's relatives, but they refused to say anything, in large part because they were so stunned about what Peggy Jo had been doing. "We had absolutely no idea," Michelle said. "We asked Helen if she knew what Aunt Peggy had been doing, and she kept saying, 'Robbing banks? Peggy was robbing banks?' "

Powell himself, realizing he had the case of a lifetime, did what he could to get Peggy Jo to talk. He wanted to know how she had learned to rob banks in the first place. He also wanted to know why she had decided to rob two banks in one day and why, before the second robbery, she didn't take the time to steal another license plate. Had she gotten so cocky that she thought the FBI would never catch her? "If she had just followed her usual routine," Powell later said, "we could still very well be wondering who Cowboy Bob really was."

But Peggy Jo wouldn't tell him anything. Nor would she say much to her court-appointed attorney, who then hired Richard Schmitt, a psychologist who specialized in evaluating criminals, to interview her. During their session, she eventually admitted that she had decided to rob a bank to pay for her mother's medications. But she certainly had no intention of robbing a second bank, she said. Or a third or a fourth, she continued, pulling out a cigarette and lighting it.

Schmitt could not take his eyes off her. Up until that point, he had interviewed approximately fifty bank robbers, all of them male. He had never before interviewed what he described as "a nice, normal-looking woman" who crossed her legs while she talked with him. "So why did you keep robbing banks?" he asked her.

But Peggy Jo never answered. She kept staring at a wall, shrugging her shoulders and shaking her head as if she wasn't sure what else to tell him.

"I guess it was hard for her to admit just how much fun she had being a bank robber," Cherry said.

Perhaps because she carried out her crimes without using weapons—or perhaps because the judge agreed with the defense attorney's argument that Peggy Jo's behavior was "completely out of character"—she received a mild, thirty-three-month sentence. Michelle later went to see her at the federal prison in Bryan. "I knew that she was unhappy, confined to a cell most of the day," Michelle said. "But she came out smiling, and she asked me all about me and my daughter. She didn't say anything to me about the bank robberies. She didn't say a single word. She just said it was something that would never happen again."

A true-crime author contacted Peggy Jo while she was in prison, asking her to collaborate on a book and perhaps sell it to Hollywood and make a lot of money, but she turned him down.

"She told me she didn't want to embarrass her family with more publicity," Cherry said. "And I think she also was determined to put that part of her life behind her."

Peggy Jo did try to put it behind her. By the mid-nineties she was out of prison and back living with her mother. To avoid the stares of their neighbors at the apartment complex, they moved to a two-bedroom townhome in Garland, 1,120 square feet in size, with a tiny backyard. She spent most of her time with her mother, whose hands by then were shaking so badly that she couldn't hold her own silverware. Every night, she gave her mother a bath and put her to bed. Then Peggy Jo sat alone in her bedroom, usually watching nature documentaries on the Discovery Channel until late at night.

For a while she worked as a telemarketer, going to an office for a few hours a day and making cold calls, offering whoever answered the phone the opportunity to receive a catalog filled with lovely home decorative items. She later found a job as a cashier at the Harbor Bay Marina, at Lake Ray Hubbard, just outside Dallas, selling customers everything from coolers to minnows to those key chains that float in the water. "She was one of our best employees," said Suzy Leslie, who was then a manager at the marina. "Not once did the money in the cash register come up short on her shift. And what I loved about Peggy Jo was that she checked on the poorer customers. She was constantly pulling out her own money to help some of the families pay for bait. She used to visit with a poor Vietnamese woman who came out here to fish off the docks for her family's supper. There was a man who came out here who was deaf, and Peggy would write down questions on a sheet of paper, asking him if there was anything he needed. And I know she used to give some money to a man out here who had been in prison and was still down on his luck. One day I asked her why she did that, and she said, 'Well, we all got a past, you know.' "

Occasionally, at the end of the day, some man at the marina would ask Peggy Jo if she'd like to join him for a cocktail at

Weekends, a little restaurant nearby that had a dance floor next to the bar. But she'd turn him down. She'd tell him she needed to get back to her house to look after her mother. Maybe next time, she'd say, giving the man an apologetic smile. Then she'd sweep the floors, take one more stroll around the docks, watch the sun set, and head for her car.

Once again, a year passed, and then another. Peggy Jo lost touch with her old friends like Cherry and Karen. Her sister, Nancy, died of breast cancer, and in December 2002 Helen died in her sleep at the age of 83. Peggy Jo was at her mother's bedside, holding her hand. "She could have put her mother in a nursing home a long time ago," said Suzy, who by then had become close friends with Peggy Jo. "But when we talked up at the marina, she said to me that she wanted her mother to be at home, to live out her last years in dignity, sleeping in her own bed. She was relieved her mother was no longer in pain, yet you could tell she was still heartbroken. She couldn't talk about Helen without tears coming to her eyes."

At Helen's funeral, Peggy Jo and her brother reconciled. She later went to the annual Christmas dinner that Pete and his wife put on for the Tallas family. "She was friendly to all of us, she loved the kids, and when I asked her what she was going to do now, she said she had some plans," Pete said. "But she never told me what they were."

IN THE SPRING OF 2004 Peggy Jo approached a man at the marina who was selling a Frontier RV. She gave him $5,900 in cash and promised to pay him $500 more at a later date. She told Suzy that the time had come to move on. "She said she was going to put some money together and head down to Padre Island or to Mexico and live on the beach like she had always wanted to," Suzy recalled. "She told me I ought to come along while I had the chance, before life ran out on us. I'll never forget her saying that. 'Before life ran out on us.' "

Peggy Jo sold or gave away all of the furniture in her townhome, and she sold an old Volvo she had been driving. She carried a few potted plants over to a neighbor's front porch, and then she drove away in her RV—"Just flew the coop," one neighbor later said. For a few weeks, she stayed at a public park near Lake Ray Hubbard, spending part of the day fishing or walking along the shore, watching the herons fly across the water. Occasionally, Michelle came out in the late afternoons to visit. She and Peggy Jo would sit on maroon folding chairs next to the RV. Peggy would drink Pepsi out of a coffee cup and smoke Merit menthol cigarettes, grinding them out in a little ashtray she held in her hand.

"Sometimes she'd turn on the radio and listen to old rock and roll from her younger days, groups like Lynyrd Skynyrd and Bob Seger," Michelle said. "She'd watch the sun set and then she'd go inside the RV and pull out a skillet and cook up some fajita meat with chopped onions. You know, it wouldn't have been the life I would have chosen for myself, but I couldn't help but admire her, doing her own thing and doing it her way. She loved being completely free."

In the late summer of 2004, Peggy Jo left a telephone message for Carla Dunlap, another friend from the marina. When Carla had developed breast cancer the previous year, Peggy Jo had checked on her nearly every day and had brought her a cap to wear when her hair began to fall out from chemotherapy. "On the message, she asked how I was doing and she said she was about to hit the road," Carla said. "And then she said, 'And no matter what happens to me, always remember that I love you.'"

Concerned, Carla's husband, John, drove out to the park to see if he could find her and perhaps give her some money, but she was already gone.

WHERE PEGGY JO WENT still remains the subject of great speculation. Months later, people would say that they had seen her at

Lake Texoma and Lake Lavon. Others would say they had seen her driving her RV through various East Texas towns. And some would say they had seen her in Tyler in October 2004, right about the time that an odd bank robbery occurred at the small Guaranty Bank on the southern edge of the city. According to the tellers, the robber was an older man with a round stomach and a scraggly mustache; he wore a dark floppy hat, baggy clothes, and gloves. He placed a green canvas bag on the counter and said, "All your money. No bait bills. No blow-up money." Then, after receiving a stack of cash (the authorities would not say exactly how much), he walked out of the bank and down a street. No one got a glimpse of his getaway vehicle.

One of the tellers did tell FBI agents that she was struck by the softness of the robber's voice; it sounded a bit feminine. What's more, the teller said, the robber's mustache appeared to have been glued on, and his stomach looked more padded than real.

Perhaps if Steve Powell was still working for the FBI, he might have had an idea who had committed the robbery. But by then he was retired, living on a ranch outside Lubbock, occasionally teaching seminars to bank employees about how to spot a bank robber. At the end of each seminar, he'd pass around a photo of Cowboy Bob and tell her story with a certain relish, like a man reminiscing about his first lover.

The agents who were investigating this robbery, however, brought in an older male suspect to take a lie detector test. After he passed with flying colors, they began investigating other men. If they had been told that their suspect was a sixty-year-old spinster who drove an RV with pretty purple curtains, they would have laughed out loud.

Peggy Jo's own family certainly had no suspicions that she had returned to her secret life. Periodically, throughout the fall of 2004 and the early months of 2005, she would call them from pay phones, telling them she was doing just fine. One afternoon, Michelle ran into Peggy Jo at a Wal-Mart in Garland where Peggy

Jo was picking up supplies—a couple cartons of cigarettes, some paper towels, and fajita meat. "She seemed to be in great spirits," Michelle said. And this past May—May 4, to be exact—Pete happened to be in Kaufman County, east of Dallas, when he heard that Peggy Jo's RV was parked next to a small lake on a farm owned by a relative. "I drove out to see her, and we spent about an hour together," Pete said. "She pulled out a bunch of family photos from a big old box, and we looked at all of them. I've got to tell you, we had a really good time, the two of us. Then she told me she was going to be packing up shortly and leaving, hitting the road, going on one of her adventures. I said, 'You okay, Peggy Jo?' And she hugged me and said she was happy, and then I said, 'See you later.' "

THE NEXT MORNING, Peggy Jo woke up and made her bed, smoothing out the wrinkles in the sheets and spreading a fake sheepskin blanket over the mattress, making sure the bottom edge of the blanket was as straight as a ruler. Nearby, hanging from two wooden rods, were her nicer clothes: a few pairs of blue jeans, a couple pairs of khaki pants, and six blouses, all of them neatly ironed. But on this particular morning, she put on a black long-sleeved shirt and a pair of black pants that she kept in a plastic drawer. From a shelf, she grabbed a sandwich baggie filled with makeup and applied some lipstick and rouge to her face, and she ran a brush through her graying hair. She looked at herself in a mirror that she kept on another shelf, right next to some photos of young children with freckles and lopsided grins—her grandnieces and grandnephews—and she then made her way to the front of the RV, where she kept a variety of sunglasses and wide-brimmed hats along with a couple of black wigs and hair extensions.

After choosing a large black straw hat that came down over her forehead and a pair of black sunglasses that practically covered the top half of her face, Peggy Jo slipped into the driver's seat and drove to Tyler, parking her RV next to a Jack in the Box, which happened to be across the street from Guaranty Bank, the very bank that had been robbed the previous October. Holding a black satchel, she stood at the street corner waiting for the traffic light to change; then she headed for the bank. She walked through the front door, past a sign in the lobby that read "You Need the Right Tools to Build Your Dreams," and said to the teller, "This is a robbery. I need all of your money. Don't set any alarms."

The teller, a young woman barely out of her teens, gave Peggy Jo everything she had in her drawer: $11,241. Peggy Jo's heart had to have started racing. This was big. This was like the robbery back in Mesquite in 1992. All she had to do was get out of there and head south, and she could finally get to Mexico and start her new life on a beach.

In her haste to get away, however, she made one simple mistake. She didn't check for a dye pack. It exploded as soon as she walked out the door, covering the money with red ink. A plume of red smoke also began to rise from the satchel as she headed back across the street, dodging traffic to get to her RV.

The smoking satchel caught the attention of a TXU crew working in cherry-picking buckets above the street. A young Tyler couple named Chris and Courtney Smith, who were driving away with their children from a nearby Wal-Mart, also saw Peggy Jo. Because of her disguise, however, they couldn't tell whether they were watching a woman or a man dressed as a woman. "I bet that person robbed a bank," Courtney said, dialing 911 on her cell phone while Chris whipped the car around to follow Peggy Jo, ordering the children in the backseat to keep their heads down.

It just so happened that a group of FBI agents and Tyler police officers were out in their cars that very morning, cruising the streets. They literally were searching for bank robbers. Three banks had been robbed recently in the Tyler area, and the authorities believed that two or three young black men were the robbers.

As a matter of fact, when the police radios crackled with the news about Guaranty Bank, Jeff Millslagle, the burly senior agent in charge of the FBI's Tyler office, had just begun to interview a young black man in the northern part of the city who had been caught driving a stolen car. Millslagle and other FBI agents raced south in their unmarked SUVs. Officers from the Tyler Police Department also came roaring toward the bank, their sirens screaming, as did state troopers from the Department of Public Safety.

Within minutes, a posse of law enforcement officers and such curious citizens as Chris and Courtney Smith and their children were right behind Peggy Jo as she headed down the highway. Because the RV was going up a hill, it was not able to get above the speed limit. Its gears grinding, it lumbered past the Colonial Hills Baptist Church, the Heritage Baptist Church, a movie theater, and a skating rink. Exhaust billowed out of the tailpipe and floated over a field of bluebonnets blooming in the highway's median.

Peggy Jo made one last-ditch attempt to get away, suddenly hitting the brakes and turning the RV into a quiet, middle-class subdivision at the edge of the city. She immediately turned again, onto the poetically named Irish Moss Drive. Before she could get to the end of that street, however, a couple of police cars raced past the RV, boxing it in. Officers in bulletproof vests leaped out of their cars, some holding handguns, a few holding rifles. One officer crouched near an azalea bush; another bent down behind a tree. One of the residents on Irish Moss Drive grabbed his video camera and stood in his doorway to film whatever was going to happen next.

The truth was that no one was exactly sure who was in the RV. The police dispatcher had reported that the bank robber was possibly a white female, but the officers could not rule out that the robber was one of their black suspects who had disguised himself as a woman. Nor could they rule out the possibility that other members of the bank-robbing gang were inside the RV, all of them wielding guns.

Minutes ticked by. Because the curtains were pulled across the windows, the officers were unable to see inside. Some of those close to the RV were saying the things that officers always say in such situations. "Come on out, now." "You're surrounded." "Just make it easy on yourself."

From what could later be determined, she sat at the RV's little kitchen table, smoking a Merit, the smoke drifting from her nostrils. On the floor next to the table was her black satchel, the money useless, almost all of it stained red. A couple of feet away from the satchel was her fishing pole, and beside the pole was her box of family photos.

Who knows what she thought about during those moments? Surely she had to have realized that she was facing a long prison sentence. Maybe, if she was lucky, she would get a couple of hours a day in a prison yard where she could feel the sun against her face. Maybe, if she was lucky, she would be released before she died.

A few more minutes passed.

Finally, Peggy Jo went back to her bedroom, where a .357 Magnum loaded with hollow point bullets was hidden underneath a pillow. But she didn't touch that gun. Instead, she picked up a toy pistol that she also kept in the bedroom. She had bought it, apparently, to carry with her in case she ever needed to threaten a bank employee in a future robbery.

She walked to the door and opened it, her hands at her sides. The police officers who had surrounded the RV could not believe what they were seeing: an unassuming woman in a wide-brimmed hat. A woman who was the age of their grandmothers.

"You're going to have to kill me," she said.

"Ma'am, you don't have to do this," replied one of the officers, a young man who would later be advised by his superiors to seek counseling for the guilt that would haunt him.

"You mean to tell me if I come out of here with a gun and point it at y'all, you're not going to shoot me?"

"Please don't. Please don't do that," yelled another officer.

But then she took a step out of the RV, and from the doorway her hand emerged, holding the toy pistol. Just as she began to lower it, four officers fired, the sound of the shots echoing off the surrounding houses and Peggy Jo's RV.

The bullets came at her all at once, hitting her at nearly the same time, and she didn't even stagger. She fell forward, like a stalk of celery being snapped.

Once she hit the ground, however, she somehow found the strength to pull off her sunglasses. For a moment, she lifted her head. That May morning, the light was like honey. A soft breeze blew across the yard. From somewhere came the sound of pigeons cooing. Peggy Jo looked up at the dense new foliage of a sweet gum tree that rose above her. Then she closed her eyes and died.

STILL ASSUMING THAT ACCOMPLICES were in the RV, a police SWAT team shot tear gas canisters through the windows and stormed through the front door, stepping over her fishing pole and box of photos and turning toward the bedroom. They stared at the bed, still perfectly made up, and at a couple of glass dolphin sculptures on the windowsill. After the "all clear" was announced, one officer found a small baggie of marijuana and another officer found her purse, which contained thirty-eight dollars in cash and her driver's license. The FBI's Millslagle ran a records check and realized that the dead woman was none other than Cowboy Bob. He called Steve Powell at his ranch and left him a message, saying he had some bad news about his old nemesis.

Powell called back. "Say it ain't so," he said almost wistfully.

"Yeah, I'm afraid we killed Peggy Jo," Millslagle said.

For the FBI, of course, the biggest question was how many other banks had Peggy Jo robbed. Some agents wondered if she had tried a bank robbery or two back in the sixties, when she was a freewheeling young woman tooling around Dallas in her burgundy Fiat. Others wondered if she had begun her career in the seventies, when she had been caught stealing the pickup. It is not an uncommon practice, after all, for a bank robber to avoid detection by using a stolen car as a getaway vehicle and then later abandoning it. Still others wondered if she had returned to robbing banks soon after her release from prison. After studying the evidence from the October 2004 robbery at Guaranty Bank, Millslagle did conclude that Peggy Jo was the robber. But that only led to other questions. Why had she gone back to that bank? Was she imitating her heroes Butch Cassidy and the Sundance Kid, who had once robbed the same train twice? And why didn't she dress as a man for that second Guaranty robbery? Why also did she decide to speak to the teller instead of handing the teller a note? Was she hoping that FBI agents would study the bank's surveillance tapes and realize she had returned?

Meanwhile, newspaper and television reporters once again hunted down Peggy Jo's relatives. But they stayed silent. "I didn't know what to tell them," said Pete, who's now retired and living in Plano. "I mean, none of it made the slightest bit of sense. Surely Peggy Jo had to know that if she was in some kind of financial jam again, we would have helped her out."

About thirty members of the Tallas family and a few of Peggy Jo's friends gathered at the Kaufman city cemetery for a private burial service. In an impromptu eulogy, Michelle told a story about Peggy Jo's adopting a wounded duck at the marina and naming it Bernice. One of Michelle's brothers read some Scripture and then said, "I am certain that in the few minutes leading up to her death, as she sat in her RV contemplating her fate, Peg was making peace with God."

There was a long silence. Michelle and Karen covered their faces with their hands and wept. "Okay, I guess we're done," said Pete, nodding at the undertaker, walking away before anyone could see the strain on his face.

Cherry Young, still living in Oklahoma, wasn't at the funeral. She didn't hear about Peggy Jo's death until August, when she called Pete to catch up. "There still isn't a night that goes by that I don't wake up and think about her," Cherry said. "Sometimes I can't get over the sadness that she's gone. But then I think about her walking out of that bank, sixty years old, that bag full of money, and I have to say that she went out doing what she loved. We'll never understand it, but she was doing exactly what she loved. I wish I could write her a note and say, 'Good for you, my sweet Peg. Good for you.' "

SKIP HOLLANDSWORTH *was raised in Wichita Falls, Texas, and graduated with a bachelor of arts degree in English from Texas Christian University. He has worked as a reporter and columnist for newspapers in Dallas, and he also has worked as a television producer and documentary filmmaker. Since joining* Texas Monthly *in 1989, Hollandsworth has received several journalism awards, including a National Headliners Award, the National John Hancock Award for excellence in business and financial journalism, the City and Regional Magazine Gold Award for feature writing, and the Charles Green Award for outstanding magazine writing in Texas, given by the Headliners Club of Austin. He has been a finalist four times for the National Magzine Awards, the magazine industry's equivalent of the Pulitzer Prize, and his work has been included in such publications as* The Best American Crime Writing *and* The Best American Magazine Writing.

Coda

Because Peggy Jo Tallas was so secretive, never telling one friend about another, hiding even the most simple details about her life from her own family, I wrote the story convinced that, as soon as it was published, I would hear from people who had known her. I thought they would tell me that I had missed certain key insights into her personality that would have helped me understand why she robbed banks. But for weeks, there was nothing. Then, six months after the article was published, I received a two-sentence letter, obviously written by an elderly person: "Mr. Hollandsworth—the Peggy Jo I knew was a gentle, loving woman who devoted her life to her mother. If the police knew her like I did, I think they would have let her keep driving."

Jeffrey Toobin

KILLER INSTINCTS

Did a famous prosecutor put the wrong man on death row?

FROM *The New Yorker*

MANY AMERICAN COURTHOUSES have a Kenneth Peasley. For years, he was the most feared prosecutor in Arizona's Pima County, which includes Tucson. He was widely known as the government lawyer who wouldn't plea-bargain, who left his adversaries seething, and who almost always won. When defense lawyers got together, they would talk about how Peasley had stuck his finger in their clients' faces, or how he wouldn't greet them in the hallway. "The defense lawyers hated him," Howard Hantman, a Pima County Superior Court judge, said. "But I always thought that was because he was so good. Watching Ken was like watching great theatre. He had an instinct for the jugular like no prosecutor I ever saw."

Peasley was more than just a local phenomenon. From 1978 until last year, he tried more than two hundred felony cases, including a hundred and forty homicides, and handled about sixty capital cases. He gave lectures around the country about how to try murder cases, and he won national awards. Steve Neely, who, as the county attorney, was Peasley's boss for eighteen years, said, "He was absolutely the most effective prosecutorial performer that I have ever seen or heard of." Peasley, a two-time state prosecutor of the year, is personally responsible for a tenth of the prisoners on Arizona's death row.

Last year, Peasley acquired another distinction: he was disbarred for intentionally presenting false evidence in death-penalty cases—something that had never before happened to an American prosecutor. In a 1992 triple-murder case, Peasley introduced testimony that he knew to be false; three men were convicted and sentenced to die. Peasley was convinced that the three were guilty, but he also believed that the evidence needed a push.

During the years of Peasley's rise and fall, the exoneration of prisoners on America's death rows has become increasingly common. According to the Death Penalty Information Center, since the mid-nineteen-seventies a hundred and seventeen death-row inmates have been released. Defense lawyers, often relying on DNA testing, have shown repeatedly how shoddy crime-lab work, lying informants, and mistaken eyewitness identifications, among other factors, led to unjust convictions. But DNA tests don't reveal how innocent people come to be prosecuted in the first place. The career of Kenneth Peasley does.

Although new evidence suggests that the co-defendants may have had nothing to do with the crime for which they were convicted, Peasley still believes that he prosecuted the right men. "I have never seen a case where I believed the prosecutors set out to prosecute someone whom they believed to be innocent," says Rob Warden, the director of the Center on Wrongful Convictions at the Northwestern University School of Law, whose staff members were involved in eleven of the eighteen recent exonerations on Illinois's death row. "They just get wedded to a theory and then ignore the evidence that doesn't fit." According to Barry Scheck, who co-founded the Innocence Project, which has won exonerations for more than a hundred and fifty convicted defendants, "After a while, some veteran prosecutors think that they can just trust their gut. Once you get to the point where you believe your instincts must be right, you quickly get to the point where you just deep-six inconvenient evidence."

One of the men Peasley prosecuted in the 1992 case is still on Arizona's death row. Unless a court intervenes, that man, Martin Soto-Fong, who was a seventeen-year-old high-school dropout at the time of the murders, will be executed, although no date has been set. The case already ranks as an extreme example of prosecutorial misconduct, but if Martin Soto-Fong is killed for a crime he didn't commit, it will stand for something far worse.

SHORTLY AFTER TEN O'CLOCK on the night of June 24, 1992, in Tucson, an anonymous caller dialed 911 and said, "Yeah, I just walked into the El Grande. It's on Thirty-sixth, and uh, there are two, uh, guys that work. . . . They laying down on the floor, and one's laying in a pool of blood, and there's no one in the store."

The operator apparently recognized the reference to the El Grande Market; the battered, one-story painted-brick store was a landmark of sorts on the desolate streets of South Tucson—a desert ghetto of vacant lots, trailer parks, and auto-repair shops. When the police arrived at the scene, they found that the caller had understated things. There were three, not two, people on the floor, two dead and one dying from gunshot wounds. They were Fred Gee, forty-five years old, the store manager; Zewan Huang, seventy-five, Gee's uncle, who also worked there; and Raymond Arriola, thirty-one, who had started at the market as a clerk the previous month. Peasley soon arrived on the scene, as did Joseph Godoy, a detective with the Tucson Police Department.

This was familiar duty for Peasley. Shortly after he joined the Pima County prosecutor's office, in 1978, he agreed to be the first lawyer called to most murder scenes, and he held on to that demanding assignment, often working with Godoy, for almost two decades. For several months after the murders in the El Grande

Market, there were no viable suspects, and pressure built in the local press for a break in the case. One headline in the Arizona *Daily Star* read, "TRIPLE MURDER HAS POLICE PUZZLED."

WITH A POPULATION of about half a million people, Tucson is one-third the size of Phoenix. The contrast between the two cities extends to politics and is exemplified by the difference between their two most famous sons, Morris Udall and Barry Goldwater. "Tucson is as far away from Phoenix as San Francisco is from Los Angeles," Bruce Babbitt, a former governor of the state, told me. "Phoenix was built on the pursuit of monetary gain, and Tucson was built around the university, which has given a kind of intellectual and idealistic strand to its politics." Tucson, however, never turned into a desert version of Berkeley or Cambridge. "There's always been a dark side to Tucson, too," Babbitt said. "The mob was a significant presence for years, with the Bonnano family living there. The drug trade, with the proximity to the Mexican border, has always been a problem."

Government, including law enforcement, dominates Tucson in the way that business, notably real-estate development, controls Phoenix. Dingy municipal buildings, not gleaming office towers, predominate in downtown Tucson. A couple of forlorn palm trees, and a cactus here and there, offer the only reminders of its desert setting. The county attorney's office long ago outgrew its quarters in the courthouse and now occupies nine floors in a dreary building a few blocks away. There, from a corner office on the tenth floor, Ken Peasley could watch storms roll in over the Santa Catalina Mountains.

Peasley would sometimes arrive at his desk before dawn to prepare for trials, which he often scheduled back to back. His appetite for trial work was matched by a compulsive streak outside the courtroom. He arranged the papers on his desk in rigidly precise piles. He chain-smoked. He drank a case of Pepsi a day. (Later, he lost thirty pounds just by switching to diet soda.) "For me, it wasn't a job," Peasley told me. "It was who I was and what I did."

Peasley was early for our first meeting, which was at my hotel's restaurant. He doesn't look like someone who could dominate a courtroom. He's on the short side, more shrunken than fit at fifty-seven, with thinning gray hair and a wispy beard, and he dresses in the civil-service uniform of white shirt, striped tie, and oversized aviator glasses. His voice, though, is a low growl that demands attention, and he talks in emphatic declarative sentences, like a man unaccustomed to interruption. The ordeal of his disbarment may have taught him a little humility, but just a little. He's more angry than sorry.

Peasley's father, a sign painter, and his mother, a legal secretary, moved from Michigan to Mississippi to Texas; they settled in Tucson when Ken was in junior high school. He attended the University of Arizona for college and law school, and served as an intern in the public defender's office. Stanton Bloom, who is still a prominent defense lawyer in Tucson, recalled, "I was supervising Ken, and we were raising an insanity defense in a case where my guy blew someone's head off with a shotgun. And we interviewed a witness who said my client was acting 'like the wild man of Borneo.' Later, I needed Ken to testify about that conversation, and he said he didn't remember and didn't have it in his notes. I could tell Ken just didn't like defending people. I told him he ought to get a job as a prosecutor, and he did."

As a deputy county attorney, Peasley thrived, finding satisfactions that had eluded him in his personal life. An early marriage ended in divorce, and Peasley does not see the two children from that union. His second wife, Elizabeth Peasley-Fimbres, was also a prosecutor, but that marriage ended after Peasley had an office romance with a college-student intern. (Peasley-Fimbres is now a juvenile-court judge in Tucson.) A third marriage also failed. Peasley and his fourth wife, a nurse, have been married for twenty years, and have teenage twin boys. "What he did for his job was his first love—more than women, more than his children," Lea Petersen, the former intern, told me. "It was his identity."

Peasley never tried to make friends in the courtroom. "I didn't believe in playing grab-ass or glad-handing during trial," he said. "If I went to trial on somebody, frankly, I was convinced that they had done something really bad and I didn't think that it was funny. So during the trials, no, I didn't kid around a lot. There was nothing to kid around about, from my point of view." Defense lawyers regularly asked judges to make Peasley stop glaring at their clients. "I was something of an asshole," Peasley said.

THE BURDEN OF THE EL GRANDE investigation fell to Peasley and Joe Godoy. Peasley and Godoy made an odd pair. Godoy is genial and outgoing, where Peasley is taciturn and severe. Godoy is thickly built, with a big thatch of black hair and a drooping mustache that curls down to his chin. When he talked about the El Grande murders, the case that led to his departure from the force, he never appeared defensive or unsure. "Joe is just totally likable, and juries loved him," Judge Hantman said. "He was very soft-spoken, very credible, very sympathetic." First thrown together at crime scenes, Peasley and Godoy started working cases as a team, and then became friends.

The courthouse crowd in Tucson flees from downtown at every chance, and at lunchtime judges, cops, and politicians line up for Mexican food at Rigo's, in South Tucson, about fifteen minutes away. Godoy doesn't so much patronize Rigo's as preside there, in both English and Spanish. "I tried to think about El Grande the way a bad guy would," he explained, as we sat in a booth at Rigo's. "You had all these people killed, so maybe it was a stranger or maybe it was someone who knew them. So I decided to find all the people who had worked at the El Grande. It took weeks, but I found everyone except this one guy, this guy named Martin. I knew he was just a kid, and I kept just missing him. He was moving apartments, staying in different places. At first, I thought it was two different people, one named Soto and the other named Fong. Then I realized it was only one guy, Martin Soto-Fong, and he had never been prosecuted, never even photographed or fingerprinted. I was looking for him, but I was always one step behind him. I needed to make him or clear him."

The situation became even more pressing for Godoy and Peasley when a similar crime took place on August 26th: in the course of a robbery, masked gunmen shot the owner of Mariano's Pizza, though he survived. "Mariano's Pizza was something similar to El Grande because they shot someone when they didn't have to," Godoy said. "I learned from these other detectives that they were going to arrest these two guys, Chris McCrimmon and Andre Minnitt, and I wanted to be part of the arrest teams. I said, 'After you're finished with them about the robberies, I want to talk to them about the homicides at the El Grande.'" McCrimmon and Minnitt, both in their early twenties, were arrested, with Godoy's help, on September 2, 1992.

BY THAT POINT, Godoy and Peasley regarded Soto-Fong, McCrimmon, and Minnitt as suspects in the El Grande murders, although there was little evidence against them. Then they discovered Keith Woods, who became the key witness in the case.

Woods, who was friends with Christopher McCrimmon, had been in prison on a drug charge. Although Woods was only twenty-one years old, he was already a three-time felon. When he was released, on August 21, 1992, McCrimmon picked him up to drive him home. A few days later, Woods was arrested for possessing cocaine, a parole violation that subjected him to a sentence of twenty-five years to life. Faced with this prospect, Woods told the detective who arrested him that he knew something about several recent crimes in Tucson, and detectives eventually steered him to Joe Godoy.

On September 8, 1992, Godoy sat down with Woods at Tucson police headquarters for an interview, which was tape-recorded. According to the transcript, Woods said that after McCrimmon picked him up from prison they met with their mutual friend Minnitt, and the two men revealed that they, along with a third man, committed the El Grande murders. In that interview, Woods said he knew the third person only as "Cha-chi," but he later said that it was Martin Soto-Fong. Woods also said that McCrimmon and Minnitt played a role in the Mariano's Pizza case. Peasley and Godoy decided not to pursue the parole-violation charges against Woods.

The use of criminal informants poses difficulties for prosecutors, because such witnesses can be extremely manipulative. Some informants lie, telling prosecutors what they want to hear, because they think they can get themselves a better deal. "You have to be tremendously careful that you don't give them ideas," says Stephen Trott, a federal appeals-court judge and former prosecutor, who lectures widely on the ethics of using informants. "They know that the best way to stay out of jail is not to hire Johnnie Cochran but, rather, to turn on someone else. At a moment's notice, they will make stuff up and give it to you. With an interested witness, you do not lay information on the table and let him snatch it and say he knew it already."

As far as Peasley was concerned, Woods solved two high-profile crimes: the El Grande murders and the Mariano's Pizza shooting. Peasley told me that he understood the risks of dealing with Woods. "He had priors. He was a drug user at the time. He had one of just about everything a witness could be impeached with," he said. "So he wouldn't have been my first choice. But he was who I had. And I was satisfied from the information he was giving that it was accurate."

Armed with Woods as a witness, Peasley brought charges against McCrimmon, Minnitt, and Soto-Fong. The first El Grande trial, in 1993, was against Soto-Fong, who had worked at the store a few months before the murders. After the tip from Woods, Tucson police investigators determined that Soto-Fong's prints matched those that had been found on plastic bags and a food stamp found at the scene. In light of this, Peasley said, "probably a third-year law student could have convicted Fong." The court appointed James Stuehringer, a respected Tucson lawyer and a friend of Peasley's, to defend Soto-Fong.

During the Soto-Fong trial, Stuehringer criticized the way Godoy had handled the evidence, especially the items with the fingerprints. Peasley defended Godoy with characteristic zeal, and, in the end, won a conviction and a death sentence against Soto-Fong. The trial deepened the bond between Peasley and Godoy. "I thought that Ken did a really good job putting everything back together and saying I'm not a bad cop," Godoy told me. Godoy was so moved by Peasley's defense of him that when he married for the third time he asked Peasley to perform the civil ceremony. (Tucson law enforcement is a small world, and Godoy's wife is also a Pima County prosecutor.)

In 1993, Peasley also won convictions in joint trials against McCrimmon and Minnitt—first in the Mariano's Pizza case and then in the El Grande murders, with Keith Woods as the key witness. Apart from Woods's testimony, there wasn't much evidence against McCrimmon and Minnitt in the El Grande case. Eyewitnesses described a gold Cadillac as the getaway car, and McCrimmon's fingerprints were found on a car that was parked a few blocks away from the El Grande; but that car was neither gold nor a Cadillac.

It was in these trials, in 1993, that Peasley started bending the truth about the evidence. He knew that a jury would have suspicions about a dubious character like Keith Woods, so he tried to enhance Woods's credibility, urging jurors to believe Woods because what he'd told Godoy was "something that Woods could get only from those people who were directly involved in causing the deaths" of the three victims. Peasley said that investigators knew nothing about the three defendants until Woods volunteered the information during his interview, on September 8, 1992. McCrimmon and Minnitt were sentenced to thirty-six years in the Mariano's Pizza case and to death in the El Grande murders. With the convictions of the three men now complete, the case vanished from the front pages of the Tucson papers and the defendants began their wait on death row.

Only a moment's hesitation by a single juror kept the case alive. Immediately after the verdicts were announced in the 1993 murder trial of McCrimmon and Minnitt, the judge did the customary polling of the jury. In answering whether he agreed with the verdict, one juror wavered, saying, "God, I can't say 'yes' and I can't say 'no.' "After further questioning by the judge, the juror went along with the verdict, but three years later, in 1996, the Arizona Supreme Court ruled that the juror had been coerced, and ordered a new trial for the two defendants. (The appeals court, however, separately upheld Soto-Fong's conviction and death sentence.) For their second trial, which did not take place until 1997, McCrimmon and Minnitt were assigned new lawyers. McCrimmon drew Richard Lougee.

RICK LOUGEE AND KEN PEASLEY could pass for fraternal twins. Both men are fifty-seven, of medium height and weight, with gray hair and a gray beard. Peasley has a slicked-back pompadour, Lougee the tousled look of an aging hippie. Though made from similar raw material, the two men come out of different worlds. Like Peasley, Lougee took a circuitous route to Tucson. He was born into a middle-class family in Connecticut, educated at Franklin and Marshall College, and started law school at Duke in 1969. At that point, he was drafted into the Army, where he served as a stateside chaplain's assistant; after he was discharged, in 1971, he went to Tucson to study Romantic poetry at the University of Arizona. But he didn't have the patience for academic life, so he returned to law school, graduated in 1977, and began a career as a defense attorney. He lived in Connecticut, New Mexico, and Key West until he remembered how much he had liked Tucson as a graduate student and returned there, with his second wife, in 1988. He spent six years with the public defender's office and opened a private practice with a friend the following year. "Because we were just starting out and didn't have any clients of our own, we applied to the county for what were called 'contract' murder cases," Lougee told me. "The first one I got was Chris McCrimmon."

Lougee and I were talking in the small adobe house, across the street from the university, where he lives with his wife, who works for him as a paralegal, and their twelve-year-old son. By the late nineties, Lougee had been a defense lawyer for more than two decades, and he had few illusions about the system, or about his own clients. "I normally don't ask my clients whether they're guilty," he told me. "Personally, I don't care. But the first thing Chris said to me was 'Dawg, I didn't do it.' Frankly, it didn't make much of an impression. I've tried hundreds of cases. I've heard it all from clients before."

Late one night, shortly before McCrimmon's retrial in 1997, Lougee started reading the transcript of Woods's first tape-recorded interview with the police, the one on September 8, 1992. Lougee noticed that, during the course of that long, rambling conversation, Woods made a brief reference to an earlier discussion with Godoy. "I said to myself, 'Holy shit, Joe had talked to him before,' " Lougee said. "I see how Peasley has been finessing this issue. He's been arguing to the juries that Woods must be telling the truth because there is no other way that Woods could have known this information. Now I see that's not true. It becomes clear to me that Woods didn't come up with those names—Godoy did."

At the last minute, in 1997, the judge severed McCrimmon and Minnitt's joint trial into separate cases. Minnitt went first, and Lougee walked into the courtroom to listen to some of the testi-

mony, because the same witnesses would also be testifying in the
McCrimmon retrial. Peasley asked Godoy about his initial interview with Woods: "When you first sat down and talked with Mr.
Woods on September 8 of 1992 . . . had you come up with the
name Chris McCrimmon?"

"No, sir," Godoy said.

"Had you come up with the name Andre Minnitt?"

"No, sir."

Godoy further testified that he had never heard of Martin Soto-
Fong before the September 8th interview.

Peasley drove the point home: "The first time you heard any of
those three names would have been in the conversation with Keith
Woods on September 8, 1992?"

"Yes," Godoy replied.

"I knew that Godoy had committed perjury in that trial,"
Lougee said.

Minnitt's second trial ended in a hung jury, and he remained
incarcerated on his conviction in the Mariano's Pizza case.
McCrimmon's retrial—Lougee's case—began within a few days of
Minnitt's. When Lougee prepared, in August of 1997, he made a
chart laying out evidence that Godoy had lied in the previous trial.
During the retrial, faced with proof that he had elicited false testimony from Godoy, Peasley responded by attacking Lougee for raising the issue.

"Peasley was leaning on the counsel table, hissing at me. His
saliva was on me," Lougee recalled. "His finger was six inches away
from my face." Repeatedly, in a series of heated conferences with
the judge, Peasley expressed shock that Lougee could question his
integrity, and dared the defense lawyer to lodge a formal complaint
against him.

"He is accusing me of suborning perjury, and if he is going to
make those accusations," Peasley said to the judge outside the hearing of the jury, "he should have filed a—"

"Hold it," the judge interjected.

Peasley later challenged Lougee directly in the courtroom: "If Mr. Lougee thought this was perjury, he should have filed a complaint. He hasn't done that."

Nevertheless, Lougee proceeded to demonstrate to the jury that, in fact, Keith Woods had not spontaneously volunteered the names of the suspects in the El Grande case. After just forty-two minutes of deliberation, the jury acquitted McCrimmon of the murders. "When the jury came back, Chris picks me up in his arms and says, 'See, dawg, I told you! I told you!' " Lougee recalled. Later that day, Lougee began drafting his complaint about Peasley to the Arizona state bar. "I didn't celebrate," he told me. "I went and filed a bar complaint"—on September 5, 1997. Lougee added, "It has cost me dearly."

But Peasley remained a power in the county attorney's office. In April of 1998, Barbara LaWall, who succeeded Steve Neely as county attorney, appointed Peasley as head of the criminal division, making him the top prosecutor in her office. (In April of 1999, Minnitt went on trial for a third time for the El Grande Market murders, without Peasley as the prosecutor, and was again convicted and sentenced to death.) Even with his new administrative duties, Peasley continued trying and winning cases, and in 1999 he received a national honor—the Association of Government Attorneys in Capital Litigation's Trial Advocacy Award. Lougee, on the other hand, found that his professional life was getting harder. "From the day I brought the complaint, I basically stopped getting plea offers for my clients from that office," Lougee said. (Pima County officials deny that they retaliated against Lougee's clients. "I think Rick Lougee suffers from considerable paranoia from time to time," LaWall told me.) Judges, prosecutors, and even defense lawyers rallied to testify for Peasley. Lougee had few supporters; among them was Richard Parrish, a Tucson lawyer and friend, who says, "This guy discovered extreme wrongdoing in a capital case by the most respected prosecutor in Tucson and brought it before judges and before the bar, and was excoriated at every instance for doing such a thing to such a great man."

Still, the bar complaint did move forward, and Peasley had to get a lawyer: he chose his old friend James Stuehringer, who had unsuccessfully represented Martin Soto-Fong in the first El Grande trial, in 1993, and who had his own reasons to be grateful to Peasley. In early 1998, Stuehringer's son Craig was arrested in Cincinnati for possessing a hidden gun while dealing drugs, a crime that carried a mandatory three-year prison term, and Peasley intervened on the young man's behalf. Peasley urged the Ohio judge to allow Craig to do community service rather than serve a prison sentence. (In the end, the judge reduced the charges so that Craig Stuehringer could receive a sentence of probation.)

JAMES STUEHRINGER, a gregarious midwesterner with a head full of carefully barbered salt-and-pepper hair, practices civil and criminal law at one of the larger firms in Tucson. The obvious question is whether Stuehringer had a conflict of interest. How could he defend the prosecutor against charges of misconduct in the very case that had put one of his clients on death row?

"I was done representing Fong," Stuehringer told me over lunch at Rigo's. "I had taken his case all the way to the United States Supreme Court, which declined to take his case. I had written him a letter saying, 'I worked my ass off for you, and I wish you well,' " Stuehringer said. "The accusations against Ken just had to do with McCrimmon and Minnitt. So was there a conflict in representing Peasley? I sat down with my partners to talk about it, and they said, 'There's no conflict, but be prepared for some shit.' "

Karen Clark, the lawyer who conducted the bar association's investigation of Peasley, tried repeatedly to get Stuehringer thrown off the case but failed. Lougee saw Stuehringer's role as symptomatic of the cozy nature of law practice in a small city like Tucson, not to mention a betrayal of a client who faced execution. "You don't take on the representation of the guy who is charged with misconduct in a case when you were the attorney for the other side unless you are basically saying, 'No harm, no foul,' " Lougee said. "By representing Peasley, Stuehringer was basically admitting that Soto-Fong was guilty. It's appalling."

Godoy and Peasley, not surprisingly, felt wronged by the investigation. "I was just really upset that I had to go through all this," Godoy said. "I was upset with the system, how far they had gone, and the lack of support from my own command staff." Because of Peasley's and Godoy's prominence in Tucson, a prosecutor from outside Pima County investigated the two men for obstruction of justice, and ultimately obtained an indictment of Godoy for perjury. The indictment meant that Godoy had to retire from the police force, though because he had twenty years' tenure he received a full pension. Godoy's lawyer, Michael Piccarreta, told him that prosecutors had offered him a plea. "They said, 'We'll give you a deal'—guaranteed probation if I turn on Ken and say that he was obstructing justice," Godoy recalled. "Now, I don't cuss that much and it takes me a while to get upset, but I told Mike, 'Fuck no.' I didn't want to lie to get an indictment on Ken." The criminal case against Godoy was finally assigned to a Pima County judge, Lina Rodriguez, who promptly dismissed the indictment on the unusual ground of an "overzealous" presentation to the grand jury. (The same judge later wrote a letter to the bar association as a character witness on Peasley's behalf.) In all, Godoy felt only modestly repentant about the experience: "Did I make a mistake or mistakes? Sure, I did. I'm not going to say I didn't, 'cause it's pretty obvious I did. Were they intentional? Did I need to do it to get somebody in prison? Of course not."

For a long time, Peasley's case stayed within the Tucson legal community. After more than a year of intermittent hearings, the bar association offered to drop the matter if Peasley would accept censure—a punishment well short of disbarment. Peasley turned it down.

He miscalculated. By rejecting the censure, he let the process continue, and as lawyers outside Tucson began to see the facts of his case the potential consequences grew. "In hindsight, of course, you're going to second-guess yourself for not taking the censure," Peasley told me. "I didn't do anything 'intentionally' or 'knowingly' wrong. I was not willing to take a censure for something I didn't think I did."

But, as the case moved forward, Peasley's defense evolved from a complete denial of wrongdoing to something more nuanced. First, he pointed out that the case against him had been built using documents that he himself had turned over to the defense in the El Grande cases. Eventually, Peasley's defense turned into a request for pity—something he rarely dispensed as a prosecutor. During the Minnitt trial in 1997, Stuehringer wrote in a brief, Peasley had "vision problems, periodic vertigo, mini-strokes, difficulties in focusing and concentration," so his "physical problems and workload were affecting his ability to function as a lawyer in the courtroom." But his health problems in 1997 didn't explain why he had put forward the false evidence in 1993. Today, Peasley doesn't exactly defend his conduct, though he insists that any mistakes he made were unintentional. "I'm the one who screwed up," he told me. "I gave them the opportunity to claim what they claimed and to say what they've said. And I don't miss that. And I'm responsible for that."

In 2002, the Arizona Supreme Court overturned Minnitt's conviction and death sentence and ruled that double jeopardy barred another trial, which would have been his fourth. "The record is replete with evidence of Peasley's full awareness that [Godoy's] testimony was utterly false," the justices wrote. "Peasley's misdeeds were not isolated events but became a consistent pattern of prosecutorial misconduct that began in 1993 and continued through retrial in 1997." Like McCrimmon, Minnitt was now left to serve out the remainder of his thirty-six-year sentence for the Mariano's Pizza shooting.

Finally, on May 28, 2004, the court, following up on its criticism of Peasley in the Minnitt opinion, ordered him disbarred, noting that his behavior "could not have been more harmful to the justice system." On behalf of a unanimous court, Justice Michael D. Ryan wrote, "A prosecutor who deliberately presents false testimony, especially in a capital case, has caused incalculable injury to the integrity of the legal profession and the justice system."

Even with Peasley's disbarment, the story of the El Grande murders was not over. Just a few weeks before that decision, the Arizona court had issued another unanimous order: a warrant of execution for Martin Soto-Fong. The defendant, the court wrote, "shall be executed by administering to MARTIN RAUL SOTO-FONG an intravenous injection of a substance or substances in a lethal quantity sufficient to cause death, except that MARTIN RAUL SOTO-FONG shall have the choice of either lethal injection or lethal gas."

THE ARIZONA STATE-PRISON COMPLEX, in Florence, sits on a barren stretch of desert about fifty miles off the main highway between Phoenix and Tucson. Inside the old prison yard is a small, one-story blue stucco structure that is identified on the outside as "Housing Unit 9." It's better known as the death house. The arrangement inside the building reflects the choice now available to Martin Soto-Fong. A carpeted room for spectators has one window facing the gas chamber and another facing the room holding the gurney used for administering lethal injections. (The only sign inside the building is an Air Quality Control Permit, issued by the Arizona Department of Environmental Quality to "the Florence Prison Gas Chamber.") Meg Savage, a genial middle-aged woman who is a warden at one of the units in Florence, took me behind the window to the gas chamber itself, where the swinging metal door was open. "You can sit in it if you like," she said.

Death row in Arizona has a dramatic history. In 1982, a condemned prisoner known as "Banzai Bob"Vickers killed another death-row inmate by setting him on fire; he soaked toilet paper withVitalis, set it aflame, and threw it between the bars of the man's cell. (Vickers was executed in 1999.) In 1997, another condemned prisoner, FloydThornton, was weeding the prison vegetable garden when his wife drove up to the fence and tried to help him escape. She started shooting an AK-47 assault rifle and a .41-calibre revolver, but both Thornton and his wife were killed after guards returned the fire. These incidents, coupled with the general trend toward ever-greater prison security, have led Arizona to establish one of the most restrictive death rows in the country.

The condemned are now housed in a new prison building, known as Special Management Unit II, about two miles from the death house. They stay in their eight-by-twelve-foot cells all day, every day. They may take three showers a week and have up to ninety minutes of recreation, also three times a week.They may not take prison jobs.The recreation facility is a cement-walled twenty-three-by-eleven-foot pen with a rubber ball and a surveillance camera. For days at a time, many death-row inmates may not see another human being. "We are right up there with any super-max in the country," Meg Savage says.

Martin (pronounced Mar-TEEN) Soto-Fong is now thirty and has been on death row for eleven years. He's about five feet six, with a slight build. His ancestry is Chinese and Mexican; he's starting to lose the straight black hair that he had when he was arrested. His voice is soft, and his English has improved during his years in prison. "He's one of the quieter guys we have on death row," Lieutenant Glenn Pacheco, a corrections officer who helps to supervise death row, said. "We never get any trouble from him." Soto-Fong was eight when his family moved from Mexico to Tucson, where his father supported the family as a construction worker. Five years ago, Soto-Fong's mother, who was of Chinese descent, committed suicide, which he attributes to her sorrow over his situation. "I can see her depression, just seeing me going through this," he told me. "I can see that it was putting her through a real difficult time. So, yeah, this had everything to do with it, I believe." As for himself, Soto-Fong said, "I just try to stay as busy as possible. Read. Work out. Write my family. I stay involved in my case a lot. I read a lot of transcripts and whatever my attorneys send me. . . . Just try to do whatever I can to keep myself busy."

He shows some bitterness toward his former attorney Jim Stuehringer, who now represents Ken Peasley. "To this day, I hold some, you know, a bit of anger towards him, and I just feel very betrayed," he said. But he also says he's confident that he, like McCrimmon and Minnitt, will one day be vindicated in the El Grande case. "I have no doubt," he said. "And I believe with all my heart that Peasley and Godoy know that I'm innocent."

Several years ago, during the bar proceedings against Peasley, Rick Lougee turned his attention to Soto-Fong. Working on his own time, along with a paralegal, Linda Lavis, Lougee became convinced of Soto-Fong's innocence and was just as obsessive on the subject as he was in pursuit of Peasley's disbarment. "My wife said this case would make me crazy," Lougee said, with a half smile. "She was right." Progress was as slow on Soto-Fong's case as it was on Peasley's, and Lougee has at times been despondent about that one, too. Two years ago, Lougee sent an e-mail to some lawyer friends that concluded, "Martin told Joe [Godoy] when he was arrested, 'You're framing me.' Martin was right. Godoy, Peasley and that prick, the ultimate prick Stuehringer, are trying to kill an innocent kid. Someone needs to stop this, but I can't do it alone. I'm tired, broke and nearly suicidal. Please help."

ONE DAY IN TUCSON, I asked Ken Peasley to take me to the El Grande Market. Reopened under new management and renamed Jim's, the market still looks much as it did in 1992, with long aisles full of inexpensive merchandise and a cash register near the front.

Standing by the entrance, Peasley narrated his version of how the murders took place, largely on the basis of the fingerprint evidence and the testimony of Keith Woods. "Soto-Fong went to the produce counter, which used to be in the back, and picked up some cucumbers and lemons," Peasley said. "He put them down on the counter, and something happened between him and Mr. Gee, the owner. Something happened between the two of them, and then it became a fucking shooting gallery. They got about three hundred dollars, a hundred dollars a body. Strange thing was, there was all kinds of money in cigarette cartons in the back, but they didn't see it or something, because it was still there after the murders.

"Fong had worked there, so he knew they would recognize him," Peasley went on. "So if he was going to allow somebody to recognize him, they were going in there with the idea of taking the money and killing the people who were there. To this day, that's what I believe happened." Fingerprints identified as Soto-Fong's were found on plastic bags (which had contained the lemons and cucumbers), as well as on a food stamp, and that helped to convict him.

Lougee has tried mightily to discredit the fingerprint evidence. At the murder scene, he says, Godoy collected and processed the plastic bags in a haphazard way, and delayed forwarding them to the crime lab. It isn't clear whether the food stamp with Soto-Fong's fingerprints is the one that appears in photographs of the scene, and there was conflicting testimony about whether it came from the cash register or had been found on the floor near Gee's body. (Since Soto-Fong had worked at the El Grande a few months earlier, it would be possible for his prints to turn up there.) At the time of the investigation, the fingerprint examiner, Timothy O'Sullivan, who had made significant errors in earlier cases, was suffering from terminal cancer and was heavily medicated, raising questions about his focus and attention. It is peculiar that O'Sullivan, who died before the trial in 1993, identified only Soto-Fong's prints on the evidence, and not those of anyone else who worked at the store. It is also odd that other produce bags at the store had a red line across the top but the one with Soto-Fong's prints, did not.

Nonetheless, by the time Peasley was disbarred, Lougee despaired of finding conclusive proof that Soto-Fong was innocent. Lougee could not look to Keith Woods, the dubious informant, for help. After testifying against the El Grande defendants, Woods moved to Nevada, where he was convicted on federal cocaine charges and sentenced to thirteen years in prison. In 2001, Woods pleaded guilty to possessing marijuana and heroin in prison and received a sentence of an additional twenty-seven months. (In response to a letter from me, Woods asked that he not be mentioned in this article.)

By now, Soto-Fong had been assigned new lawyers for a final appeal in federal court, so Lougee was ready to turn the files over to them. "I was so obsessed that my wife was getting ready to leave me," he told me. "I thought to myself, I don't need this anymore. I decided to take another murder case from the county, a woman named Carole Grijalva-Figueroa. Simple case. Shooting at a Circle K. And then one day Carole says to me, out of the blue, 'Do you remember El Grande?' "

TO LOUGEE, the government's theory of the El Grande murders—that it was a botched robbery—never made much sense. The perpetrators allegedly stole just a few hundred dollars, and they left thousands more in cash lying around the store. Photographs from the night of the murders show several cigarette cartons full of cash that had been left in plain view. Peasley said that he thought the killers panicked and forgot to take the cash—or that they never saw the money in the first place—but the motivation for the murders had never been entirely clear.

The South Tucson neighborhood was full of drug dealing and, in the early nineties, a great deal of drug violence. In the days following the murders, Peasley and Godoy seem to have investigated the possibility that the murders had a drug connection. Godoy received a tip that a man named Ernest King, who had ties to the Tucson drug world, might have been involved in the murders at the El Grande. Godoy interviewed King, checked his prints, and gave him a lie-detector test, which he passed.

"We can tell when somebody's lying. We can smell these things," Godoy told me. "King was clean." Once Keith Woods appeared on the scene, the investigation of a drug connection was dropped.

Carole Grijalva-Figueroa, who is thirty-four, was arrested in January, 2004, for her role in a fatal shooting outside a Circle K convenience store in Tucson. As part of a religious awakening, Lougee says, Grijalva-Figueroa has told him of her association with the city's drug underworld, and that included a connection to the El Grande murders. According to a transcript of a statement that Grijalva-Figueroa made to a private investigator, which she acknowledges in a brief telephone interview, the murders were a revenge killing over drugs. Grijalva-Figueroa said that, in June, 1992, a friend learned that about sixty-five pounds of cocaine that he partly owned had been stolen—and that "the El Grande guy" had tipped off the people who took it. As a result, her friend and two other men went to the store on the night of June 24th to exact retribution. "I was supposed to be the lookout," she said, adding that she waited in a gold Cadillac while three men went inside.

"I sat and I waited. Heard a bunch of yelling. And I heard shots," she said, according to the transcript. She drove the three men from the scene, and heard one of them say, "Did you see I got that motherfucker point-blank?" As for Martin Soto-Fong, Chris McCrimmon, and Andre Minnitt, Grijalva-Figueroa said that she didn't know them.

Grijalva-Figueroa's version of events raises many questions, as Lougee acknowledges. It is, for example, hard to square Grijalva-Figueroa's version with Soto-Fong's fingerprints on the plastic bags—if those bags were really the ones found by the register and those prints are really his. "I know it seems impossible that, out of all the cases in the world, I happen to get this woman out of the blue who solves the one case I've been obsessed with for years," Lougee said. "I know there will be people who think that I fed it to her, or she didn't say it, or that it's just too pat. I can't help it. But I believe her story is true." Grijalva-Figueroa, who is in protective custody, fears for her safety, and, according to Lougee, has said that she may deny any knowledge of the El Grande case if she feels that testifying will jeopardize her further. "How do you present a case like this to a jury?" Lougee said. "You're better off as a defense attorney if you can just point to a single lie or a couple of them. No one will ever believe you if you say the whole thing is a lie."

KENNETH PEASLEY ISN'T THE only prosecutor who has got into trouble in Pima County lately. David White, who preceded Peasley as the head of the criminal division, failed to disclose more than eight hundred pages of potentially exculpatory documents to defense lawyers in a first-degree-murder case; the county was compelled to dismiss the charges. (White died in 2003.) In July, the Arizona Supreme Court suspended the law license of a third veteran prosecutor, Thomas Zawada, for six months and a day, because he made false accusations against defense lawyers in yet another first-degree-murder case.

In October, a prominent local doctor, Brad Schwartz, was charged with hiring a hit man to kill a former colleague, who was stabbed to death. Schwartz had been romantically involved with a onetime Pima County prosecutor, and had social ties with her former office; last month, LaWall fired a deputy county attorney and suspended three others who had apparently delayed sharing relevant information about the case with the police. In recent months, at least eight other prosecutors have retired or resigned—extraordinary turmoil in an office of only about sixty prosecutors. Still, in

LaWall's opinion nothing is amiss. "I don't think any of the conduct of any of these men reflects on the office," she told me. "This is a good office."

The three men convicted in the El Grande case remain in prison. In 2004, the International Court of Justice, in The Hague, ordered the United States to grant new hearings to several condemned Mexican nationals, including Martin Soto-Fong, but it's not clear how that ruling will be applied. Through his new attorney, Gregory Kuykendall, Soto-Fong is seeking a writ of habeas corpus in federal court in Tucson, a case that would appear to be his final hope of avoiding execution. McCrimmon and Minnitt, incarcerated on Keith Woods's testimony in the Mariano's Pizza case, will not be eligible for release until about 2023. Lougee hopes to challenge McCrimmon's conviction in that case as well, but no appeal is yet pending.

Joe Godoy and Ken Peasley, still close friends, have joined forces in the private sector, working out of the historic downtown house that serves as the law offices of Brick Storts, a prominent Tucson defense attorney. Godoy is now an investigator, and Peasley is a consultant and a paralegal. (They are collaborating on Schwartz's defense.) Godoy is characteristically effervescent about his new role. "I have to work nights sometimes, just to keep up with my work. And I have a couple of guys working for me, and, gosh, I just got too much work," he said. "The people that know me know that I'm not a bad cop and that I'm not a bad person."

The lawyers in Storts's building have spacious offices in the front, but Peasley is wedged into a small room in the back, next to the parking lot. The papers on his desk are still arranged in orderly piles, and his prosecutor-of-the-year plaques hang on the stucco walls. While we were talking, a secretary came in to say that one of the lawyers was heading back from court, and Peasley almost sprinted out to the parking lot, to make sure that my car wasn't blocking the lawyer's way. "He hates when someone gets in his space," Peasley said.

For now, Peasley is collecting his pension and marking time. He had a heart attack and quadruple-bypass surgery in 2003, but he has kept some of his old habits. "Cigars is what I do. And I shouldn't even do that," he said. "I shouldn't have done a lot of things. And, unfortunately, the reason I had the heart attack is I probably did everything that was bad for you for so many years it was inevitable that something was going to happen." He is not ready for the El Grande case to stand as his legacy. "It's disappointing," he said. "And the reason is, I worked real hard and, frankly, every case I handled was prosecuted with integrity. And for twenty-seven years I did it, and one case, basically, is the definition of what I've done. I mean, the best that I can hope to be remembered as is the guy who screwed up the triple-murder case." Peasley plans to apply for readmission to the bar as soon as he is eligible, in about four years.

JEFFREY TOOBIN, *a staff writer at* The New Yorker *since 1993, is the senior legal analyst for CNN. His fifth book, about the Supreme Court, will be published in 2007.*

Coda

On March 1, 2005, during the week after "Killer Instincts" was published in *The New Yorker*, the Supreme Court ruled, by a vote of five to four, that states could no longer execute defendants who committed their crimes before they turned eighteen. The ruling meant that seventy-two juvenile offenders in twelve states would leave death row. One of them was Martin Soto-Fong, who was seventeen at the time of the murders at the El Grande Market.

After the Supreme Court's decision in *Roper v. Simmons*, Soto-Fong was returned to Tucson for resentencing and for a hearing in his petition for a new trial under Arizona's habeas corpus law. At those proceedings, his lawyer, Gregory Kuykendall, raised many of the issues discussed in the article—including Kenneth Peasley's misconduct and Carole Grijalva-Figueroa's alternative account of the murders. Judge Clark W. Munger could have given Soto-Fong a new trial, or he could have imposed concurrent sentences that would have made Soto-Fong eligible for parole at the age of sixty-eight. Instead, on February 21, 2006, the judge denied the request for the new trial and sentenced Soto-Fong to consecutive terms in the triple-murder. As a result, Soto-Fong, who is now thirty-one, will be eligible for parole when he is one hundred and forty-three years old. Soto-Fong is again appealing.

The lifting of Soto-Fong's death sentence has improved his life in prison. For his twelve years on death row, he was allowed just three showers and three ninety-minute recreation periods per week. Now that Soto-Fong has returned to the general population, he has greater freedom of movement within the prison, and he is eligible to get a job. At the time of the murders at the El Grande, Soto-Fong was attending Lamaze classes with his future wife, Betty. His daughter, Ashley, was born after his arrest. "Once again I want to be able to hold my family and have a better relationship with my daughter," Soto-Fong said after the Supreme Court's ruling. "Back in 1995, we were allowed contact visits once every six months, but then they stopped those. She's twelve now, and I've only held her twice in my life."

Robert Nelson

ALTAR EGO

FROM THE *Phoenix New Times*

IT IS 1988 IN MCALLEN, TEXAS. Irene Garza's portrait hangs in the living room of her aunt's home. The fair-skinned girl is hauntingly beautiful.

Another family member stops by the house for a visit. Noemi Ponce-Sigler happens upon the portrait and looks into the eyes of the girl. She gets the feeling Irene's looking back.

And a question comes into Noemi's mind that has been troubling her since:

"Who killed you, Irene?"

IT IS THE FRIDAY FOLLOWING GOOD FRIDAY, April 1960, in McAllen. Police come to the door of Josephina and Nick Garza's home. They are there to tell the couple that their daughter, Irene, has been found dead in a nearby canal. She had been beaten. It appeared from bruises inside her thighs that her attacker had tried to rape her.

Josephina's body spasms. She collapses to her knees.

And out of her mouth comes a sound so mournful that it has become the stuff of legend in this border town.

"They said it was this long, awful moan from deep inside her body—almost like the howl of a wolf," a niece of Josephina's describes. "They said it was like nothing they had ever heard or ever heard again."

The family's parish priest, Joseph O'Brien, comforted Josephina by telling her that Irene died in a state of grace. After all, she was last seen alive on her way to confession.

The fact was, though, O'Brien had no idea if the cleric Irene saw, Father John Feit—a visiting priest at O'Brien's parish—ever gave her confession.

O'Brien held back another important fact from the Garzas that day: He was confident he knew who had killed their daughter.

POLICE HAD THE MCALLEN CANAL, in which Irene's body was found, drained a few days later.

They found a nearly new slide projector just feet from the spot where the young woman's body had been dragged into the canal. Police told local newspaper reporters they believed this was the clue that would break the case. Clearly, the murderer had used the heavy chunk of equipment, complete with a long cord, to sink Irene's body to the muddy floor of the canal.

After a headline story in the McAllen paper about the projector, area newspapers never mentioned this clue again.

Police sought the owner of the projector. Eight days after Irene's body was found, they received this note:

This viewer belongs to Fr. John Feit (Order of Mary Immaculate), of San Juan, Texas.

It was purchased in Port Isabel, Texas, in July, 1959, at Freddies Professional Pharmacy.

Terms—cash.

Price—I don't remember.
April 29, 1960.

Police already knew the young priest was the last person to see Irene Garza alive.

John B. Feit later became the prime suspect in the Garza murder, as well as in an attempted sexual assault of a young woman in a nearby Catholic church three weeks earlier.

Feit wound up pleading no contest to assault charges in the earlier case. He was fined five hundred dollars.

But Feit was never charged in the murder of Irene Garza.

Instead, according to one of his supervisors, the Archdiocese of San Antonio and the Order of Mary Immaculate "shipped him away" for "rehabilitation" at a series of monasteries in Texas, Iowa, Missouri, and, finally, New Mexico.

Feit left the priesthood ten years later to marry a young AT&T worker he met at a church in Albuquerque. In the late 1970s, Feit, his wife, and three children moved to the Arcadia district of Phoenix, where the family became active in the nearby St. Theresa church.

As a layman in Phoenix, John B. Feit has, by all appearances, become a model citizen. For much of that time, he has been a lead organizer of charitable programs for the Phoenix chapter of the Society of St. Vincent de Paul, where longtime coworkers describe him as a tireless advocate for the poor.

Phoenix Police Department investigators tell *New Times* there are no cold-case files in the Valley that match the modus operandi in the Irene Garza murder or the 1960 aggravated assault in which Feit pleaded no contest.

Even in retirement, Feit spends much of his days counseling and helping the infirm or disadvantaged. At his local parish, Feit is one of the organizers of the JustFaith program, an intensive educational program designed to help Catholics put their belief into action on social justice issues.

But this angel in Phoenix remains a devil in McAllen, Texas.

There—with renewed interest in the murder of Irene Garza, along with new evidence in the case—citizens are clamoring for an indictment of John Feit.

The old evidence, much of which has been reviewed by *New Times,* makes a strong case that their quest for justice is warranted.

The new evidence—which includes testimony from two of Feit's closest associates, who say the ex-priest confessed to them that he killed Irene Garza—seems to make a case against him a slam dunk.

Yet the district attorney in south Texas, in whose jurisdiction the murder occurred, seems content to let things die.

Feit also wants the case to die. He has said, "I did not kill Irene Garza."

In that sentence begins an even deeper mystery, one that may only be solved by understanding a brilliant man's own concepts of faith, contrition, justice, and personality.

When asked by a reporter at his Arcadia home if he should be considered a danger to the community, he yelled: "Look at my record for the last forty-five years!"

Irene Garza's body was thrown in a McAllen canal on Easter Sunday, 1960—forty-five years and two months ago.

THE WEEK BEFORE EASTER, 1960, had been unusually hot along the Texas-Mexico border. With highs already touching the nineties, residents of the valley surrounding McAllen were predicting a long, dismal summer.

Throughout the week, young adults raised in the area were streaming back to McAllen from college or new jobs. The Easter vacation was a time to see old friends, maybe even to rekindle or start a love affair.

The scuttlebutt among some returning young men was that Irene Garza was no longer seeing Sonny Martinez.

This was big news. Irene, as one unrequited suitor wrote, "was the closest thing to an angel" he'd ever met.

So bright, so beautiful, such a sweetheart, such a good heart.

Irene was the first in her family to go to college. After graduation, she returned to do what she had set out to do: teach disadvantaged children in McAllen.

She taught second grade at a school south of the railroad tracks, the line between the haves and the have-nots, the Anglos and the Hispanics, the longtime Mexican Americans and the new immigrants.

She spent her first paycheck on books and clothing for her students. She spent early mornings, late evenings, and weekends giving her students extra learning and fun. She worked with the local PTA.

Her students, she admitted in letters, were becoming her children, her life. She wanted her students to be able to cross the tracks if they chose to.

Like she had done. Irene Garza had become the first Hispanic twirler and head drum majorette at the Anglo-dominated McAllen High School, just a year after her parents' prospering dry-cleaning business had allowed them to afford a house north of the tracks.

Irene was Prom Queen and Homecoming Queen at Pan American College. She was Miss All South Texas Sweetheart 1958.

The catty teenage girls in her old neighborhood blamed her success on her light skin and bone structure and on her Doris Day–style clothes. She was tall and thin, as well as proper and dainty in pillbox hats and high heels.

To some of the little girls in her old neighborhood, though, she was a goddess.

"I can still see her," says Noemi Ponce-Sigler, the cousin of Irene's, who was ten when she died. "She was so beautiful and so good to us kids. [To] a little girl, she just seemed like everything you'd want to be."

Irene Garza, though, never saw herself in such a positive light.

She was humble to a fault, so humble that she sometimes floundered in self-doubt. As she gained confidence in her mid-twenties, she came to believe that her longtime boyfriend, Sonny, was a smothering force in her life. In her breakup letter to him, after providing a lengthy list of her own faults ("Extremely sensitive," "withdrawn," "jealous," "fearful," "serious," "my proportions"), she explained how Sonny made her "feel inferior and insecure." She even made a list of what she believed Sonny needed in a girl:

"A self-confident female, a happy girl, a girl with just a little jealousy that's enough to feed your ego, a girl not easily hurt, a girl who makes your burden easier to carry."

And, apparently, from the girls Sonny had liked to ogle when they were out together: "A girl 38-22-38."

Sonny admitted his frustration at having a flat-chested girlfriend who, instead of having sex with him, wanted to talk about children and God.

It was true that Irene was attending church more often, seeking, she told friends in letters, "to better understand and serve God's will." As for men, she told friends she wanted to marry and have a big family, but she wasn't going to push the issue. And she wasn't going to let Sonny define her anymore.

Irene wrote to a friend just before Easter that she had gone on a few dates with two men, one of whom she described as "this Anglo boy—not real handsome, but cute and religious (which is important). He is a member of the Legion of Mary and goes to Mass and receives Holy Communion every morning."

When she disappeared, police first assumed she had run off with a man. Police interviewed dozens of young men who had shown interest in dating her.

Her family and friends knew better.

When she borrowed her father's car the Saturday night before Easter, she said she was going to church for confession and that she would be right back.

Irene always did what she said she would do.

Besides, she was dressed casually. She had taken none of her possessions.

Irene was helping plan the Easter egg hunt the next morning for the children of the parish. Her family speculated that she may have had to talk to a priest about the logistics of the event.

Family members believe that is why she telephoned the church before leaving the house, asking to meet with a priest.

Father John Feit, a guest priest at the church helping out with the pre–Easter confession crunch, answered the phone.

Irene Garza then drove the twelve blocks to the church to meet with Feit.

Feit's story of what happened next changed several times over the following weeks and years. Now, he refuses to speak about that meeting or the critical hours and days that followed.

Two years ago, after the case had been reopened, a Texas Ranger called Feit at his Phoenix home.

The Ranger asked Feit to speak to him about his role in the events that Easter weekend in 1960. Feit's answer was as opaque as it was potentially illuminating:

"That man doesn't exist anymore," he said, hanging up the phone.

JOHN B. FEIT GREW UP on the south side of Chicago in a devoutly German Catholic household.

It was in the rough and vibrant Chicago of the 1940s, and Feit lived in a neighborhood of working-class families.

Much of the neighborhood was Irish, much of the priesthood was Irish. He developed an accent that faded from south-side Chicago to Irish brogue.

His uncle, also named John, was a priest in Detroit. His parents hoped that one of their sons would become a priest.

At age thirteen, John was sent to San Antonio to begin his religious education. He became a priest in Texas in 1958 within the Order of Mary Immaculate. A year later, he began a one-year internship program based out of a pastoral house run by the Oblate Fathers in the valley town of San Juan, Texas.

From that house, Feit and several fellow OMI priests took classes at nearby Pan-American College and helped fill in at parishes in nearby McAllen and Edinburg.

Father Feit often helped Father Charles Moran at Sacred Heart Church in Edinburg. Through the spring of 1960, he also often stopped by the rectory in Edinburg for coffee with Moran and the church secretaries.

Easter weekend of that year, Father Feit was asked to help Father Joseph O'Brien and his two associate priests give confession and offer Mass at Sacred Heart Church in McAllen.

Like every Easter weekend, it was a hectic time for priests. Confession lines and pews were bloated with visitors, children back for holiday and the multitude of Catholics who practice their faith only at Easter and Christmas.

The three priests and the visiting priest gave confessions that morning, then from 3:00 to 6:00 P.M., Saturday afternoon.

At 6:00 P.M., they returned to the rectory for dinner. The priests would resume confessions in the church at 7:00 P.M. Irene Garza phoned the church rectory and spoke to Feit just before 7:00 P.M.

Witnesses saw Irene walking from her car to the church about 7:00 P.M.

Witnesses saw three of the four priests return to the church from the rectory at 7:00 P.M. The visiting priest, Feit, thin, dark-haired, with distinctive horn-rimmed glasses, was not with them.

Witnesses said they then saw Irene Garza walking to the rectory.

At 7:20 P.M., Irene was seen walking from the rectory.

She was last seen by witnesses about 8:00 P.M. outside the church.

———————

TWO DAYS AFTER IRENE DISAPPEARED, one of her high-heeled shoes was found alongside a road on the edge of McAllen.

Her purse was found the next morning.

At that point, it was obvious she hadn't run off with a lover.

By midweek, her disappearance had already sparked one of the largest investigations in McAllen-area history.

Seventy sheriff's department posse members scoured the region on horseback looking for her body. Sixty-five National Guardsmen were called in. Investigators followed dozens of leads, most pointing toward ex-boyfriends, unrequited admirers or transients.

Skin divers dragged irrigation canals. They just dragged the wrong ones.

On a balmy Thursday morning, four days after Easter Sunday, Irene's body rose to the surface of the Second Street Canal and was spotted by several passersby.

Frightened valley residents began locking their doors. The search switched to a manhunt. There was a murderer on the loose.

In the days after Irene's disappearance, investigators learned of an attempted sexual assault three weeks earlier inside another Catholic church in Edinburg, a nearby town in the valley. Again, the victim, Maria America Guerra, was a young Hispanic female.

Investigators quickly linked the two attacks. And investigators in the Garza case began digging deeper for information on the Edinburg attack.

They re-interviewed the victim. She repeated that her assailant was a white male with horn-rimmed glasses in a light-tan shirt and dark trousers—clothing she assumed was that of a priest.

At the time, police were looking for a serial rapist who seemed to lurk around valley Catholic churches preying on attractive young light-skinned Hispanic women. Perhaps the rapist was masquerading as a priest?

The same day Irene's body was found, police investigating the Edinburg case made a stunning discovery:

The priest who last saw Irene Garza alive not only was at the Edinburg church the day of the earlier attack, he matched the victim's and another witness's description of the attacker.

As police continued to publicly state they had no hard leads, they quietly began zeroing in on Father John Feit.

Catholic leaders dreaded the possible fallout if one of their own was the culprit. Not only would it bring scandal to the church, it would give fodder to already deep prejudices within the Protestant community.

Bridges between Anglos and Hispanics, Protestants and Catholics, were just beginning to be built in earnest in deep south central Texas (Irene Garza was seen as an ambassador in that effort).

The investigation of Feit would be kept as quiet as possible.

After Irene's body was found, police spoke again with Feit's supervisor, Father Joseph O'Brien from Sacred Heart Church in McAllen—who admitted something he had kept quiet from police:

Feit was his prime suspect too.

MARIA AMERICA GUERRA HAD returned home in the late afternoon of March 23, 1960, after attending classes at Pan-American College.

At 4:30 P.M., the pretty, light-skinned twenty-year-old had gone to the outdoor bathhouse behind her home in Edinburg to get cleaned up.

As she walked outside, she noticed a man watching her from a parked car adjacent to the bathhouse, which sat directly across from Sacred Heart Church in Edinburg.

In her April 1960 statement to police, Guerra described the young man as having black hair and horn-rimmed glasses.

He was sitting in a blue-and-white 1955 or 1956 model car.

Later, after dinner, Guerra said she left the house to go across the street to pray in the church.

As she left, she noticed the same car parked between her house and the church. The man with the horn-rimmed glasses was not in the vehicle.

She entered the church through the main doors and walked to the communion rail.

"As I entered the church, I noticed a man sitting alone in one of the rear benches on my left," she said. "This man also had black hair and horn-rimmed glasses, and the thought that it was the same man that I saw earlier entered my mind. But being in a house of God, I dismissed any thoughts of foul play."

Another lady was in the church praying as Guerra knelt to pray. That lady, whom Guerra did not know, soon stood and left the church.

Moments later, Guerra said, she heard the footsteps of someone coming from the back of the church toward the front.

"I looked to see who it was and noticed that it was a man, the same man sitting at the rear of the church when I entered. I noticed that he was wearing a light beige T-shirt and black pants."

Guerra said the man walked to a side door, looked out in both directions, then quickly walked back in her direction.

"The next thing I know, he had turned very quick, come to my rear and grabbed me around the head.

"He placed a small cloth over my mouth, and I fell backward to the floor. I began to scream now as when I fell, the rag fell free from my mouth. Then while I was on the floor, he tried to cover my mouth with his hands to stop me from screaming and when he did this, one of his fingers went into my mouth and I bit it very hard. I know that I bit it very hard because I could taste blood in my mouth.

"When I bit him, he threw me toward the south side door of the church and ran out the north side door."

Guerra ran to the rectory and rang the doorbell. Father Charles

Moran, who was inside taking a shower, yelled for her "to wait a minute."

As she was ringing the bell, a young woman came up to her and asked what had happened. The woman had heard her scream. Guerra told her she had been attacked in the church. The woman then walked away.

Guerra, afraid that the man might still be lurking, decided to head quickly back to her home.

She noticed the blue-and-white car was gone.

The woman who asked her what had happened was Maria Cristina Tijerina, who was walking past the church on her way to work at 6:20 P.M.

"As I passed the front door [of the church], I heard some screams coming from inside the church," she said. "I became interested and started trying to see what was happening. I kept walking while I was looking because I was late for work.

"As I passed the side door of this church, a young man about twenty-nine or thirty years old came out walking very fast like he was in a hurry. When I saw the man, I didn't hear any more screams. He was dressed in black pants and had a white T-shirt on. In his hands, he was holding a towel about the size of a face towel."

Tijerina saw the man enter the door to the church sacristy. She saw Guerra leave the church and head toward the rectory. Tijerina said she then went to ask Guerra what had happened.

In early May, Guerra was taken to the McAllen police station by a deputy sheriff. Investigators wanted her to see the lead suspect in the Irene Garza case.

"I looked at this man, and I [said] that I thought he was the one [who had attacked] me. Later that night, I told my mother this was the man who attacked me."

Guerra wrote in a statement two weeks later, "I saw this same man not long after in the library at Pan-American College, but I saw him dressed as a priest, and I was surprised to see him dressed as a priest, as this was the same man I had seen at the Police Station in McAllen. The minute I saw him I felt afraid of him.

"I want to state that this same Priest that I have seen [at the] College and that I saw at the Police Station in McAllen is the same man who attacked me in church in Edinburg. I am positive he is the same man."

The man she identified was Father John Feit.

THE INTERNING PRIEST FROM SAN ANTONIO admitted he had visited Father Charles Moran at Sacred Heart Church the afternoon Guerra was attacked. Feit also admitted that he went into the church to pray, but said he exited the building by 5:15 P.M. to talk to Father Moran about "the personal problems of a boy from Edinburg." He said he then returned to San Juan in his blue-and-white 1956 Ford Tudor in time to "ring the 5:30 bell for Adoration."

Moran, however, remembered nothing of a conversation with Feit about a boy's troubles. He just remembered Feit coming "for no good reason I know of." Moran remembered Feit was dressed in black pants and a light-tan shirt with his usual horn-rimmed glasses.

Other witnesses said Feit didn't ring the 5:30 bell in San Juan.

Feit then gave a second police statement in which he tried to explain the contradictions.

"I believe I hurt my cause by trying to be too specific and detailed about my doings on that afternoon of March 23. Frankly, it was just another routine day, and it is very hard to recall my exact whereabouts, actions or what have you at any exact time."

Regarding the bell-ringing: "I left the rectory and drove to San Juan, arriving in time to ring the bell, for supper or chapel service? I don't know for sure."

Besides the victim's and the chief witness's identifying Feit—

besides witnesses contradicting his story—the most damning evidence was Feit's mangled left pinkie finger, which several fellow priests and church workers noticed in the days after March 23.

In Feit's initial statement to police, he explained that his finger had been injured in a church mimeograph machine the day before Guerra was attacked.

"In trying to make the stencil ink better, the little finger of my left hand caught between the revolving drum and the frame breaking the skin and causing a severe bruise."

Feit wrote that on Tuesday night, the day before Guerra was attacked, he asked a Father Houlahan for some rubbing alcohol to soak his finger.

Feit wrote that he also went to the secretary at the Edinburg church on the morning of March 23 asking for a bandage for the injury. Feit said, "She asked me how I hurt my finger, and I said I hurt it in the mimeograph machine."

Father Houlahan, in his statement, said that Feit came to him later in the week regarding his wounded finger.

And a secretary at the church in Edinburg was adamant in her statement that Feit came the morning after the Guerra attack asking for a bandage. And she was vocal in her suspicion that her mimeograph machine could not have done the damage to Feit's finger.

That secretary, Cleotilde "Tilly" Sanchez, still lives in the McAllen area. And she says she still vividly remembers the events of March and April 1960.

She remembers walking in as the church's other secretary, Leonila Sanchez, was putting iodine on Feit's finger.

"I didn't just ask Feit what happened to his finger," she tells *New Times.* "I asked, 'Who bit your finger?' It had teeth marks on it. It was as clear as day.

"Feit said, 'It isn't a bite.' I said, 'Well, it sure looks like a bite. You can see the mouth shape on it.' "

Sanchez says she had come to know Feit well during that

spring. Feit was often over visiting Moran. Feit, she says, was always calling the church asking for Moran or for help with some issue.

"Pretty early on, [Feit] wouldn't have to say his name when he called," she says. "His voice was that distinctive, and he was calling that much."

In late April or early May of that year, after Irene Garza's body was found, after Sanchez had made her statements to police, a call came into the church that chills her to this day.

"It was a Friday," she says. "The phone rings, I pick it up and a man says, 'You're next, Tilly.' I said, 'What?' And he says, 'You're next!'

"It was Feit," she maintains. "I knew his voice immediately. Father Moran walks in, and I tell him Father Feit just called and said, 'You're next,' and Father Moran just says, 'Oh, Tilly, it couldn't be Father Feit.' By that point I was just scared to death."

She quit her secretary job soon after.

Investigators were confident they had an ironclad case against John Feit in the Garza killing.

But they held off pushing for charges. They wanted to have something to offer Feit.

The deal they came up with was this: If Feit would confess to Irene Garza's murder, they wouldn't bring a charge in the Guerra case. He wouldn't have to face two trials.

In reality, it wasn't a very big carrot. Avoid an assault-related charge by confessing to rape and murder?

Feit refused to confess that he killed Irene Garza. In the summer of 1960, Feit was charged with the attempted sexual assault of Maria America Guerra.

Even without a confession, though, investigators felt confident they had more than enough evidence to charge John Feit with the murder of Irene Garza.

That never happened.

———

ON MAY 3, 1960, two weeks after Irene Garza disappeared, police asked John Feit to give a sworn statement of his whereabouts on Easter weekend.

At 7:00 P.M. on the Saturday before Easter, he told authorities, he and Father O'Brien were leaving the rectory heading for the church when the phone rang.

Feit said he returned to the rectory to answer it.

He said a woman was on the line asking to see Father Junius, who was already taking confessions in the church.

Feit said he told the woman that Father Junius would be busy until 10:30 P.M., but that he could talk to her if she hurried down to the church.

Irene Garza, whom Feit says he didn't know, arrived five minutes later.

"She was a light-complected girl, apparently of Latin American extraction—good-looking. She spoke perfect English," he told police.

"For ten minutes she discussed a personal problem of hers with me, the nature of which I do not feel justified in making public since it involved my obligation of professional secrecy as a clergyman and Catholic priest."

However, Feit did let on that the issue wasn't too serious.

"Her overall attitude and comportment during our brief conversation led me to believe that she possessed a very delicate conscience."

Feit said he sent Garza to the church so she could go to confession.

Feit said he left the rectory, locked the door behind him, and headed to the church to help the other three priests give confession.

Feit said he last saw Garza "standing on the sidewalk, in front of the church, arranging a scarf or handkerchief on her head."

At 8:00 P.M., Feit said he left the church for a short break. He saw Father O'Brien talking to some men outside the church. He went to O'Brien and asked for the keys to the rectory.

From this point on, Feit's story begins to differ from the evidence and the statements of witnesses.

He said he returned to the church at 8:15 P.M. He said he left the church again at 9:00 P.M. to go to the rectory "because my voice was beginning to give out." There, he said, he had a cigarette and a 7UP and returned to the church to give confession.

However, a host of witnesses within the church said Father Feit's confessional line stopped moving about 8:00 P.M. As Father O'Brien later told police, that was a sign there was no priest in the confession booth.

Feit said that at 9:50 P.M., near the end of confession, a screw in his eyeglasses came loose and fell out. He told Father Busch that he would have to go to the pastoral house in San Juan to get his other pair of glasses.

The next day, O'Brien and the other priests noticed that Feit's hand was injured.

Feit explained that injury away:

"Upon arriving at the Pastoral House in San Juan, I found all the doors on the ground floor locked." So he said he placed a wood barricade against the building and climbed up and through a second-story window.

"While entering the house in this way, I scraped the back of my right hand slightly, and the index finger and middle finger of my left hand more severely on the brick wall."

He said he changed clothes and headed back to McAllen for the 11:00 P.M. service.

He said he went to bed at 1:00 A.M. with a "severe headache," which he assumed was caused by his second pair of glasses. He said the spectacles "never fit me as well as the first" pair.

The next morning, Feit gave Mass at 9:00 A.M., then asked Fathers Busch and O'Brien if he could use Busch's car to go to San Juan to get his glasses fixed.

Feit said he worked on the glasses "for five minutes," but had no luck. Then, he said, "I drove straight back to Sacred Heart Church."

At 12:40 P.M., he asked another priest to drive him to the Pastoral House in San Juan, where he said he stayed until about 4:00 P.M.

He returned to Sacred Heart to give 5:30 Mass. Shortly after 7:30 P.M. on Easter Sunday, he said, he was given a ride back to the Pastoral House by Father O'Brien.

Feit said he immediately realized he had left some of his belongings at Sacred Heart, so he borrowed a car and drove back to the church.

There, he said, several priests were talking about the "missing girl." As he stood there, the phone rang. Father Junius answered. It was Irene Garza's parents wanting to speak with the priest who had spoken with her the night before.

The parents came over, and Feit said he spoke with them. He said they asked him if he "had perhaps said anything which might have upset or disturbed their daughter."

In fact, Garza family members say, Nick Garza asked Feit, "What have you done with my daughter?"

Feit said, "I could see the parents were very disturbed and upset themselves, so I sent them home as quickly and as quietly as possible.

"I then picked up my coat, collar, and laundry and headed for home. It was about 9:15 P.M. But I did not go straight home. My talk with the girl's parents had disturbed me. Perhaps I had said something, unintentionally, that might have upset that girl? I was worried, and drove around aimlessly for a while."

He said he stopped at a nearby Whataburger, got a malt, then drove back to San Juan in time for the 10:00 P.M. news.

According to investigators, Irene Garza's body was probably thrown into the canal on Easter Sunday evening.

SEVERAL DOZEN YOUNG MEN were considered potential suspects early in the investigation of Irene Garza's death.

One by one, all proved to have credible alibis. And all passed lie-detector tests administered by state police investigators from Austin.

All except John Feit.

Nobody could vouch for Feit's whereabouts at critical times during the weekend. And time after time, Feit attempted to control his breathing as critical questions were asked during the polygraph examinations.

A lengthy report detailing the exams by Texas authorities, then by John Reid—arguably the top polygraph examiner in the country at the time—paints an ugly picture of Feit.

The tests "definitely implicated him in both crimes," the report said.

"It is the opinion of the examiner, based on this subject's polygraph test, that [Feit] is purposefully attempting to defeat the recordings."

In fact, each time Feit was hooked up to a polygraph machine, he began taking exactly ten breaths per minute, "indicating that he was purposefully controlling his breathing even though he had been given warnings and instructions throughout."

Examiners secretly monitored Feit's breathing rate during normal conversations. On average, they said, he inhaled and exhaled 16 to 20 times a minute when he didn't believe he was being monitored.

Reid went on to describe Feit's demeanor throughout the tests.

"The examiner pointed out in detail to the subject that he should make an effort to tell the truth concerning his implication in these crimes so that the church and the priesthood would not suffer when evidence definitely implicating him is turned up at a later date.

"The subject, in very deliberate and explicit words, stated there will never be any evidence turning up in the future of this case.

"He also pointed out to the examiner that there are two . . . murders in the area [that] had gone unsolved, one for 15 years and one for 20 years, and that this case, like those, will soon be forgotten."

When asked why he entered the priesthood, Feit answered, "I just wanted to give it a try."

When asked about the attack on Maria America Guerra, Feit's answers bordered on the absurd. At one point, he claimed that Guerra's true attacker had actually confessed to him.

"The subject was queried as to where the confession was obtained, and [Feit] told the examiner that it was not in the confessional box, not in the rectory but out in the open some place and was very vague as to where the open place was."

When asked if the lie detector was incorrect when it indicated that he committed these crimes, he answered, "Your machine is probably functioning correctly, but these men from Austin have told me that I have a vague respiration and a bad heart."

What everyone knew—Feit's attorneys, the examiners themselves—was that polygraph exams weren't admissible in court.

In effect, the stated belief by examiners that Feit was "concealing the truth" would mean nothing in a courtroom.

Feit had been taken to Austin and then Chicago for the polygraph tests.

Each time, he was escorted by Father Joseph O'Brien, his supervisor at Sacred Heart Church.

It was clear that O'Brien had been placed in charge of Feit by his superiors within the Order of Mary Immaculate.

PROSECUTORS FINALLY DECIDED to first move forward with the attempted sexual assault case against Feit.

When charges were filed, John Feit became a household name.

It was the biggest story in the McAllen valley in years. And as leaders had feared, it tore the community apart.

Feit remained confident. As he told investigators, he "had the best attorneys money can buy."

The trial was moved to Austin. It was believed Feit couldn't get a fair trial in Hidalgo County.

His trial ended with the jury deadlocked 9 to 3 in favor of conviction.

Rather than face a second trial, Feit pleaded no contest to the reduced charges of aggravated assault and was ordered to pay the five-hundred-dollar fine.

No murder charge was ever filed.

The assumption in McAllen was that a deal had been struck to avoid both further embarrassment to the church and a prolonged fight between the church and elected officials in this predominantly Catholic town.

Documents in the case seem to support the assumption.

Indeed, it is clear that the church promised to ship Feit away from the valley and lock him up in the monastery system.

Irene's aunt, Herlinda de la Vina, remembers Father Joseph O'Brien telling her as much.

"He told us that the church's punishment was greater than any sentence handed down by the courts, and we believed him."

Father O'Brien told the family that Feit would be sent to a monastery and kept there so he would be unable to hurt anyone else.

And that's what happened. For the next decade, Father O'Brien essentially served as John Feit's probation officer, as well as the liaison between civil and church authorities in the matter.

O'Brien was even named a "special investigator" by the city manager of McAllen.

O'Brien's role in the case ended with a short letter sent to McAllen police in December 1971:

"Dear Chief:

"I have just received notice that John Feit has left Denham Springs, New Mexico, and is now living in the Chicago area. He is seeking employment as a layman and will no longer function as a priest. This was his own decision and was not due to a problem.

"If any further information is needed please feel free to call upon me.

"Father Joseph O'Brien, OMI."

NOEMI PONCE-SIGLER WAS ten years old when Irene Garza was murdered.

The cousins, part of a close-knit extended Mexican-American family, were often at the same homes, the same family parties, the same town events.

To a ten-year-old girl, Irene Garza seemed to be everything a woman should be.

"She was beautiful, so graceful, so loving," Ponce-Sigler says.

In 1988, Ponce-Sigler was visiting the house of her aunt, also one of Irene's aunts, when she suddenly felt as if someone were watching her. Nobody was in the room. But on the wall was a large portrait photo of Irene.

"I don't know, I'm sure it was the light or something, but it seemed like she was staring at me," Ponce-Sigler says. "I stared at her photo, and just began asking myself questions about what happened to her. From that visit on, I've just continued to knock on doors asking questions."

She contacted Sonny Miller, then a detective with the McAllen police force. Miller was still interested in the case. He pulled the old files on Irene's murder and began digging again.

He found more new evidence. Still, the local district attorney had no interest in filing charges.

"Everything said this guy Feit was as guilty as sin," Miller, who is now retired, tells New Times.

Besides loads of evidence, Miller says he discovered something else. In the year following Irene's murder, it seemed like everyone lost interest, or was told to lose interest.

Police even later found candlesticks near where Irene's body was thrown into the canal that had come from Sacred Heart Church. But, Miller says, investigators never tried to match them to the wounds on her head.

Miller talked to several of the investigators from the time of the murder, as well as to the daughter of then–police chief Clint Mussey. It became clear that from the turmoil caused just by Feit's sexual-assault trial, the powers that be at the time didn't want to see a priest tried for murder in the valley.

"It frustrated the hell out of the people who knew [that] Feit was the guy," Miller says. "Justice was not done."

In 2002 the Texas Rangers reopened the case.

By 2004 the Rangers and the Garza family believed that justice might finally be had.

And by last year, Noemi Ponce-Sigler believed she finally knew what actually happened to Irene Garza.

"Once I was able to talk to Dale Tacheny and Father O'Brien, it was all pretty clear," she says. "The only thing left is justice for the killer."

DALE TACHENY WAS A GUILT-RIDDEN young man. When he left the U.S. Army in the late 1940s, he decided to become a monk to save his eternal soul.

"It was a very selfish decision," says Tacheny from his home in Oklahoma City. "I wanted to save myself. I wasn't thinking about others."

Forty years later, it was guilt, Tacheny says, that finally led him to speak publicly about his involvement with John B. Feit.

Tacheny began his religious training in 1949 at age twenty.

By twenty-seven, he was already something of a golden boy in the Trappist order.

In the fall of 1958, Tacheny, known as Father Emmanuel, was sent to Rome for two years of study. When he returned to the

United States, he was promoted to second in command at Our Lady of Assumption Abbey in Ava, Missouri.

Tacheny was Novice Master. As such, he was the abbot's right-hand man and the priest in charge of all of the abbey's newest postulants.

He was a sort of spiritual drill sergeant for seven to ten young men seeking to become monks within the Order.

In 1963, Tacheny says, he was given his strangest assignment ever.

"The abbot called me in and said, 'There is a priest who murdered a woman who is in the guest house. He wants to become a monk. We are instructed to take him in.' "

Tacheny was told that the priest had been sent to Assumption Abbey from New Melleray Abbey in Dubuque, Iowa, where, a month earlier, he had attempted to attack a woman as she got into her car outside the abbey.

This attack, he was told, had followed similar attacks in Texas, one of which had led to the death of a young woman.

Tacheny says he then went to the guest house, where he met Father John Feit.

In the days that followed, Tacheny started his new novice down the quietly arduous path to becoming a monk.

The novices rose at 2:00 A.M., and their day included classes, meditation, manual labor in the fields surrounding the abbey, and vespers. They were to be in bed by 8:00 P.M.

Once a week was the Office of Faults, when novices professed or found themselves accused of sinful thoughts or actions. The novices then self-flagellated for one minute by beating their bare shoulders with a knotted rope.

Tacheny met with each of his novices weekly to explain, or be told, how they were doing.

Tacheny remembers Feit having trouble adjusting to the abbey and his fellow novices. For one, he didn't fit in. He was an ordained priest in his late twenties. The others were barely out of high school.

It was during one of their weekly meetings, Tacheny says, that he finally began asking Feit about his past.

"I just asked, 'Why are you here and not in prison?' " Tacheny says. "It was very matter-of-fact.

"Feit said, 'The church is behind me.' Feit said that any time the authorities would get close to anything, he would just say he couldn't speak because of confessional secrecy."

Then, Tacheny says he remembers asking Feit why the church *would* stand behind him.

"Feit said he was told by his superiors that they didn't want the faithful to be scandalized," Tacheny says.

"To be honest, at the time, it all didn't seem that strange," Tacheny says. "Over the whole issue was our belief that we could help him more than some prison and that he wouldn't be a threat because he was locked up in a monastery somewhere. Civil justice wasn't part of the equation at that time."

As the months passed, it became clear that John Feit would not be able to handle the monastic life. Tacheny says Feit himself asked to be transferred.

Tacheny was then told that it was his job to prepare Feit to return to society.

Tacheny had studied psychology, but he admits he was completely unqualified to "try to cure him, whatever that means."

At that point, Tacheny says, his relationship with Feit changed. It was now his job to probe Feit's mind, get the truth about "this murder" and break Feit of whatever impulses led him to attack women.

Tacheny says he did his job. And he still believes he was successful.

But in the decades that followed, as he left the abbey, then the priesthood, Tacheny again became eaten by guilt.

He increasingly felt as though he was an accomplice to murder and that he may have unleashed a dangerous man on society.

In 2002 Tacheny sent a two-page letter to the Texas Rangers. In it, Tacheny laid out to detectives what he remembered being told by Feit in 1963.

The problem: Tacheny wasn't ever told where the murder took place or on which Easter it had taken place. Since he knew Feit had been shipped to the Midwest abbeys from San Antonio, Tacheny says, he assumed the murder Feit described to him had taken place in San Antonio the year Feit came to Assumption Abbey in 1963.

The Ranger who received the letter, Detective George Saidler, went hunting through records of unsolved murders in San Antonio. Nothing matched. So he moved on.

Late in 2002, another Ranger, Rocky Milligan, stopped by Saidler's office to talk about an investigation. During that conversation, Milligan went on to talk about the Rangers' cold-case unit, which, he said, was working on cases more than forty years old.

"[There's] one out of the [McAllen] valley that dates all the way back to 1960," he told Saidler. "A woman was murdered on Easter weekend, and the main suspect was a priest."

The Rangers called Tacheny.

ONCE IT WAS CLEAR that John Feit was not going to be a monk, Dale Tacheny says, it was his job to make sure Feit would not be a danger once he left the monastery.

"We were very concerned," Tacheny says. "By that point, he had a history of attacking women. We needed to get to the bottom of his problem and help him control it."

There was the mindset within the Trappist order at the time, he says, that priests could be healed. The order was intent on forgiveness. It would hate the sin, not the sinner.

If sin and sinner continued to live as one, punishment was better meted out by God than some secular judge, in purgatory or hell rather than a Texas prison.

The idea of justice here on Earth was of no concern. It was many years later before Tacheny began ruminating over the plight of the victims and their families.

He now believes he did the wrong thing. That, he says, is why he is talking now.

At the time, though, he firmly believed he was doing the right thing.

Which began, he says, by getting to the bottom of what happened in the slaying.

"I remember [Feit] said it happened Easter weekend," Tacheny says.

"Feit said he was hearing confessions with several other priests, four to six priests. He said a woman came, and he suggested going to the rectory to hear confession. He took control of her somehow. He told me the only thing he did sexually was take her blouse off and fondle her breasts.

"He said he tied her up, took her to the basement, then went back to the church to hear confessions. That night, he said, he took her back to someplace where the [interning priests] were staying. Feit said he put her in a room and locked her up there until the next day. He told me he went to Sunday services, then came back . . . for lunch in his room. Before he left, he said, he put a bag or something over her head and put her in a bathtub.

"I remember Feit saying that, as he left, the woman says, 'I can't breathe,' but he goes on anyway. He said that when he returned, he found her dead in the bathtub."

Tacheny says Feit would never say the woman's last name. He just called her "Irene."

Tacheny says Feit then explained how he disposed of her body: "That night he put her in a car and drove her to a canal. I remember him saying he patted her on the chest as he drove, saying, 'Everything is okay, Irene.'

"It was very disturbing, I had never had to deal with anything like this," Tacheny says.

But Feit, he says, talked about Easter, 1960, as if it was any other weekend.

"He was usually very nice and cooperative, but it was chilling that there didn't seem to be any remorse," Tacheny recalls.

Tacheny says he then began questioning Feit about "the things that bothered him."

"Feit said one thing that really bugged him was the 'click, click, click of women's heels on solid flooring,' "Tacheny says.

"Which led to discussions about whether he believed he would have a problem leaving. At that point, he tells me he sometimes has this urge to attack women from behind. Especially as they are kneeling. A compulsion. So we began working on that. We talked it through."

Tacheny says they finally got to a point in the therapy when Feit said he thought he could control his urges in the future.

So, Tacheny says, Feit was sent on a mission.

Amazingly, Feit was told to go to several churches—in St. Louis and then in his home of Chicago—and see if he could stand behind women without feeling a compulsion to attack them.

"He came back and said he had accomplished the task," Tacheny says. "So I made a judgment after that that he could go back into the world."

Tacheny says he remembers hearing that a priest who knew Feit before he came to the monastery was arguing that he should not be allowed to leave. Tacheny later found out the priest was Father Joseph O'Brien.

Feit was then transferred to Jemez Springs, New Mexico, to a treatment center for troubled priests run by the Order of the Servants of the Paraclete.

That treatment center (and Feit himself, who rose to the position of superior at Jemez Springs) later became notorious for quietly sending pedophile priests back into communities around the country.

While in New Mexico, Feit met a young light-skinned Hispanic woman in a church in Albuquerque. Her Spanish ancestry dated back to the 1600s in northern New Mexico.

They fell in love. In 1971, Feit sent a letter to Rome asking that he be released from his priestly duties.

He headed back to Chicago with his new wife to start a family. He bounced through several jobs in the Midwest before finally moving to Phoenix and into the parish where his brother was a pastor, St. Theresa.

NOEMI PONCE-SIGLER COULDN'T BELIEVE what she was hearing when she picked up the phone last year. It was the voice of Father Joseph O'Brien.

He was calling from a nursing home for retired priests. He had decided it was time he told the family what he knew before his mind slipped or his body failed.

By 2004 both O'Brien and Tacheny were willing to become vocal about Feit's role in the Irene Garza case. They were also willing to talk about their frustration with Hidalgo County District Attorney Rene Guerra.

It was Guerra's job to consider charges in the reopened case against Feit in the slaying of Irene Garza.

For years, Guerra avoided the case. In 2002, when asked if he would pursue charges now that evidence seemed overwhelming in the old case, Guerra told the *Brownsville Herald*: "I reviewed the file some years back; there was nothing there. Can it be solved? Well, I guess if you believe that pigs fly, anything is possible."

He concluded, "Why would anyone be haunted by her death? She died. Her killer got away."

Guerra's comments naturally angered the Garza family, which

still includes more than a dozen first cousins, aunts, and uncles (her parents passed away in the 1990s). But it did not surprise them.

"Guerra is just known to be politically motivated, pretty dang bad at his job, and also arrogant as hell," Noemi Ponce-Sigler says.

He is also part of a powerful Catholic family in the McAllen valley.

In 2003 the Texas Rangers submitted information from the agency's new investigation into the case to Guerra, but the D.A. refused to present the findings to a grand jury.

Leaders and media across Texas jumped on Guerra. Finally, in 2004, he agreed to let grand jurors consider the case.

Incredibly, though, Guerra refused to call witnesses such as O'Brien and Tacheny. And Guerra continued to trash the case even as he presented it to a grand jury.

In fact, Guerra called only one witness, a secretary from Sacred Heart Church in McAllen who had served as a defense witness for Feit in the 1961 assault trial.

The grand jury came back with a no bill, meaning Feit was off the hook again.

To investigators, witnesses, family, and many in McAllen, it was clear what was happening.

"[Guerra] didn't want to stir this up again," says retired McAllen detective Sonny Miller. "He badly wants this thing to die."

Soon after the grand jury decision, Father Joseph O'Brien called Noemi Ponce-Sigler to get some things off his chest.

With O'Brien's consent, Ponce-Sigler recorded O'Brien's comments for posterity:

Noemi: "Feit told you that he had killed [Irene]?"
O'Brien: "Yes."
Noemi: "Oh my God!"
O'Brien: "I suspected him from the very beginning."
Noemi: "What happened that night? You're the only one who knows besides him."

O'Brien: "It was Easter week. We had a lot of confessions. After the Mass, we sat down and [Feit's] hands were all scratched. He gave me two different reasons. 'Well,' I said, 'okay, something is wrong here.'

"So, then, Father Busch—he's dead now—[and I] searched the attic for her. That's how suspicious we were."

Noemi: "She did go to church?"

O'Brien: "Yes. She went to the rectory. I was in the church. Father Busch was in the church. [Feit] went back to answer the phone. We went and heard confessions. [Feit] goes back to the rectory. [Feit] took her to the pilgrim house in San Juan, kept her overnight.

"I'm just speculating that he hit her in the head with the candlestick."

Noemi: "Was [the candlestick] found in the canal?"

O'Brien: "Yes."

Noemi: "When in the world did he ever tell you about the murder?"

O'Brien: "To be honest, I sort of tricked him. I said, 'How can I help you if you don't tell the truth?' I kept asking him the question, over and over. Then he came at me. I said, 'Oh, this is great, one more step and [I'm] dead.' Then he went back to reading the prayer book he was reading. Then he finally admitted it."

Noemi: "When he admitted that he killed her, did he say, like, 'Sorry'?"

O'Brien: "No. Well, I don't know if he did later. I imagine so. We took him to Chicago to John Reid, the guy who literally wrote the book on polygraph tests. He said, 'This man is guilty.'

"What happened is, we knew he was dangerous, okay? We shipped him off to [monasteries]. Stayed ten years. Then he got married."

O'Brien is currently in the hospital. His health appears to be failing.

But the Texas Rangers have his complete story on tape. Now they just need a prosecutor.

MORE THAN A MILLION MEALS GO OUT to the needy each year from the Society of St. Vincent de Paul's sprawling kitchen and warehouse facility in south central Phoenix.

The Society would be unable to feed the city's disadvantaged, as well as offer them clothing, medical aid, and numerous other forms of assistance, if it was not for the charity's six thousand volunteers in the Valley of the Sun.

From the 1980s to 2003, it was John Feit's job to recruit and coordinate the activities of the Society's volunteers. There are thousands.

The Society's Steve Jenkins and Steve Zabilski were asked to talk about the John Feit they know.

"He was phenomenal at reaching out to the community and teaching volunteers what it meant to grow closer to God through charity," says Jenkins, a longtime coworker and friend. "He is so clearly a man who has a genuine love for serving others."

"John often went beyond what anyone would remotely imagine a man doing," says Society executive director Zabilski. "He truly lived his beliefs. And his passion motivated many others to do more than they otherwise would have done."

The man they described is humble, deeply charitable, wise, kind, and gentle. Their John Feit has a mind that is nimble with history, scripture, and philosophy.

Their friend is nothing like his alter ego, the lead suspect in the brutal slaying of Irene Garza.

"It's black and white," Jenkins says. "We knew nothing about these past issues. We've only seen the white."

Feit began volunteering for the Society soon after joining the parish of St. Theresa near his home in the early 1980s. In the mid-eighties, Jenkins says, Feit was asked to join the Society's staff to liaise with volunteers.

"He was perfect for the job," Jenkins says. "He spoke with such passion and clarity about the mission of the Society."

Jenkins and Feit worked countless hours together, including during a trip into Mexico to do the charity's work. There, he says, Feit was the interpreter: "He speaks fluent Spanish."

Zabilski, director of the Society since 1997, says Feit's personal charity "knew no bounds." Several years ago, Zabilski says, one of Feit's co-workers was facing financial difficulties trying to support a family.

"So John comes to me and asks that I reduce his salary and give the other person the money," Zabilski says. "He's the only person in my twenty-five years of doing this who has ever done that. His only request was that I don't tell anyone where the money came from."

Feit also was instrumental in raising fifty-five hundred dollars to purchase and renovate a house for a poor couple trying to raise their twelve grandchildren. It was the first time the Society "got into the extreme makeover business," Zabilski says.

Feit retired from his Society job in 2003.

Jenkins and Zabilski were asked to read through the evidence and allegations from the 1960 cases.

"This is simply not the John Feit we know," Zabilski says. "To us, it's like two completely different people."

A VISITOR COMES TO JOHN FEIT'S DOOR asking for information about the JustFaith program he's involved with at St. Theresa's church.

Feit opens the door to the guest with a broad smile. He says he would be pleased to tell the visitor more.

Feit's hair is no longer black, the glasses no longer horn-rimmed. His thick shoulders are somewhat hunched, but he is vibrant and expressive. He still has that south Chicago accent tinged with the Irish brogue.

On the wall of his small condo is a picture of his two daughters and his son.

His wife, Mary, is at the store. On the wall is a knitted plaque: "Dull Women Have Immaculate Homes."

Feit shows the visitor something he wrote about JustFaith to the pastor at St. Theresa: "My experience," Feit wrote, "has been that Stephen A. Covey's observation—'The enemy of the best is the good'—applies in a peculiarly perplexing way in Catholic parishes. Too often a 'Put on your blinders, hunker down and do your own thing' mentality divides rather than unites the community."

Feit discusses the Catholic Church's early history in Rome and its original concepts about charity to the poor.

Near the end of the conversation, he observes, "You know, we all [would] like to write the story of our life. And we all like happy endings."

In Texas, investigators and the Garza family are fighting to have a special prosecutor brought in to review the murder case. They hope state and federal officials will work around the local D.A. and get all the information in the case to a grand jury for a change.

For Garza's family and many others in south Texas, the happiest ending they could hope for would be seeing Feit sitting in court facing charges in the murder of their beloved Irene.

On a return visit, Feit implores the visitor to judge him by his last forty-five years of service to his church and community. Remember, he told that Texas Ranger two years ago that the Father John Feit who lived in south Texas in 1960 no longer exists.

"Perhaps we're all operating with different ideas of justice," says Noemi Ponce-Sigler. "All I know, though, is [about] the pain this has caused so many people.

"All I know is that Irene was murdered, and that nobody has seen justice."

ROBERT NELSON has been a writer for the Phoenix New Times for six years. In that time, he has won the Thurgood Marshall Journalism Award from the Death Penalty Information Center, has been twice a finalist for Arizona Journalist of the Year, and has twice won the John Kolbe Award for political writing. In 2003 he won the Association of Alternative Newsweeklies' first-place award for political commentary. Nelson is finishing his first nonfiction novel, Bleeding Arizona, *which follows a clan of violent abolitionists from the fight for a free-state Kansas to the postwar battle for the soul of the wild new territory of Arizona.*

Coda

John Feit has yet to face charges in the murder of Irene Garza. But the fight for his indictment continues in southern Texas, where the Garza family and former law enforcement officials are pushing for the ouster of District Attorney Rene Guerra, who has failed to prosecute the case in the face of compelling evidence pointing to Feit. Feit continues to live in Phoenix, Arizona, and continues to help the city's underprivileged and elderly.

S. C. Gwynne

DR. EVIL

FROM *Texas Monthly*

ON JUNE 8, 2003, A FORMER POPEYES COOK from Houston named Cecil Viands died following routine spinal surgery at Vista Medical Center Hospital, in Pasadena. The cause was a massive infection. Under normal circumstances, Viands's death might have been seen as a bit of horrifyingly bad luck, the sort of thing that happens to one unfortunate patient in a million. But luck had little or nothing to do with it. The immediate assumption in much of the local medical community was that Viands had died because of the incompetence of his doctor: an orthopedic surgeon and one-man surgery mill named Eric Heston Scheffey.

Viands's death was only the latest episode in a long, grim tale of malpractice stretching back more than a decade. Scheffey had performed five surgeries on him since 1992. In complex and largely unjustified procedures that few orthopedists would ever have attempted, he'd methodically removed a large portion of Viands's lower spine, taking out six vertebral disks, a good deal of bone, and alternately inserting and removing intricate arrays of screws, rods, bone-graft cages, and electronic growth stimulators. His activities went well beyond what consulting doctors had recommended or what the patient had authorized. In a single operation, he'd cut into Viands's spine in seven different places—virtually unprecedented except in cases of severe accidents. He'd removed bone in order to decompress fourteen nerve roots—again, something most surgeons would never have even considered. According to an orthopedist who later reviewed the case for the Texas State Board of Medical Examiners, Scheffey's surgical failure rate over those five surgeries was 100 percent. And almost all of them were entirely unnecessary. By the time the infection killed him, Viands was already facing life as a disabled person.

As disturbing as Viands's case is, it was by no means unique or even unusual for Scheffey. There was Ed Gonzalez, for example, an auto body repairman from Humble who'd hurt his back lifting heavy equipment. Scheffey operated on him four times between 2001 and 2003, cutting out disks and bone and busily installing and removing hardware. After each surgery, Gonzalez's back pain got worse. He is now unable to walk around the block, unable to sleep, and in pain twenty-four hours a day. He says that he might have killed himself if his father had not hidden his shotgun. A person identified only as B.P. in public records, a school custodian on whose spine Scheffey operated three times between 1998 and 2000, now has a condition called drop foot in which her foot hangs limply in a vertical position. She must wear a brace to walk. She has lost all bladder control and has to wear diapers. According to a later finding by a judge, not only did B.P. not consent to the surgeries, but they too were completely unnecessary. There is a long list of such people. Many, like B.P. and Viands's widow, have sued Scheffey; many have not.

By almost any measure of medical performance, including the sheer number of his patients who are crippled, maimed, or in constant pain, Scheffey ranks as one of the worst doctors in American history. He is easily the most sued. Since 1982 he has had seventy-eight malpractice claims filed against him, a total that does not count what one attorney estimates to be more than 150 people who would have sued him if they had not been beyond the legal statute of limitations or if lawyers had been willing to take their cases. He has settled forty-five of those suits for more than $13 million. At least five people have died as a result of Scheffey's surgeries, though doctors, attorneys, and former patients will tell you that the actual, unreported number is much higher. At least four of Scheffey's patients have committed suicide because of the pain they were in or because of the depression brought on by the massive doses of narcotics the doctor prescribed or a combination of the two. One of those patients was so miserable that he committed suicide *after* he'd received a cash settlement from Scheffey.

Oddly, Scheffey's litigation-stained career has been anything but anonymous or low profile. It has been splashed all over Houston newspapers, magazines, and television news reports, which have been fascinated by his spectacular cocaine bust, in 1985, and by the multiplicity of lawsuits against him. There was also Scheffey's flamboyant lifestyle, which featured multimillion-dollar mansions in River Oaks and Shadyside; a house full of expensive, big-name art; a collection of Ferraris; a private jet; and status as a favorite son of Houston's art community. He has been the subject of five legal actions by the state medical board to either restrict or revoke his license. Viands's death led the board to suspend Scheffey's license in 2003. In February 2005, after twenty-four years, it was finally revoked, and he was fined $845,000.

Scheffey did not respond to several requests to be interviewed for this story, but if his own estimate in a deposition is correct—that his three thousand spinal procedures represented 20 to 30 percent of his total surgeries—then he may have performed eight thousand or more total operations on knees, ankles, hands, and shoulders, as well as spines. Yet what makes his story even more startling is that all were done with the explicit consent of a vast medical, insurance, and governmental bureaucracy, which, even after he became notorious for injuring patients, approved and funded every unnecessary surgery he did.

Like Viands, Mary Tywater believed she was going into the hospital for a routine operation. On the Thursday before Memorial Day weekend in 1985, Scheffey operated on the forty-three-year-old Daisetta housewife to remove several disks in her back and fuse several vertebrae. He was in the midst of that surgery when he lost control of her bleeding. Some four hours into the operation, Tywater was dead. There was blood everywhere in the operating room. The anesthesiologist's report is nearly illegible because it is smeared with Tywater's blood. Scheffey was thirty-five at the time, and this was the first fatality to take place in his operating room. But what should have been the unique horror of watching a patient bleed to death had seemingly little effect on him. He spent the holiday with his girlfriend and another couple at his large house in Baytown on Cedar Bayou. They rode golf carts around the property and drove golf balls into the water, went waterskiing, and swam in his pool.

Scheffey was used to the good life, and his career can be understood as an ongoing, if highly unconventional, attempt to maintain it. He was born in Dallas in 1949 and grew up in an affluent family with a brother and two sisters. His father was a decorated World War II pilot and a successful lawyer who once ran for mayor of Dallas. The family was wealthy enough to buy Eric a Jaguar XKE for his sixteenth birthday. He attended W. T. White High School and then the University of Texas, graduating in 1972. He began his medical training at the University of Texas Medical Branch at Galveston before transferring to the University of Texas Medical School at San Antonio and finishing in 1976. The year before, he had married Liza Goodson, a former Highland Park High School cheerleader from a well-to-do Dallas family. The marriage ended in divorce in 1979, for undisclosed reasons. He completed an internship and a four-year residency in orthopedic surgery at the Medical University of South Carolina. In 1981 he moved to Baytown, just east of Houston, home to the blue-collar industries that line the booming Houston Ship Channel.

Baytown, and east Harris County in general, is an orthopedic surgeon's paradise. People who do manual work for a living are frequently injured, and their most serious injuries usually involve backs, knees, shoulders, elbows, and hands—the domain of orthopedics. Most of these people also carry generous amounts of state-regulated workers' compensation insurance, which involves a sort of bargain between the laborer and the employer: A worker gives up the right to sue if he is injured in exchange for long-term medical care and disability benefits, including partial replacement of lost wages. Each year workers' comp in Texas covers roughly 200,000 injuries, for which 240 insurers pay out some $2 billion in benefits. The workers themselves pay nothing, and there is no limit to how much medical care they can receive. Most of these patients have real injuries. But a small percentage engage in what is known euphemistically as symptom magnification (i.e., faking it or exaggerating pain) to take advantage of the system. It is a bitter irony that many of them ended up in the offices of Eric Scheffey, who would one day become the largest single biller in the program. In later testimony, Scheffey recalled that in Baytown his practice "took off like a rocket and continued along that vein. . . . A lot of workmen's compensation patients predominated my practice and continued to do so, at least ninety percent." Under workers' comp rules, Scheffey was required to get a second opinion for every surgery. He always managed to find one.

He established his surgical practice at three Baytown hospitals: Humana Hospital Baytown, Gulf Coast Hospital, and San Jacinto Methodist Hospital. He was immediately popular. A strikingly handsome man, with olive skin, brown eyes, and a thick shock of dark, wavy hair swept back from a widow's peak, Scheffey had a soft voice, a Texas accent, and a warm, engaging manner. His patients and colleagues found him friendly, charismatic, and very persuasive, particularly when talking a patient into an expensive surgery. In the words of one patient, he "could talk a monkey out of his last peanut." He had a way of saying just the right things. According to Margaret Pieske, a former patient, Scheffey once held an X-ray up to the window, saying, "We'll use God's light." "I immediately liked him," she said, "because I thought he believed in God."

Still, the hospitals where he worked soon started to notice his odd work habits. At San Jacinto Methodist, for example, he repeatedly canceled scheduled surgeries. He also failed to keep appointments with patients or keep accurate medical charts. Internal hospital memos from as early as 1983 show that the medical staff was worried that Scheffey's erratic behavior might be the result of drug use. And he was not always the well-mannered and charming young doctor. In one nurse's report from 1984, he was described as "very ugly and sarcastic toward me." The nurse added that "his speech was very slurred and irrational."

Even more disturbing, Scheffey came to be known as a surgeon whose patients lost a great deal of blood. "The losses were massive," says Priscilla Walters, an attorney who has been involved in twenty lawsuits against Scheffey. "Sometimes almost all of the patient's blood had to be replaced. The surgeries he was performing, in the hands of a competent surgeon, did not result in much blood loss—usually about one hundred cc's, or three ounces. One of my clients lost four thousand cc's [more than a gallon] during a back surgery." Scheffey so often emerged from the operating room covered with blood that he earned a nickname: Eric the Red.

Scheffey was woefully ignorant of one of the most important areas of surgery: hemostasis, or the control of bleeding. In depositions from lawsuits, two of Scheffey's former colleagues said that since he did not know how to use conventional techniques to control bleeding, Scheffey resorted to primitive ones, notably the wildly liberal use of bone wax and Gelfoam sponges. Bone wax is a substance used to stop bone from bleeding. Gelfoam sponges are soaked in a coagulant called thrombin and are used to stop general bleeding. Most surgeons require less than one tube of bone wax during an operation. Scheffey often used ten. In a single operation, most surgeons might use one or two five-by-seven-inch Gelfoam sponges. Scheffey once used seventeen. "Since he did not know how to control bleeding, he used bone wax like Bondo," says Hartley Hampton, a Houston attorney who has represented more than a dozen of Scheffey's former patients. The application of bone wax in those quantities, according to a 1992 deposition from Dr. Baltazar Benavides, who had assisted in many of Scheffey's operations, can create a breeding ground for bacteria that cause the sorts of infections that plagued so many of Scheffey's patients.

Tywater's death was thus a logical outcome of Scheffey's incompetence. But it was also related to another of the doctor's personal quirks. On the day after Memorial Day, a security guard at Montgomery Ward found Scheffey in green surgical scrubs, with shoe covers, a cap, and a lab coat crammed with hundred-dollar bills and reported that he was "pacing real fast, swearing and cussing, pulling things off the shelves." Trailed by the security guard, Scheffey then went to the cash register and put eight toy dolls, four hundred-dollar bills, and his car keys on the counter and walked out of the store. Scheffey, as it turned out, was out of his mind on cocaine. Police later found thirty grams of the drug—about $3,000 worth—in his Jaguar. He was arrested, pled guilty to criminal possession of cocaine, and received a ten-year probation and a $2,000 fine. The state medical board restricted his license and put him on its own ten-year probation, which included drug tests, counseling, and the requirement that he be monitored by other doctors. Shortly after the incident, Scheffey checked himself into a California drug rehabilitation center.

The story, in all of its lurid detail, made the newspapers in Baytown and Houston. Though reporters never drew a direct connection between Scheffey's arrest and the death of Tywater four days earlier, the two events were connected. In a later deposition, a doctor who had worked with Scheffey testified that the staff at the hospital where Tywater had died believed that Scheffey was taking drugs and that nurses had struggled to wake a drugged Scheffey in the doctors' lounge just before he operated on her. Scheffey admitted in a medical board interview in 1986 that he had been using cocaine for eighteen months prior to his arrest.

His promising career quickly unraveled. Scheffey lost his hospital privileges at the three Baytown hospitals. The number of medical malpractice suits against him (including one from Tywater's husband) was steadily rising, from one in 1982 to thirteen in 1986. By that same year he had, for the third time, flunked a test that would have made him a board-certified orthopedic surgeon. Meanwhile, word had spread in the tight-knit medical community that he was an inept surgeon who performed unnecessary surgeries. At the age of thirty-six, he was a professional pariah. His career should have been over.

UNTIL THE EARLY 2000S, doctors in Texas were rarely removed for lack of medical competence by the Texas State Board of Medical Examiners. They were frequently reprimanded and probated, as Scheffey was, for substance abuse. They could lose their licenses for committing crimes (though at one point the state had nineteen felons practicing medicine). But they almost never had their licenses suspended or revoked for what is known in the industry as a "standard of care" violation. In fact, a doctor could be sued, as Scheffey was, dozens of times, and be the subject, as Scheffey also was, of wave after wave of complaints and still keep his license.

Which is exactly what Scheffey did. Only six months after his spectacular downfall, he even managed to find a hospital that would let him operate: a small facility in inner-city Houston called

Medical Arts Hospital. Scheffey went to work there in November 1985, embarking on what would become the most productive, lucrative, and destructive phase of his long career. He was now cocaine free; his condition was monitored by frequent urine tests ordered by the state medical board. Whether this was good or bad news for his patients was debatable. A drug-free Scheffey quickly turned into a workaholic Scheffey. Almost immediately, he became the hospital's main revenue producer, accounting for more than half of the patients at the hospital. His new private clinic in Channelview was soon jammed with people waiting for appointments. By the end of the decade, as many as ninety people a day would pass through his office.

A good example from that era was William McDuell, a Houston truck driver who came to Scheffey with a broken wrist. Scheffey operated on McDuell at Doctors Hospital-Airline, in Houston (where he received privileges in 1986), set the wrist, and had it put in a cast. Soon afterward, according to McDuell, his wrist "split open" from an infection. Scheffey operated again to fix the wrist and then somehow persuaded McDuell, who had merely mentioned to Scheffey that his leg had once locked up, to undergo back surgery in order to fix his leg. Scheffey performed the operation, after which McDuell was forced to stay in the hospital, in pain, for two weeks. Ten months later, McDuell was still in pain, and Scheffey operated again. This time McDuell's back went numb, and he could neither get out of bed by himself nor walk without falling. Scheffey operated a third time on his back, after which McDuell found that he could not swallow. A fourth surgery left him in constant pain, and he had been unable to sleep well since his ordeal had begun. When Scheffey then told him that he needed a fifth surgery, he consulted another doctor. (McDuell later sued, and Scheffey settled out of court.)

Why would Scheffey operate five times—or fifteen times in another case—when it probably wasn't necessary? As far as anyone can tell, the answer was, very simply, money. He propped up his lavish lifestyle by performing anywhere between 250 and 350 surgeries annually, some of which could cost as much as $50,000 each. In 1988 he sold his house in Baytown and bought a twelve-bedroom, eight-thousand-square-foot, $2.75 million mansion on West Lane, in River Oaks. And while he ran his high-volume surgery mill out of his medical clinic—from which he took in more than $3 million a year—he plunged into the glittering social life in the heart of old-money Houston.

The next few years of Scheffey's life are a testament to the fluidity of wealth in Houston and to the lack of social barriers for anyone with a great deal of money and a resolute willingness to throw it around. Tan, fit, rich, handsome, and extremely eligible, Scheffey began courting wealthy Houston women and was soon showing up in the society pages. He had a long relationship with socialite Francesca Bergner Stedman. According to the *Houston Press,* it led to the end of her marriage with Stuart Stedman, the grandson of real estate and oil tycoon Wesley West. Together they hosted receptions for the Houston Symphony and the Houston Art League and threw parties at his house. Scheffey was on the board at the Contemporary Arts Museum Houston and gave generously to many local arts organizations. He socialized with the likes of art collector and heiress Dominique de Menil and arts patron Sue Rowan Pittman.

His lifestyle was not just lavish but quite public as well. His multimillion-dollar car collection was perhaps the best example of this. The July-August 1991 issue of the Houston fashion magazine *Intrigue* described the collection as "a dizzying array of red, white and black sports cars that includes seven Ferraris, a Porsche, and a BMW 750il." They were all housed in a specially built, brick-paved, climate-controlled garage with mirrored walls. By all accounts, the interior of his house, which he had renovated over a seventeen-month period at huge expense, was stunning. "Dr. Eric Scheffey's River Oaks house is positively jam-packed with eye-popping, mind-boggling, big-time, famous-name art," gushed

Houston Metropolitan magazine in the fall of 1991. That art included works by Frank Stella, Robert Rauschenberg, and Salvador Dalí. Almost every piece of furniture in the house—like the 1945 rosewood-and-aluminum Brunswick-Balke-Collender pool table—was special in some way. Scheffey, who was a music aficionado, had installed a $250,000 stereo system, which was featured in another magazine story. He also co-owned a private plane. To many people, it looked very nearly like a perfect life.

WHILE THE FAILURE OF either the Texas State Board of Medical Examiners or the Texas Workers' Compensation Commission (TWCC)—which had to approve every surgery—to put a stop to Scheffey was ongoing, he didn't entirely escape the notice of the medical community. In 1985 a Houston neurosurgeon named Martin Barrash began to see former patients of Scheffey's and became alarmed at the condition that many of them were in. "I started seeing people with the most god-awful complications I'd ever seen in my life," says Barrash. "One woman I saw had a piece of her ureter taken out during a disk [operation]. I had to go look in the literature. I had never even heard of it. . . . The patient's belly filled up with urine. He didn't know what the hell he was doing." Barrash also says he saw patients who were, as he puts it, "plunged on," meaning that Scheffey had slipped with a bone-biting instrument. The result: People being treated for minor back injuries ended up having trouble walking. "He would get in the spine and get lost," Barrash says. Barrash became one of a very small group of doctors who both testified in malpractice suits against Scheffey and notified the state medical board about botched surgeries.

Many of the injuries Barrash saw over the years involved the spine. Scheffey's hallmark operation was the spinal fusion in the lower, or lumbar, area of the back, which usually involves removing a ruptured, herniated, or severely deteriorated disk, installing a bone graft (usually from the pelvis) where the disk was, and securing it with screws and rods. While many orthopedic surgeons regard fusion at even a single level (there are five lumbar levels, corresponding to each vertebra) as something of a last resort, multilevel spine fusions were Scheffey's principal source of profit. He would commonly do something that few other surgeons would do, or even find necessary, which was to reoperate on a patient in order to remove the screws and rods he had put in. "Routine removal is medically unnecessary," says George "Buddy" Tipton, an Austin orthopedic surgeon who testified against Scheffey before the medical board. "In all the cases I reviewed, he took out screws and rods for no reason. Even an experienced surgeon risks nerve injury, and that can result in permanent paralysis and loss of bowel function, bladder function, and sexual function." There are other risks of fusion as well: The more the back is fused together, the more pressure there is on other disks and vertebrae and the greater the likelihood that those parts of the spine will fail or become unstable too.

The result for Scheffey was, by the early nineties, litigation on a scale that has rarely been seen. By 1995 fifty malpractice suits had been filed against him for unnecessary or incompetent surgeries, overprescription of drugs, and other issues related to his bizarre willingness to perform operation after operation on people who apparently did not need them. One of those cases was that of Pete Dunstan, whose 1988 lawsuit offered another window into the strange and lethal medical subworld of Eric Scheffey.

When he began treating Dunstan in 1985, the patient was a healthy, athletic forty-four-year-old whose only problem was that he had strained his back. Scheffey told Dunstan that a disk in his back was about to rupture and performed a three-level fusion. A few months later Scheffey performed a two-level fusion on Dunstan's neck, this time telling him that another disk was about to rupture. The fusions failed, leaving Dunstan crippled and in constant pain. His condition at the time he left Scheffey's care can be summarized as follows: He had atrophy and weakness in his right hand due to an ulnar nerve Scheffey had damaged and difficulty urinating. He was impotent, severely addicted to painkillers, in unremitting pain, and, according to his doctors at the time of his deposition, would never work again. Scheffey settled out of court with Dunstan for $2.6 million, but Dunstan's crippled, pain-racked condition suggests a reason why two other Scheffey patients in those years, Benny Norton and Charles Webster, committed suicide. (Both families sued Scheffey.)

By the mid-nineties Scheffey had already been deposed an astonishing ninety times, but the videotapes from some of those sessions offer few hints that he felt any remorse. When challenged, his approach was almost always to retreat into medicalese, droning on for hours about the more technically complex points of his surgeries. One video deposition from 1992 is typical: Scheffey, with a guardedly neutral expression on his face, answered questions with a sort of impenetrable, emotionless objectivity. He conceded nothing. One of the few press interviews he ever gave (to the *Houston Chronicle,* in 1995) suggests a deeply adversary cast of mind. "They [insurance companies] set out on a plan . . . They have kept me in hot water with the board with complaints about patients," he said. "They managed to have me sued a number of times in such a manner that it made it difficult for me to get malpractice insurance . . ." Scheffey backed up such claims by mounting his own legal attacks against those whom he perceived to be harming him. He sued Barrash for slander three times. He sued an insurance company, whom he said had slandered him, winning a whopping $11 million in 1993. He also sued the media that had covered him, including NBC and the *Houston Press,* whose 1992 "Eric the Red" story was harshly critical of him. The *Press* settled out of court.

Yet none of his legal trouble seemed to deter Scheffey or make him change his behavior. His biggest problem was finding anyone to insure him at all. In 1993 he had appealed to the state Commissioner of Insurance to force the Texas Medical Liability Insurance Underwriting Association to suspend a surcharge they had imposed on him that would have required him to pay $537,931 in addition to his usual premium of $63,286. Such a surcharge meant that the insurance company would be charging $601,217 for what amounted to $600,000 of insurance. Scheffey lost the appeal. If state regulators had not quite figured out who Scheffey was yet, the insurance companies certainly had.

Where were the regulators? Why, with so many lawsuits filed, a track record known to a large segment of the medical community in Houston, and continual coverage in the press, was he allowed to continue performing surgeries in the state of Texas? In 1989 the state board had filed an informal complaint against the doctor based on a long list of patient injuries and other problems collected by Barrash, who by now was spending a good deal of time trying to expose Scheffey. But it was not until 1993 that the board mounted a full-scale, heavily-documented effort to revoke Scheffey's license in an administrative law court. Hearings in that case coincided with news of yet another Scheffey disaster: In 1994 his patient Ancel "Bud" Freeman, who had gone in for his third back operation, lost four quarts of blood and died after a seven-hour surgery. In 1995 a judge did what everyone expected: She recommended that Scheffey's license be revoked, not just for malpractice but also for excessive charges. But the board ignored that recommendation and voted instead to give Scheffey a five-year probation that would let him continue to practice but with some restrictions: To operate, for instance, he would have to have a written consultation from another doctor. "I was extremely distressed and disgusted at the board's action," says then–executive director Bruce Levy, whose staff mounted the case. "I came close to resigning."

Scheffey immediately appealed the ruling in a state district court and won a temporary injunction. Later, the court reversed the board's decision, allowing Scheffey to proceed as though nothing had happened. It was not until 1997 that an appeals court reversed the district court, but by then Scheffey's probation had less than three years to run. It is likely that Scheffey had started to believe, with good reason, that his medical license was legally invulnerable.

THUS BEGAN WHAT AMOUNTED to a second professional golden age for Scheffey. In the late nineties he went to trial with five lawsuits and won them all, including one by the family of Freeman. The number of lawsuits filed against him dropped: From 1997 through 1999 only three suits were filed; from 2000 to 2002 there were only six. And he was making more money than ever. According to filings in one lawsuit, Scheffey's gross income from his practice in 1998 was $4,032,292. By 2002 it had risen to $5,453,361. Four entries from his 2002 profit-and-loss statement suggest the sort of life he was leading: Entertainment and meals: $238,927; Legal [fees]: $259,013; Travel and convention: $389,419; Charter expense [aircraft]: $448,260.

In the wake of all the bad press in 1994 and 1995, however, Scheffey had begun to lose friends in River Oaks, especially in the old-money set. "Oh, this guy was playing big, trying to date girls of the old Houston circle," says a woman who runs in those circles but asked not to be identified. "The problem was that old Houston never liked him and was always suspicious of him." Says *Houston Chronicle* society columnist Shelby Hodge: "People absolutely stopped seeing him. People cluck-clucked all the time, especially in the medical community." But in 1999 Scheffey had done something that had greatly improved his social standing: He'd married a young society woman named Kendall Thomas, who was eighteen years younger than he was. She was pretty and well connected and part of the young social set in River Oaks. A year before he married her, he had moved into a $5.8 million, ten-thousand-square-foot house on Longfellow Lane, in Shadyside, near Rice University. The place was so spectacular that its landscaping and elaborate flower beds were featured five years later on the cover of *Texas,* the *Houston Chronicle*'s Sunday magazine.

With Kendall there were parties and social invitations, even though many people wondered, as one acquaintance put it, "what she was doing with him." But he never quite made it back inside: "I went to a party at their house, one of those art groups," says the friend. "I just remember that it was a big party with big money but kind of sleazy people. Girls with surgeries, like they might have had a background in exotic dancing. You know what I mean."

Through all this tumult, both social and professional, there is no evidence that Scheffey altered even a small part of the work behavior that had caused him so much trouble. It seemed that Scheffey's practice had never operated quite so efficiently, relying upon an elaborate network of enablers that included fellow surgeons, nurses, radiologists, anesthesiologists, and a system of insurance and workers' comp approvals that was easily gamed. The TWCC, which, in effect, controlled 90 percent of his revenue, not only allowed him to continue but failed to challenge him when he was asking for approval (in one case, for the fifteenth surgery on a patient). Once the TWCC approved it, there was little anyone could do.

Scheffey had also found the perfect home for the sort of work he did: a facility in Pasadena called Vista Medical Center Hospital. Vista was owned by a publicly traded Houston company called Dynacq Healthcare, whose main line of business was high-volume surgery. Dynacq, in fact, made both the Forbes and Fortune lists of the one hundred fastest-growing companies in 2002 on the strength of its astounding 47 percent annual growth rate over a three-year period. In a 2003 article in *Barron's*, company spokesman Jim Baxter boasted that "a very active surgeon might be able to do five spinal surgeries in a day." It is unclear if he was referring specifically to Scheffey, but he may as well have been. In one deposition, a Vista nurse said that Scheffey would often have two operating rooms going at the same time. So dependent was Vista on Scheffey that when his license was later suspended, in 2003, his absence led to dropping profits, which had a direct impact on Dynacq's bottom line.

Vista was also remarkably undiscriminating in whom it allowed to use its facilities. In 2001 Vista became the last hospital in Houston (of twenty at one time or another) to let Scheffey operate. According to a 2004 report by the Texas Department of State Health Services, Vista not only failed to check on its doctors' records and on lawsuits against them but also knowingly allowed Scheffey to perform surgeries in 1999 and 2000 as the main surgeon and without a monitor, in violation of his probation. In response to a detailed and lengthy written query from this magazine, Dynacq spokesperson Christina Gutel would say only: "Dr. Eric Scheffey was licensed by the Texas State Board of Medical Examiners during his tenure at Vista Medical Center Hospital. As soon as that board suspended his license, his surgical privileges were revoked at Vista Medical Center Hospital."

All the while, of course, the list of Scheffey's victims only grew longer. In 2001 he'd operated on Thomas T. "Buddy" King after King had injured his back in a truck accident. Instead of the four hours the operation was supposed to have lasted, it took fourteen hours. King lost large amounts of blood. When it was over, he had severe pain in his legs. On the third day after the surgery, on his way to the bathroom, King dropped dead of a blood clot. Another patient, Jennifer Springs, was a fast-food cashier who had injured her back in a fall in 1995. Scheffey had operated on her back eight times between 1996 and 2001, telling her that if she did not have the operations, she would eventually be unable to walk. She got worse and worse, at one point staying in the hospital for three months. She now has severe leg and back pain, far more intense than when she started out. She can walk only short distances. Patient Mary Garcia lost a large amount of blood in a 2002 operation on her back. Now she too has severe pain in her legs and back, can't sleep because of the pain, and can walk only short distances.

She will never be able to work again. She sued Scheffey last year. "I try not to take too much pain medication," she says. "I prefer to cry."

With such a constant flow of patient complaints, Scheffey ought to have attracted (yet again) the attention of the state board. But the lesson of 1995 was that even if the board mounted a large and competent case, it was still impossible to get rid of Scheffey for reasons of malpractice. In 2002 *Dallas Morning News* reporter Doug J. Swanson published a sweeping indictment of the medical board as an incompetent, do-nothing agency. "It has refused," wrote Swanson, "in the last five years to revoke the license of a single doctor for committing medical errors." Nothing was different at the workers' comp commission either: The agency still resolutely refused to throw out bad doctors.

Things finally began to change at the state board under president Lee Anderson and new executive director Donald Patrick. In 2002 the number of informal "settlement conferences"—where doctors come before the board to defend themselves against complaints—rose from 172 to 477, the number of disciplinary actions jumped from 187 to 277, and the financial penalties more than doubled. Budgets increased. Government funds flowed. Bad doctors had their licenses taken away for standard-of-care violations. "We, the agency and the board, began to see our mission differently," says Patrick. "There is a lot of fearlessness, because we've got nothing to lose. We said, 'Let's do as good a job as we can to try to protect the people of Texas,' because we were aware that we had not been doing that." The same thing was happening, at a much slower pace, at the TWCC, where medical adviser Bill Nemeth had instituted an "approved doctor" list, prompting howls of protest from the Texas Medical Association, the doctors' trade association.

Taking out Scheffey was one of the reformers' top priorities. In 2003, after the death of Cecil Viands, Scheffey's license was temporarily suspended by the state medical board. The following year, the board brought a second case against him that was based on twenty-nine surgeries on eleven patients and the testimony of six surgeons. On the recommendation of that court, Scheffey's license to practice was revoked in February 2005. He has appealed it, though it seems unlikely that he will win reinstatement.

Though Scheffey would not comment for this story, his long-time lawyer, Ace Pickens, said he felt that there was no basis for either the revocation of Scheffey's license or for the $845,000 fine. "If you look at the Board of Medical Examiners' records for administrative penalties over the last five years," Pickens says, "[and] you add them all up, it would not amount to this one case." He also pointed out that almost all of Scheffey's surgeries had been supported by second opinions: "They took eleven patients, ten of whom had been subject to second opinions, and said that second opinions by board-certified orthopedic surgeons were no good and that the surgery should not have been performed. Even if that is so, at least he went through the system and should be given the benefit of the doubt. He did not go about maliciously performing surgery. He got a second opinion for everything he did." Pickens, who has known Scheffey for more than twenty years and says the two are friends, also vouches for Scheffey's character. "Dr. Scheffey has absolutely been a lightning rod because he is an advocate for patients," says Pickens. "He is a good man. I don't believe he is an ogre or that he is evil."

SCHEFFEY NOW APPEARS to be completely out of business. Two months after his license was revoked, a corporation he owned called Harris County Bone and Joint Clinic Association pled guilty to a third-degree-felony charge of "securing execution of a document by deception"—fraudulent billing—and paid penalties of $25,599. He sold his mansion in Shadyside and moved back into the smaller mansion in River Oaks, where he still officially resides and where he was served with litigation papers as recently as April. According to Harris County records, he still faces roughly twenty malpractice suits, all filed since 2000. Though he was recently investigated by the FBI for workers' comp fraud, the agency says that that investigation is now complete. It produced no indictments. In its 2004 complaint, the state medical board also charged Scheffey with practicing medicine with a suspended license, a third-degree felony punishable by up to ten years in prison. According to the complaint, Scheffey had continued to practice medicine even after his 2003 suspension, using his partner Dr. Floyd Hardimon as a front. When the board temporarily suspended Hardimon's license later in 2003, it did so in part because it found that Hardimon "associated with and aided and abetted [Scheffey] in the practice of medicine after [Scheffey's] medical license had been suspended."

In the absence of any criminal charges, Scheffey is, remarkably, free to do everything but practice as a doctor. There is little doubt that he has an enormous amount of money. The talk among the Scheffeys' old social crowd in River Oaks is that Eric and Kendall have purchased a home in Geneva, Switzerland, where they have moved with their two children. "One day Kendall called me and said, 'We are moving to Geneva. Here is my number. Please call,' " says one friend who asked not to be identified. "She said, 'People are so mean-spirited. We are sorry we are leaving on such a negative and sour note.' " But very likely not as sorry as patients like Mary Garcia and Ed Gonzalez. Indeed, one of Scheffey's hallmarks is his ability to move blithely through his life, as though there were not an enormous trail of human wreckage behind him. And he feels no apparent need to hide or disappear into anonymity. Friends say that he and Kendall rented a big house for the summer in one of the richest and most celebrity-filled resort towns in America: Aspen, Colorado.

S. C. GWYNNE *joined* Texas Monthly *as an executive editor in June of 2000. Prior to that, he was Austin bureau chief for* Time *magazine, responsible for its coverage of Texas, Louisiana, Arkansas, and the Mexico border. He moved to Austin in 1994 from Time's headquarters in New York where he was a senior editor in charge of the business section. He first joined Time in 1988 as a correspondent in the Los Angeles bureau covering California and the western states. He was later Detroit bureau chief and national economics correspondent in Time's Washington, D.C., bureau. Gwynne was co-author of Time's first cover story on George W. Bush. Subjects of his Texas Monthly stories include Tom Craddick, Karl Rove, terrorism in Houston, and Big Bend. Gwynne is a 1974 graduate of Princeton University and received a master's degree from Johns Hopkins University in 1977.*

Coda

The idea for "Dr. Evil" came out of a short article in the *Houston Chronicle* that was based on the news that Scheffey's medical license had been revoked. The reporter recapped the essentials of Scheffey's career—the lawsuits, the huge settlements. I had never heard of Scheffey before, but I was amazed that he had been able to continue to practice in spite of the huge number of complaints, lawsuits, and patient deaths. The $845,000 fine was impressive but it begged the question: Why hadn't the state medical board gotten rid of him years before?

Six months of reporting later, I finally had the full answer to that question. Why six months? Mainly because of the volume of legal material that I had to wade through. I have done a lot of investigative stories in my career but none that required as much slogging through depositions, court transcripts, pleadings, summary judgments, administrative law proceedings, and medical records. Scheffey was a monster of litigation. He sued everyone and was sued by everyone. The good part about this was that all these meticulous court records made it possible to track his thirty-year career in a fairly minute way and without his cooperation. The difficult part was sitting in regulatory and legal offices, week after week, reading thousands of pages of text. I estimate that I read or at least cast my eyes on more than 20,000 pages. I spent almost three weeks camped at a desk in downtown Austin at the medical board, as various board staffers brought me box after box of legal proceedings and medical records. From there I went to a plaintiff's lawyer's office in Houston where I spent another two weeks reading more than seventy lawsuits against Scheffey, including dozens of lengthy depositions.

The story has an interesting ending. While I was reporting it, I suspected that the Harris County (Houston) district attorney's office was investigating Scheffey, but they had denied this and I could not prove it. Then I managed to find out that Scheffey was not in Switzerland, as everyone assumed, but in Aspen, Colorado. Suddenly I was on the phone trading information with the Harris County district attorney. They told me that they were after Scheffey for practicing without a license and had a sealed indictment. The only reason they had not arrested him was because they believed he was out of the country. My information changed that. They put out warrants to the Aspen police, and Scheffey was arrested in Aspen about a week after my story came out. (I agreed not to spill the beans about the indictment, which almost certainly would have tipped Scheffey off and might have caused him to leave the country.) He agreed to return to Houston, where he was arraigned and charged with a felony. He is now mostly confined to his house in Houston, awaiting trial.

Paige Williams

HOW TO LOSE $100,000,000

FROM *GQ*

ON CHRISTMAS DAY 2002, Jack Whittaker, a fifty-five-year-old contractor from Scott Depot, West Virginia, won $314,900,000 off a $1 Powerball ticket and became the biggest lottery winner of all time. Lucky Jack.

But for certain guys, winning the lottery can be just about the worst thing to ever happen. You might as well hand them a grenade. Plenty of winners have blown their dough in the post-payoff delirium, but no one has done it quite like Big Jack. One minute he was a good Christian husband, father, grandfather, and businessman, just another respectable old dude in a cowboy hat living his West Virginia life, and the next he was sitting on a curb outside a titty bar, complaining to the cops that an ex-stripper named Misty and her boyfriend drugged his cocktail, busted out the window of his truck, and made off with a half-million of his dollars. And things were only starting to get ugly.

AT ITS BEST, WEST VIRGINIA is as green as Jack Whittaker's millions, but in March it is muddy-river brown. Windowless factories line the Kanawha River, and in between stand forgettable little towns, drab mountain pockets of overworked humanity, connected by interstates. Every other restaurant is a Biscuit World. Fog hangs on the river and on the bare branches of trees. Rain falls on tobacco barns, boatyards, and coal trains, and on the lonely gold dome of the capitol. It's hard not to wonder how this affects a fellow's psychology. A man might be driven to do just about anything in the brown months of West Virginia.

Jack lives now, as he did then, in one of these little interstate towns, called Scott Depot. His house is a two-story brick number, like countless others in these parts. He owns a construction business, Diversified Enterprise Inc., which builds water and sewer systems across the state. He's been working since age fourteen and has been with his wife, Jewell, about that long, too. Supposedly, his company was grossing more than $17 million for a while but ran into some problems, and Jack had to lay off twenty-five of his 117 employees. His adult daughter, Ginger McMahan, has been battling lymphoma. Jack's own health isn't tip-top, either. He loves his teenage granddaughter, Brandi, so much, he named his office building after her: the Brandi Building. Millionaire or not, Jack liked to play the lottery.

Right before Christmas 2002, the Powerball prize climbed to record size. People in twenty-three states, the District of Columbia, and the U.S. Virgin Islands fattened the pot in anticipation of the televised drawing Christmas night. On the morning of December 23, Jack stopped by C&L Super Serve in the town of Hurricane, where Brenda Higginbotham cooked the food that sat under the heat lamp. Like most mornings, she fixed Jack a bacon-and-tomato biscuit to go, pulling out the biscuit guts to help him with his cholesterol. She called him her "cowboy man" and knew him about as well as you can know anyone who stays long enough to order breakfast and comment on the weather. That morning, along with the biscuit, Jack bought $100 worth of lottery tickets.

By Christmas Eve, the pot reached beyond $280 million, and by Christmas Day, $314.9 million. The odds of winning were 120 million to 1. When the winning numbers were announced, Jack had all but one. He went to bed Christmas night thinking he'd won five grand. The next morning he learned that the TV had misreported it. He and Jewell checked and checked again—Jack had the sole winning combo: 5-14-16-29-53, Powerball 7.

Jack took the onetime payment of $170 million and walked away with $113 million post-tax. He accepted his easy money before a battery of cameras, dressed in a black outfit and hat, as Jewell, Ginger, and Brandi stood alongside him. The governor handed Jack the big poster-board check and said what a good ambassador Andrew Jackson Whittaker Jr. would make for the state of West Virginia. And for a while, that's what Jack was. Right away, he thanked God for giving him the right numbers. He immediately pledged $17 million to several franchises of the Church of God; then he started giving away millions to various charities. Jack bought people houses and cars and college educations, gave money to old people and poor people and Little Leaguers. He was feted and filmed and generally hailed as the pride of West Virginia but "real down-to-earth," which is just about the best thing one West Virginian can say about another.

You could hardly turn on the TV or open a newspaper without seeing Jack in his big black cowboy hat playing the role of Christian do-gooder with down-home brio. He went on *Good Morning America* and *Today* and let the perky morning-talk-show hosts slobber over him; then he went back to West Virginia and impressed his friends and neighbors by working the same long hours at the same old job.

He cut checks to the churches as promised. He bought Higginbotham, the biscuit-maker, a three-bedroom home and a used Jeep Grand Cherokee, and did about the same for the clerk who'd sold him the winning ticket. He promised Brandi he'd spend more time with her and do his best to help her fulfill her dream of meeting the rapper Nelly. He set up the Jack Whittaker Foundation and started handing out what his staff says was $60,000 a month in food, clothing, and household items to needy families across the state, which seems implausible until you remember Jack Whittaker won enough money to give away $1 million a year for the next 113 years. He started getting so many letters of need, he had to hire people just to open them. His neighbors had to deal with extra traffic because half the state wanted a look at the home of an honest-to-God dream come true. Jewell told CNN she literally got sick when Jack won the Powerball but has since decided the money is a good thing because of all the people they can help. She has said her greatest desire is to visit Israel so she can see "where Jesus walked," but other than that, all of this just made her want to run and hide. Jack, on the other hand, decided to come out and play.

FROM A FRONTAGE ROAD WEST OF CHARLESTON, near a carpet outlet and the local Bob Evans, the club with the hot-pink awning calls out to the road-weary, marriage-weary, flesh-starved men of Interstate 64. One night Jack Whittaker heeds the call. He strides right into the Pink Pony and throws about $50,000 on the bar. It's New Year's Eve 2002, and he is six days a megamillionaire.

Mike Dunn, the Pony's general manager, runs a smooth establishment and is not the kind of fellow who needs trouble spelled out for him. He takes one look at that wad and decides to have a word with Jack. He goes over, introduces himself to Jack, says, Glad to have you here, sir, but please be a bit more discreet with the dough. He secures Jack a limo and a guard and gets him and his fifty grand home safe and sound. Jack stops throwing around fifty grand but at his subsequent Pony outings still flashes enough cash to make it clear he's a big shot.

It's a summer Monday evening, and Jack has a hankering for vodka and a briefcase full of scratch: $245,000 in $100 bills and three $100,000 cashier checks. He gets rolling at Billy Sunday's, a bar near his office that has a note on the door asking its patrons to please leave their knives and whatnot in the truck. It's a good place to catch a wet-T-shirt contest or a NASCAR race. The staff didn't know Jack before he won the lottery, but they know him plenty now. Sometimes he shoots pool. Sometimes he just sits and drinks his Absolut and orange (or tomato) juice—doubles, if they recall. If he's feeling generous, he might throw down a good tip or give a cute young bartender a gold Rolex pen right out of his pocket, just for the hell of it, because he can, because he's Big Jack. He tells people he's a martial-arts expert and sometimes gets up to do a few karate kicks to prove it.

By the time he gets to the Pink Pony, it's around 2:00 A.M. and he has had, by his own count, seven or eight drinks. He leaves to drive to the Motel 6 to meet a friend, but the friend doesn't show, so Jack drives back to the Pony. He parks his Navigator alongside the front door and locks it with the engine running. The half-million-dollar briefcase is on the front seat.

The kitchen manager, Jeffrey Caplinger, is in charge for the night. Jeff dates Misty Dawn Arnold, an ex-dancer who gave up the pole upon getting pregnant. The other strippers pay her to help them with their scheduling and outfits and hair. According to the club's bartender, the whole thing went down like this: At some point, Misty walks Jack out to the Navigator—maybe he needs more spending money or aims to dazzle Misty with the contents of the briefcase. Whatever it is, Misty comes back inside, says somebody needs to rob that dude.

Jack orders a vodka and tomato juice, but they're out of tomato juice so they make him a vodka and Hawaiian Punch. According to the bartender, Misty dumps a couple of blue capsules in Jack's drink. The bartender says: Misty, what gives? And Misty says: Don't worry about it; Jeff's outside breaking into the Navigator. Pretty soon Jack can't hold his head up, so they let him lie down in a back room. Toward dawn he staggers outside and discovers one smashed window, zero briefcases. There's a lot of yelling. Jack and Jeff get into it, and pretty soon Jeff's got a cut on his nose and the Pink Pony is crawling with cops. Jack summons his own security man, who finds the purloined briefcase stashed behind the Dumpster with the money still in it. The bartender later testifies to all of this at a West Virginia Alcohol Beverage Control hearing on whether to pull the Pony's liquor license, a hearing that culminates in an attorney asking Jack if it's common knowledge that he totes around so much cash, to which Jack responds: "You know, I did win the biggest lottery in history."

IT DOESN'T TAKE LONG FOR PEOPLE to start talking about Jack's predilection for loose cash and naked strangers. Christians come out of the cracks to call him a hypocrite, but Jack keeps on being Jack. One November night, at Billy Sunday's, long past last call, they're shepherding stragglers to the door. Among them the management remembers Jack and a woman they know as his girlfriend. Jack seems to get the idea that people are disrespecting her, so on the way out he tells one of the owners, Billy Browning Jr., to knock it off. Browning tells Jack it's simply time to go home. According to Browning and a witness, Jack says something about having Browning killed. Browning tells him not to come back. But a few months later, Jack's back.

Todd Parsons, the manager at Billy's, takes him aside, asks him to leave. " 'You don't want to do this,' " Parsons remembers Jack saying. " 'You don't want to put me out of here. I'll kill you and your family for this. I've got enough money now to where I can have y'all killed and nobody would ever know.' " Parsons, twenty-eight, who has a wife and two young kids, takes this rather personally. He tells Jack he can either go now or talk to the law. Jack swings. Parsons puts him out. The cops come and charge Jack with assault; according to a police report, a security-camera tape backs it all up.

Jack, meanwhile, is still driving the Navigator. A couple of weeks after the Billy's incident, he leaves $100,000 in a bank bag in the Navigator in his driveway, and naturally, someone takes it. The cops are getting sick of telling Jack to put his money in the bank. They've been spending half their time either writing him up or hunting down his loot. Jack installs security cameras overlooking his front porch (bare but for brass planters full of cigarette butts) and over the driveway and garage (silver Rolls, an Escalade, a muscle car missing a wheel or two).

So Jack's starting to become everybody's favorite joke, but while they're laughing they're also crying, because it seems unfair that God or whoever had handed a life-altering sum of money to a guy who not only already had plenty but who leaves it lying around like trash.

Eight days after the $100,000 goes missing, the state police report finding Jack slumped over the wheel on the side of I-64, not far from the Pink Pony. They wake him up and give him some DUI tests. He fails the follow-the-finger, the walk-and-turn, then he blows nearly twice the legal limit on the Breathalyzer. It's 5:30 in the afternoon.

But this snowball's still rolling. Weeks later, someone breaks into Jack's office and swipes $2,000. That same afternoon, Jack gets sued. The plaintiff is Charity Fortner, a young floor attendant at Tri-State Racetrack & Gaming Center, a greyhound track and slots casino down the road from the Pink Pony. Jack is a regular in the High Rollers Room, where the bet limit is $5. Charity's job is to change out the empty coin hoppers. Jack was gambling one day alongside a "lady friend," and when Charity bent to refill the hopper, Jack grabbed her ponytail and shoved her head toward his crotch. So alleges her suit. Fortner declines to comment, but her

lawyer, Scott Segal, says, "The fact of the matter is, if someone
doesn't take on men who act this way, it becomes acceptable conduct. Will it be an easier verdict to collect [because he's rich]? I
hope it will be. But the way the man's behaving, he may lose every
last cent before this case is over. He might as well be throwing it in
the river."

It didn't take long for Jack to lose some more dough. Two days
after the lawsuit is filed, another $85,000 disappears from the
Navigator, again from Jack's driveway. The new security cameras
record a man and a woman calmly taking the stash before driving
off in a van. The cops begin the hunt for a whole new batch of
missing money. Jack tells a local TV news crew: "I'm ready to kill
somebody." The feeling is now rather mutual. "There's been a lot of
unfortunate things," says Raymond Peak, the soft-spoken mayor of
Hurricane, where Jack scored his lucky ticket. "Carrying around so
much money entices people to want to rob him. People think he's
nuts. As a public official, it makes it difficult to condone. But it's his
money. I guess he can do what he wants."

BY NOW THERE'S NO TELLING how many people are em-
broiled in the seamier side of Jack Whittaker's good fortune. This
fall, a dead guy was found in one of Jack's houses. His body was discovered around the time police were investigating a burglary of the
house by two other men, one of whom committed the crime in
drag. The dead guy had been a friend of Brandi's, but apparently
the Whittakers didn't have anything to do with his death. This is
one of the sadder facts of Jack's life now: The trouble he used to
invite now sort of lurks in the shrubs. He was even thinking of
polling county residents on their opinion of him to see if he could
get a fair trial there.

To be sure, a whole tragicomic parade of formerly anonymous
people have lined up to testify for or against him in the criminal
and civil courts of West Virginia. In addition, several adult-

entertainment professionals have lost their jobs, and little roadside churches have had to defend themselves for accepting tithes from a guy who's been treating metropolitan Charleston like his private saloon. His own granddaughter has lost friends because she can't decide whom to trust. "She's the most bitter sixteen-year-old I know," Jack told the Associated Press.

At last check, Misty and Jeff and two separate trios of accused thieves were awaiting trial; the cops were still trying to track stolen Whittaker dough; prosecutors were preparing assault and DUI cases against Jack; two more women had sued, alleging that Jack had sexually affronted them between slot pulls; the owners and managers of Billy Sunday's had hired lawyers to defend themselves in a suit Jack Whittaker brought against them; two other, completely different fellows had now sued Jack over another incident at another club (Jack supposedly became enraged over losing a coin toss or something); bartenders dreaded seeing him walk through the door; and Mike Dunn was still trying to get the Pink Pony's liquor license back.

Robby, the Pony's former cook, wound up behind the bar of another gentlemen's establishment, in a mini-mall next door to a boarded-up adult bookstore. He looks a little wistful there one afternoon as he tends the empty club and its trio of strippers, who alternately work their poles and holler at him to turn up the fucking jukebox and to get them another Wild Turkey, goddammit. Robby misses the Pony. He liked his job, liked his boss, and probably would have kept on there if not for Jack's shenanigans. Like most everyone else, Robby doesn't say too much, because nobody cares to bad-mouth a guy with a load of lawyer money. "Besides," Robby says, "in West Virginia, rats get hurt." He did offer this, though: "People think money gives them power. But it don't."

The huge sign over the C&L Super Serve (THE BIG ONE SOLD HERE!) now seems less celebratory than ironic. Even Jack's preacher, whose little Tabernacle of Praise is $7 million richer, doesn't defend Jack so much as pretend he doesn't exist. When asked about the drinking and fighting and strippers, pastor C. T. Mathews said, "I don't know what you're talking about." Then, "What he does is his business. Here, we talk about our business and the Lord's business."

Lots of people around Scott Depot wish Jack had taken his business elsewhere. "I'll tell you what he should have done: He should have taken that money and gotten the hell out of West Virginia," one bartender said. "That's what I'd have done. I'd have bought me an island."

Jack's biggest mistake, though, was probably a gross deficit of subtlety. In flashing his cash, it's almost as though he wanted people to take it. Maybe he felt he didn't deserve it. Or maybe the money made him feel invincible, like the badass he always suspected he was—or wasn't. Maybe he was trying to simultaneously redeem and punish himself. Maybe he broke beneath the burden of divine good luck. But here's the thing. Even though he has been arrested, sued, banned from bars, robbed, and ridiculed, is down $155,000 in Navigator losses alone, and stands to lose thousands more in legal fees, Jack Whittaker has another $100 million or so to lose. So if he should decide to go ahead and blow everything, he'll have a hell of a long way to go.

God help West Virginia.

PAIGE WILLIAMS *is a nomadic writer who currently lives in New York. Her story "The Accused" appeared in* The Best American Crime Writing 2003.

Coda

On the surface this seems like a laughable story, the misadventures of a country goofball. I can say country because I'm from Mississippi and I can say goofball because maybe it takes one to know one except that I don't go to titty bars or have half a million dollars to leave around in a truck. I'm drawn to stories, though, of people whose dark need for respect or drink or vengeance or redemption (it's all the same monster) brings out their most interesting demons. Southerners are particularly good at this. We dig our graves with the most colorful shovels.

These are often tragicomic figures worthy of Shakespeare, to be pretentious about it, and while some might consider a story like Jack Whittaker's a cautionary tale I would say no; we learn our own lessons by our own hand and simply note—with pity, awe, compassion, resentment, gratitude, whatever you're made of—the fatal flaws of others. Jack's fatal flaw, I believe, was a need to stand big—to be reckoned with, to be awed. In America but especially still in the rural or uneducated or undereducated American South nothing does this quicker than dollars. Everyone may not understand the rest of the known world, or want to, but a particular band of Southerners relates solidly and with Pavlovian reliability to money. A Ph.D. means nothing, and an MD everything. John Grisham is a literary hero for his zeroes. I could tell my family this story appeared in *GQ* and they would say, "That's nice." I could tell them *GQ* paid me $25,000 for it (which they certainly did not) and my family would love and celebrate me forever. A price tag legitimizes—or illegitimates—everything.

I wish I could say everything worked out for Jack Whittaker but I'm not sure that will ever be true. From the time we closed on this piece and the day it hit the racks, Whittaker's life got perhaps predictably worse. An eighteen-year-old friend of his granddaughter Brandi Bragg overdosed at Whittaker's house; the kid's father is suing Whittaker for not having had better "control" over Brandi. (A lot of people thought Whittaker spoiled her. He paid her $109,000 a year to work at his construction company. She was seventeen.) Then, Whittaker was charged with yet another DUI, and with carrying a pistol concealed in his left boot, after his Hummer hit a concrete median off the West Virginia Turnpike. He had $117,000 in cash on him at the time.

Some said winning the Powerball was the worst thing that ever happened to the guy but then the worst thing actually did happen. Brandi was found dead. Her body was discovered the day our issue appeared on newsstands. The timing was sickening. It took months for the details to emerge but basically Brandi and her boyfriend partied one night with cocaine injections and methadone pills and Brandi died in the boyfriend's bed. The boyfriend freaked. He wrapped Brandi in a sheet and a tarp and dragged her out to the yard and left her beneath a junked van. She lay there all through the manhunt, for two long weeks. Finally the boyfriend showed the state police where he'd put her.

They buried Brandi on Christmas Eve, nearly two years to the day Jack Whittaker won big.

As for the Pink Pony debacle, that one apparently has yet to be resolved. In the Billy Sunday's case Whittaker pleaded no contest to misdemeanor assault but later asked the judge if he could take it back and stand trial because he decided the sentence of unsupervised probation and weekly AA meetings was too harsh (answer: ah, no).

And on it goes.

Big Jack apparently now lives in Virginia yet has been gilding and gilding the little Tabernacle of Praise, which isn't so little anymore. It's grown from a $4 million church to a $10 million 13.5-acre "campus."

Not long ago he told the *Beckley Register-Herald*: "I don't have nothing to live for since my granddaughter's dead." But then he said he will use his millions to establish West Virginia rehab centers for teenage girls (Brandi twice went to rehab, out of state). He told the *Charleston Gazette*: "That's what I'm spending my life doing." I suppose we'll see.

Mary Battiata

BLOOD FEUD

FROM THE *Washington Post Magazine*

THE WORD WAS, PERRY BROOKS'S BULL—all 2,000 fence-bending pounds of him—was loose again. And the word, as is sometimes the case in a small farming town, was right.

On that Saturday, Wick Coleman, a farmer and friend, had seen Brooks cruising the edge of the Food Lion parking lot in his old, gold pickup, where the lot bordered Brooks's fields. He had his head out the window, and he looked worried, Coleman said. One of Brooks's beagles was along for the ride, and it peered out the passenger window, as if it were searching, too.

There was nothing new about this. At seventy-four, Brooks was retired from full-time farming. He'd sold most of his cattle, and his remaining herd of twenty didn't seem enough to keep the herd's bull at home. From time to time, the bull, a black-and-white mongrel known as a "hundred-percenter" for its breeding prowess, would throw its front legs up against the pasture fence and slowly rock it to the ground. Free at last, it would lumber off in search of fresh female companionship.

Over the years, Brooks's wandering herd had become a source

of entertainment among some of his neighbors around Bowling Green, Virginia, an hour-and-a-half drive south of Washington.

"Perry would call and say, 'I've lost a cow, would you keep an eye out for it?' " said Frances Hurt, a neighbor. "It was a riot. We'd call each other and say: 'Where's Perry's cow today? Is he in your yard?' 'No, is he in yours?' "

Once the prodigal had been located, Brooks's habit was to fire up his truck and go retrieve it, loading it into the back or just tapping it home on foot with the aid of an old hoe-handle and whoever was around to help. That could be a sight to behold. Brooks was worn and bent as an old tree root by decades of hard labor. In recent years, he'd endured open-heart surgery and two hip replacements and had crushed his right hand in a front-end loader. To keep his hip from popping out of joint, he sometimes wore a complicated plastic brace over his dungarees. In combination with the tattered clothing he favored, it gave him the look of Jed Clampett crossed with the Tin Man from *The Wizard of Oz*.

But this time, on the third weekend in April 2004, Brooks's bull had crossed into the 675-acre purebred cattle operation of Brooks's neighbor and longtime nemesis, John F. Ames.

Ames, sixty, a Richmond lawyer and CPA turned part-time cattle breeder, had spent more than a decade developing a large herd of prized, pedigreed Black Angus cattle. In the years since he'd come to Caroline County, Ames had acquired a reputation as an exacting and ambitious cattleman, a demanding, somewhat aloof figure. Most people who knew him in Caroline were keenly aware that he'd filed more than a dozen lawsuits (and threatened more) against neighbors and business associates since taking over Holly Hill Farm. That reputation for litigiousness left many of his fellow townspeople wanting to keep clear of him.

The bad blood between Perry Brooks and John Ames, however, was in a class all its own. The sheriff's department policed it, the newspapers covered it, the local court was openly weary of it, and the families of at least one of the men had learned to tiptoe around it. The feud had even led Ames to apply for a permit to carry a concealed weapon. In his application, Ames told the court that he needed the gun, a Czech-made 9mm semiautomatic pistol, because he carried large amounts of cash for business, but also because he was afraid of his neighbor.

The feud started like this: In 1989, about four years after he'd arrived in Caroline, Ames sent each of his neighbors a registered letter announcing his plans to build a new fence. He informed them that, under an 1887 fence law, they would be required to pay for half of whatever section of it ran along their shared property line. Some neighbors would be on the hook for $6,000, some for $12,000. Perry Brooks's share would be more than $45,000.

The first reaction among the neighbors—several of them retired schoolteachers and nurses living on Social Security and pensions, who kept no livestock—was consternation. "What kind of a person moves to a small town and starts suing his neighbors?" said Hurt, whose elderly mother, aunt, and cousin all received bills.

Each neighbor wrote to Ames, formally declining to participate. When that didn't end it, the neighbors banded together and hired a lawyer to challenge the fence law. They also asked their state delegate to take the matter up with the General Assembly. But the legislature declined to get involved. A lower court sided with the neighbors, but Ames appealed to the Virginia Supreme Court, and he won. Two of the justices dissented, saying that the fence law amounted to "economic favoritism" for large landowners and was "woefully lacking" in protection for their neighbors. But the majority found the law to be constitutional.

Eventually, all of Ames's neighbors paid up, except for one. "Perry was the only one who refused to roll over and play dead," said Brooks's friend Paul Orlett.

Brooks's defiance earned him some admiration around Bowling Green and surrounding Caroline County, but it would prove costly. As the fence matter and related lawsuits proceeded, Brooks and Ames went to war. There were two battlegrounds. One was the courtroom, where Ames had the upper hand. He sued Brooks to collect his $45,000, and eventually a lien was placed on Brooks's farm. Brooks, in turn, sued Ames, claiming that Ames's property line was in error. Down along the disputed border, a second battle was waged, with shouting, shotguns, security guards, and even a detention on the premises with handcuffs. These incidents spawned more lawsuits—Brooks sued Ames for $2 million, and Ames sued back for $8 million, each alleging trespass and claiming emotional distress.

But a top-of-the-line fence was built, at the not-modest price of $22.20 a foot (more than three times the average cost of such a barrier, according to Tommy Tabor, a Virginia fence builder who has consulted on fencing materials for experts at Virginia Tech).

John Ames's new fence was just over five feet high, with nine strands of smooth, high-tensile wire stretched between posts sunk three feet into the ground. There were two additional strands of old-fashioned barbed wire, one of which was capable of being electrified.

High-tensile wire is made to withstand several times the amount of pressure that regular barbed wire can take. Struck head-on, by a bull or a truck, it is supposed to stretch, not break. But the new fence did not contain Perry Brooks's bull. At least twice before, in 1994 and again in 1995, the bull got through. (Generally, farmers and fence builders say, only an electric fence is guaranteed to restrain a bull.) On its second outing, the bull mounted at least one of Ames's purebred heifers, and Ames sued Brooks for more than $450,000, for costs and "intentional disregard" of the law. The lawsuit also alleged that Brooks had cut or damaged the fence on at least five occasions.

However relaxed some of Brooks's neighbors were about his wandering herd, the law treats bull trespass seriously, as do cattle breeders, for whom control of the herd bloodlines is crucial. Virginia's fence law gives those trespassed upon the right to demand a minimum of $500 for damage, board, and veterinary costs, such as testing for contagious disease. In cases of repeated trespass, the courts have allowed the aggrieved neighbor to take the offending animal to market and sell it in the name of its negligent owner.

After the second trespass, Brooks was ordered by the court to put up a $500 bond against future trespass. But the larger issues of the $45,000 for the 3,600 feet of fence, and the several-million-dollar lawsuits, were unresolved. And there were signs that everyone's patience was fraying. In 1995, six years into the feud, an exasperated substitute judge (the local judges had recused themselves from the matter) ordered Perry Brooks to stay off Holly Hill Farm and had the old farmer put up a $2,000 bond to help enforce the ban. The judge also admonished both men. "The parties are hereby cautioned by the Court to maintain peace and order between their persons and properties," warned Circuit Court Judge L. Cleaves Manning. The words "No Contact!" are handwritten in the margin of the order.

But on the morning of Monday, April 19, 2004, for reasons that his family and friends can only speculate about, Perry Brooks decided to flout the court order, go onto Ames's property, and bring the bull home himself. He asked his wife, Evelyn, to go along, but she refused. His son-in-law was unavailable. So was Wick Coleman, his son-in-law's uncle, who, like a number of farmers in Caroline, worked a second job on the railroad.

In the end, Brooks recruited Michael Beasley, a farmhand who lived in a trailer on a far corner of Brooks's farm, and Paul Orlett, a retired Marine infantryman and fishing buddy of thirty years. Orlett looked after his two-and-a-half-year-old grandson during the week. Having no one to leave the boy with that morning, Orlett brought him along.

The three men and the child drove over to Holly Hill Farm using a path that ran between the two properties alongside the CSX railroad tracks. They arrived at a paddock where the bull had been penned. Brooks and Beasley got out, and Orlett slid into the driver's seat. He turned the truck around and drove about fifty feet back in the direction from which they'd come.

Brooks was carrying an old, gray stick, about four feet long, that he used to guide his cattle. The plan was that Brooks and Beasley would walk behind the bull and drive it forward, while Orlett would lead the way in the truck.

Brooks and Beasley had just let the bull out of the pen, Beasley testified later, when Ames "pulled up fast in his truck." He was wearing his gun under his suit. He got out of the truck and confronted the men, Beasley told Orlett later, saying: "Put the bull back in the pen." Brooks drew his stick back by his ear in reply, Beasley testified. The entire confrontation lasted no more than ten seconds, he said. Brooks never said a word.

"He didn't get a chance," Beasley said.

Ames opened fire with a pistol. He shot six times, according to Beasley's testimony. The first shot, Beasley said, hit Brooks in the face. It entered Brooks's right cheek, according to the coroner, hitting his palate and exiting left, between his upper and lower jaw. Five more shots followed, hitting Brooks in the torso, piercing his heart and spinal cord. Two bullets hit the back of his upper right arm.

In the moments that followed, according to later court testimony, Ames walked to his truck and put the pistol on the seat beside a Winchester rifle. He picked up his cell phone and made several calls, including one to the sheriff's department, which in turn notified the state police. When the law arrived, Ames said only this: "I'm not making a statement. He's over there if you want to try to help him."

WHAT WOULD YOU HAVE DONE?

That is the question that has rattled around Bowling Green in the year since the shooting. What would you have done, if you'd gone to bed one night master of your domain and awakened the next morning to find a registered letter in the mailbox, informing you that you owed $45,000 to pay for your neighbor's new fence?

And if you did not pay up, your neighbor was entitled to slap a lien on your property. This, even though your neighbor had three times your acreage and many times your cattle. And one more thing: Your neighbor was a lawyer, which meant that you would be fighting on his battlefield. (During the feud, Ames often served as his own attorney.)

Where was the justice? According to his friends, and his daughter Kim Brooks, that's what Perry Brooks wanted to know.

Brooks's instinct was to fight. His opening volley was a handwritten note, formal in tone, dated January 25, 1989. "Dear Sir: In response to your letter of Jan. 3, at the present time my finances do not permit me to participate in the fencing project. However, at some future date, if the need for the fence arises, I will be more than glad to participate. Sincerely yours, O. Perry Brooks."

By 1993, four years into the feud, Brooks's stance had hardened. "Dear Sir," he wrote his neighbor. "I wish to inform you that nobody from holly hill farm [sic] is allowed on my property. This includes you, your wife, your sons or daughters, your farm hands. Anybody associated with you is forbidden." He signed the letter "O. Perry Brooks, owner."

Brooks's friends—Bobby Lakin, Wick Coleman—and others say that at its core, the feud was not so much about money or class differences (though those played a role), but something more intangible and fundamental. It was about respect.

"He didn't treat my father as a human being, as an equal, as someone you would talk to," said Kim Brooks.

During the trial over the disputed boundary line, Perry Brooks was asked if it was true that he had once fired a shotgun in the general direction of John Ames. Yes, Brooks testified. And was it true that he had done so in part to "needle" John Ames? Yes, Brooks said again. And why did he want to do that, Ames's attorney asked him.

"I think he needed it," Brooks replied. "Let him know some-body else was around besides *hisself*!"

PERRY BROOKS AND JOHN AMES MET, according to Brooks family accounts and court testimony, at a public auction for Holly Hill Farm in June 1985. Holly Hill, a former plantation turned dairy farm, had fallen onto hard times. The auction was not a bank-ruptcy sale, but the widow of the owner was selling by agreement with the farm's creditors. Farmers around the county were in attendance that day. Ames, visiting from Richmond, approached Brooks to ask if there were any problems with the property. Brooks, Ames testified later, said no. The property was sold to Ames for about $442,000. Ames added the word "Corporation" to the farm name. Farm stationery listed Ames as vice president and his wife as president and treasurer.

According to testimony by both Ames and Brooks, they met again in January 1989 near their shared property line. Brooks had received the registered letter from Ames but had not yet formally replied. They talked about the cost of the fence, fencing materials, and the need to keep their herds separated. At some point, Ames reportedly remarked on the beauty of Brooks's land and said that his own cattle "sure would look pretty on it." The two men dick-ered. Ames offered to swap the fence bill in exchange for some of Brooks's land. Brooks said no. Brooks suggested Ames just tie in this new fence to the one hundred yards of Brooks's existing fence. Ames said he would agree, but only if they put the deal on paper and filed it at the courthouse. Brooks said no.

Brooks also told his neighbor that Ames's proposed fence line was in error. It included a 1.87-acre triangle of land that actually belonged to him, Brooks said, by virtue of an old plat drawn up after the Civil War. That map, which used landmarks such as old sycamore stumps and white pine trees, gave him clear possession of that triangle of land, he asserted. In addition, he and the previous owner of Holly Hill Farm had made a handshake deal about the triangle years ago.

No, Ames replied, he had more recent legal surveys showing the land was his. The meeting ended with Brooks storming off, according to testimony.

At least three times in the months that followed, Brooks drove his tractor down to the disputed boundary line and nudged the new fence down, Ames alleged. He picked up posts and even a gate and carted them back to his barn, saying the materials and the new fence were over his property line and so belonged to him. On one of those occasions, Ames called out to him and demanded that he stop. Ames later testified that he had reminded Brooks then that they had talked about fencing the disputed section. Brooks replied, in so many words, that he didn't care.

On another occasion, Brooks showed up at the offending fence line with a single-barrel shotgun.

"What you got there?" Orlett said Ames shouted over to Brooks that day, a query that Brooks heard as a taunt.

"I'll show you," Brooks reportedly called back, and he discharged the shotgun in the air, according to court and other accounts. No one was hit, but Ames was frightened enough to take cover behind a tree, and later contended in a lawsuit that he believed Brooks had been aiming at him and that the incident caused him "severe emotional distress."

The feud reached a new intensity in March 1989, when Brooks drove down to the fence and found himself face-to-face with a six-foot-three security guard. The guard, a former Army Ranger, was carrying a .357 magnum. The two men scuffled, and Brooks's face was bruised. The guard testified later that his gun had hit Brooks while the guard was trying to kick Brooks's shotgun out of reach. Brooks said the guard had pistol-whipped him. The guard handcuffed Brooks and took him up to the main house, where Ames was in view. On seeing him, according to Ames's subsequent complaint, Brooks began to bellow, shouting that he was going to come back and "kill everyone on the place."

(Both Brooks's widow, Evelyn, and John Ames declined to comment on any aspect of the feud. Evelyn Brooks has filed a $10.3 million wrongful death suit against Ames, which is scheduled to be heard in civil court after the murder trial in September. In turn, Ames filed an $11.3 million countersuit, accusing Evelyn Brooks, her daughter Jacqueline Coleman, son-in-law Matthew Coleman, and three John Does of a series of crimes including trespass, infliction of emotional distress, assault and battery, conspiracy, fraud, obstruction of justice, breaking court orders, and "terrorism." Ames later dropped the terrorism count after questioning by a judge and then dropped Evelyn Brooks from the suit entirely.)

Brooks was detained for a while, then uncuffed when he complained of chest pains, according to court records and Kim Brooks. He was arrested by sheriff's deputies and charged with trespassing. At the county jail, he was taken to the medical ward, then transferred to a hospital in Richmond, where he stayed for a week.

After that, Brooks told daughter Kim and others that he "wanted the war to be over." Kim Brooks, a nurse, remembers talking with her father at the time.

"I scolded him," she said. "I told him: 'What's this I'm hearing about shotguns? I don't ever want to hear about you murdering someone. You made us go to church all our lives, and then you act like this?' " Kim Brooks remembers that her father was contrite and made no further assaults on the fence.

The ground war at the fence line was subsiding, but the bull's wanderlust was not.

THE FENCE THAT SEPARATES Holly Hill Farm from the Brooks farm is a door through time. On one side is John Ames's Farm Corporation, with its spreadsheets and cold-storage tanks for bull semen and calf embryos. On the other is Perry Brooks's 246 acres, which, by choice and temperament, he husbanded with methods and tools that in some cases harked back to Colonial times.

Like many farmers in Caroline County, Brooks was cash poor and land rich. Caroline is the last truly rural redoubt on the booming Interstate 95 corridor between Washington and Richmond, but, in recent years, housing subdivisions have begun to appear. The paper value of Brooks's land soared, but he rarely had more than $1,000 cash to his name. He lived on $400 a month in Social Security income, rent from a small second house on the property, and what he raised selling his vegetables at the farmers' markets in Northern Virginia. Most of his farm equipment was rattletrap and bore the marks of his welder's torch. He spruced up for church on Sunday but otherwise often dressed in tattered clothes.

"Perry was a little rough around the edges, but he had a heart of gold. He'd do anything for you," said McGann Saphir, a Virginia farm extension agent for Caroline County.

Brooks may have been a character, but he was nobody's fool. He could be fierce, and he was notably stubborn. "With Perry, it was, 'I may not always be right, but I'm never wrong,' " said friend Orlett.

Except for two years in Korea during that war, Brooks had lived in Caroline his whole life, as had his father before him. He was the youngest of several children. His mother suffered bouts of severe depression and was hospitalized for it several times. She once tried to drown herself in a creek, according to family members. Perry was cared for by his oldest sister, Ellen. When Ellen married and moved away, responsibility for his mother's care fell to him.

In his own old age, Brooks had leased all but ten acres of his land to his son-in-law, Matthew Coleman, to farm. The chores that remained to him he carried out less by brawn than canny use of gravity. "He could do what he needed to do. It might take him three times as long, but he would get it done," said Kim Brooks.

In his earlier years, he sawed his own boards with a sawmill he kept in the woods. He salted herring and smoked ham with a smoker he'd built himself. He hung beef in linen bags for aging. His two daughters learned to run a grader and feed the livestock— fifty head of cattle, as well as pigs and chickens. They gathered eggs, weeded the watermelon patch. When the combine harvested the corn, the children walked the rows after, picking up scrap to grind into feed. "Nothing was wasted," Kim Brooks remembered. "He was very old-school that way."

Slaughtering day at the Brooks farm was typical. Neighbors and family all helped, in exchange for meat. "It was a big mess, but we made a party of it," said Kim Brooks. "We worked all day, and then at night there would be a barbecue, with hamburgers."

None of it was very profitable. "We were all half-busted half of the time," said Bobby Lakin, Brooks's friend and Bible study teacher, who gave up farming in favor of the electrician's trade. "Perry could've sold the whole place and been a millionaire. *All* farmers could sell out. But that's not your purpose in life. Perry liked farming."

In semi-retirement, Brooks's chief pleasures remained what they'd always been: rabbit hunting with his beagles and daytrips for fishing in Deltaville, two hours southeast, where the Rappahan-nock River meets Chesapeake Bay. In winter, when farm chores eased, said Lakin, Brooks liked to sit around the fire, "smoking a pipe, laughing, and talking."

Still, he could square off like a bull, taunting and unyielding, when he thought he'd been wronged. Several days before he died, Brooks drove his truck over to the second house on his property to have it out with a tenant who was several months behind on the rent, according to the tenant. The tenant had recently moved his daughter's family into the house over Brooks's objections. Brooks was suing for the back rent. The tenant in turn claimed that Brooks owed him almost as much money for improvements the tenant had made to the property.

Brooks drove down the driveway and blocked the tenant's car as the man returned from work. As the two men began to shout from their car windows, the tenant's wife and teenage daughter emerged from the house, cell phones in hand, screaming and threatening to call the sheriff. The women surrounded Brooks's truck, and the tenant jumped out of his car, he said in an interview. Brooks, outnumbered and still behind the wheel, began to back up slowly. As he did, the women, standing behind his truck, redoubled their screaming. One jumped onto the back bumper, and the other was flung clear by her husband. The dispatcher at the sheriff's department, mindful of the fence feud and not sure what was going on over at Brooks's farm, sent several deputies.

When the law arrived, the incident was over. The women complained of leg pain but drove themselves to the hospital, where no injuries were diagnosed, according to hospital records.

Brooks was arrested, however, charged with hit and run and held for two days in the county jail. On his bail form, he listed his total cash assets at less than $1,000, put the value of his land at $1 million, and asked for a court-appointed lawyer. Kim Brooks said her father sounded abashed when she spoke to him after his release. "He said, 'Can I just stay in jail?' " His daughter said she thought he sounded tired and unlike himself. "I remember thinking, if they could just keep him in jail for two weeks, everything would be okay."

IF PERRY BROOKS WAS OLD-FASHIONED by temperament and financial necessity, John Ames's money and ambition put his farm on the cutting edge of twenty-first-century animal science. Many novice Angus breeders bail out after their first five years. But Ames beat the odds. He hired full-time farm managers and built an Angus herd that some experts rate in the top 20 percent for quality, nationwide. His bull calves have brought as much as $35,000 at sale.

Ames, by all accounts, is a hands-on cattleman, rising at 4:00 A.M. most days to see to his herd, then leaving for his law and CPA offices in Richmond around 9:00. He shovels feed in winter and helps dip the cattle against ticks in summer.

He was no greenhorn when he took up the country life at Holly Hill. As a child, Ames said in an interview, he spent time at his grandparents' five-hundred-acre working farm near Newport News. His grandparents migrated to the city to work for the Navy during the Second World War, he said. Ames's father made his living as a lawyer and accountant, but the family lived on an eighty-six-acre estate near Yorktown.

Although some in Bowling Green see Ames as a powerful squire on the hill, in reality he seems less powerful than powerfully aspiring. His college was Norfolk's Old Dominion University, known as a commuter school. His solo law practice is in a small gray house in a suburban office park on the outskirts of Richmond. His mother's house in Virginia Beach was collateral for his $100,000 bail on the murder charge.

Ames kept a low profile in Bowling Green. He was seen at the barbershop and the post office, but seldom elsewhere. He is not a member of the local bar association, and lawyers and others in the town's small professional class say they have had little contact with him. The same is true at the Virginia Angus Association, where several former board members and employees, as well as several breeders, say Ames was seldom seen at association meetings or social events. Part of that, one association official said, might have been a simple time crunch. Ames was conducing three professions simultaneously, leaving little time, perhaps, for socializing. But an additional factor in his seeming isolation may be found in the files of the clerk's office in Caroline County Circuit Court, where thousands of pages of filings document the ongoing saga of *John F. Ames, Esq. v. the world*.

In 2002, Ames sued the giant CSX Corp. for more than $6 million, accusing the railroad of breaching his property line and damaging his fields. The case is pending. In 1999, he sued a Midwestern cattle operation, Profit Maker Bulls. The case was settled out of court. In 1997, Ames sued the Frederick, Md., company that serviced his farm silo for $100,000, accusing it of breach of contract and other offenses. That suit is pending. In 2001, he sued a former client for $87,000 in unpaid fees and other damages.

Other times, Ames just made threats. In the mid-1990s, he threatened to sue the Virginia Angus Association over a disagreement about sales commissions, according to several association officials. In the early nineties, a state employee with business at the farm accidentally ran over one of the Ameses' dogs while leaving the property. Ames, who was not home at the time, responded by telephoning the man late at night several times over a period of a few weeks to berate him, the state employee said, stopping only when the man threatened to call the police with a complaint of harassment. Ames demanded $100,000 in damages. The man's personal insurance company paid a couple thousand dollars to settle the matter. (Ames did not return phone calls requesting comment on this incident or any lawsuits he has filed.)

Sometimes Ames was the one being sued. In 1990, one of his neighbors took him to court when he refused to stop using their property as a shortcut to some of his fields. He lost. He was sued by a leading cattle magazine, *Angus Topics*, for refusing to pay an advertising bill. He sued back, but the magazine prevailed.

In 1997, Ames was charged with reckless driving, obstruction of justice, and assault after a state trooper, who stopped him for making an illegal turn while driving his tractor, alleged that Ames had driven the tractor straight at him. The charges were dismissed in a plea bargain after Ames agreed to do community service.

Most of the several dozen people interviewed for this story—cattle breeders, former Ames employees, fellow lawyers, business associates, state and local officials—declined to comment about Ames publicly, saying they feared being sued.

A few associates, however, defended him. "With John Ames, it's like this," said Tom Burke, a Midwest cattle auctioneer who is conducting a sale for Ames at Holly Hill Farm next month. "If you do what you say you are going to do, and you don't take any shortcuts and you don't make excuses, then everything will be fine. But if you do take those shortcuts, well, then you are going to be in for a long afternoon."

Farm life, perhaps, offered a respite from those pressures.

"You can't sue a cow," said Saphir, the extension agent, who knew both men. "They obey orders, and they don't challenge you.

"Now a bull, a bull is a different story," Saphir added. "A bull is untamable. If a bull wants to go somewhere, it'll go." That, he speculated, could be part of a deeper, psychological truth behind the shooting death of Perry Brooks. "Here [Ames] is, this hugely respected Angus breeder, and some guy's mangy old bull comes over and breeds with two or three of your heifers? . . . It's like your daughter got raped."

J. Benjamin Dick, Ames's co-counsel in the upcoming murder trial, said people underestimate the threat that Perry Brooks posed. Brooks was old, Dick said, but don't be fooled. He was strong, with forearms "like Popeye."

"I think Perry Brooks was at the farm that morning to do great harm—there's no doubt in my mind," said Dick.

In the aftermath of the shooting, before lawyers and the county prosecutor had been allowed to examine the physical evidence in the case, Dick said that Brooks had gone to Holly Hill Farm on the morning of April 19 armed with an electric cattle prod. But after a preliminary hearing at which the rumored cattle prod turned out to be what Dick described later as a "half-broomstick," he seemed to backtrack.

"It's a tough case," he said. "No doubt about it, it's a tough case."

IN ROBERT FROST'S POEM "Mending Wall," the narrator laments a farmer who wants to build a fence between the narrator's apple orchard and the farmer's stand of pine. A fence is hardly necessary, Frost's narrator thinks. After all:

There where it is we do not need the wall:
He is all pine and I am apple orchard.
My apple trees will never get across
And eat the cones under his pines, I tell him.

But in the poem, the laconic New England farmer seems to know better: "He only says, 'Good fences make good Neighbors.' " But fences create conflict, too.

"Fences, it's *always* fences," said Cora Jordan, a lawyer and author of an authoritative guide to the area of jurisprudence known as neighbor law. Complaints about noise are the most common problem between neighbors, she said, but fence conflicts are the most likely to spiral into physical violence. "Judges can't stand these cases," Jordan said. "Lawyers don't want to take them, and law enforcement doesn't want any part of it."

"I get lots of phone calls about fences," agreed Leon Geyer, a law professor specializing in agricultural law and environmental economics at Virginia Tech. "It's a very hot subject." Since Brooks's death, Geyer has been in demand by farmers eager to educate themselves about the intricacies of Virginia's fence law.

Most states require that cattle owners fence in their livestock. Virginia is one of only three states, with Arkansas and Oregon, where responsibility for fencing changes by county, Geyer said. In some rural counties in the commonwealth, the burden is on farmers to fence the neighbor's cattle out. Elsewhere, as in Caroline, cattle farmers bear the responsibility to fence their herds in. In both settings, however, the fence law, until recently, dictated that the cost of fencing would be shared. In January, Virginia's General Assembly, chastened by the Brooks slaying, amended the fence law to exempt landowners without livestock from the burden of paying for a neighbor's cattle fence. The change would not have affected Brooks, a cattle owner.

(In most of Virginia's suburban counties, the "pay half" provision is superseded by local regulations, Geyer said. But in other parts of the country, according to Jordan, even suburban neighbors often are liable for the construction and maintenance costs of their shared fence lines.) Some state legislatures have tried to head off problems by writing laws that dictate fence wire gauges and post diameters. Virginia's law does not do this.

Every neighbor dispute is different, Jordan said, but often the two principals in a long-running feud are "two extremely stubborn people," neither of whom is willing to take a first step that professional mediators call "unilateral deescalation."

Translation? "Choosing to do nothing when it is your turn to do something extremely nasty," Jordan said.

IT WAS EMBRYO-FLUSHING DAY at Holly Hill Farm, and John Ames had agreed to let me on the property for a visit. Ames had declined all media contact since the shooting, but in a brief conversation about cattle breeding outside the courtroom before his preliminary hearing, his lead attorney, Richmond defense lawyer Craig S. Cooley, by his side, Ames had volunteered that he thought the cattle business was on the eve of a revolutionary leap forward, a day when cattle breeders might produce enough cattle, at a low enough price, to end world hunger. If there was one thing that bothered him, Ames added, it was the thought of children starving in a world of abundance.

He also had an unusual, wired energy that day. John Ames is small-boned, of medium height—five feet ten inches, according to court records—but he has the lean build of a marathon runner and appears younger than his sixty years. His skin that day was ruddy from outdoor work, and his salt-and-pepper hair was shorn close to the scalp. His bright blue eyes blazed with an expression both inquiring and imperious, and his voice had the mild twang of his native Tidewater.

With Cooley's blessing, Ames was willing to allow the visit, on one condition: There were to be no questions about the shooting, the feud, or Perry Brooks.

Holly Hill Farm is a big piece of real estate. Its rolling hills run alongside Route 207, just outside the town limits of Bowling Green, for a good mile and a half, until the property ends at the low-lying highway bridge that spans the Mattaponi River. The farm's main entrance is flanked by two formal brick pillars, and the long driveway—a half-mile or so—is paved in rough-cut gray gravel. The drive cuts through a sweeping bowl of open pasture. In the fields, large, ink-black rectangles of cattle stand motionless except for an occasional shake of a massive, ear-tagged head. Up at the house, the only sign of life is one red horse in a paddock and the sound of barking dogs coming from behind the house's tall front windows and thick white columns.

On the first of two visits, Ames appeared in a long-sleeved dress shirt and suit trousers, having come straight from his office in Richmond. He led a tour of the barn area, and talked about his love of farming. "Once it gets in your blood, it never leaves you. And you have to do it for love," he added, chuckling, "because there's no money in it." He opened a gate and called to four of his prize-winning cows. "Come on, girls," he said, and stopped to scratch one on the back.

Ames's specialty is bankruptcy law, which tends to attract people who enjoy crunching numbers. During my visits, he displayed a keen command of the statistical side of his cattle operation, explaining the intricate spreadsheets by which serious breeders track data such as intramuscular fat ratios and weight gain. He rattled off his top cows' eight-digit identification numbers with the ease of a man reciting his phone number, and in a small workroom, he unscrewed liquid nitrogen tanks where bull semen was stored in plastic straws as narrow as swizzle sticks, each painted with tiny numbers.

On the table there was a DNA sample kit that would take tissue

scrapings from the ears of two of Ames's best females and be mailed
to a lab in Iowa for storage until the price of cloning comes down.
Artificial insemination is commonplace in the cattle business. DNA
sampling for future cloning, however, is not, and the kit identifies
Ames as a serious player in the breeding game, as does the practice
of treating genetically desirable cows with fertility drugs so they
produce multiple, rather than single, embryos.

On the morning of my second visit, dozens of such embryos
were to be "flushed" from four cows with the help of saline solution, plastic tubes, and a fertility specialist vet who was driving
down from Pennsylvania. The embryos were to be stored briefly,
until they could be implanted into recipient cows that would ges-
tate them to birth. As he waited for the vet, Ames, his hair
unbrushed, looked cheerful and relaxed. He was dressed in worn
bluejeans, scuffed boots, and an old red sweater. Once the vet
arrived, the two men, with the help of a farmhand, began herding
the cows, one by one, into a metal squeeze chute. For the next several hours, as the vet worked, Ames kept up a stream of cheerful
conversation about his visits with some of the cattle industry's top
scientists and his contacts with senior executives at the country's
largest meat-packing plants.

At one point, with the vet's right arm buried up to the shoulder
in a cow's reproductive canal, and Ames's own arms draped with
plastic tubes attached to sacs of saline solution, Ames explained the
packing industry's plans for "vertical integration," for expanding its
business from the slaughter and packing to include cattle breeding.
"We want to take 'em from squeal to meal!" Ames said approvingly,
quoting an executive from Smithfield Foods.

Throughout the morning, he told stories about successful cattle
shows, mentioning a man who, when I telephoned him later,
painted a bleaker picture. "John had a couple of [cattle] sales in the
past where nobody showed up," said John Hausner, a herd manager
who has worked for Ames in the past. "Obviously, he's made somebody mad. I felt sorry for the man."

As Ames and the vet worked, I looked across a green field and saw a large silo, a small ranch house, and some paddock fence. Is that where Brooks and Ames faced off? Or was it there, on the gravel drive outside this barn? Standing there, trying to get my bearings, I felt the full force of what had happened. It was everywhere and nowhere—the idea that right there on that ground, where a white cat perched on a stall post, where the cows shifted and clanked in their chutes with hypodermic needles planted in their backs, as the vet remarked on the unexpected difficulty of the morning's work, Perry Brooks was shot dead at close range by his neighbor.

PAUL ORLETT BELIEVES HIS FRIEND was aiming to avoid confrontation on the morning he died. "[Ames] told Perry's people to come over there before 9:00 A.M., with five hundred dollars to bail out the bull, but Perry said: 'Hell no, we'll wait 'til ten. He'll be gone to Richmond by then.' "

This echoed an earlier episode, when Brooks, learning that his bull was over at Holly Hill Farm, called the farm manager in the middle of the night and suggested the two of them free the bull. "No need to tell the boss," Brooks advised. When the manager refused the offer, Brooks hung up.

Brooks did not appear to regard this new expedition as risky, Orlett recalled. "Perry said he was going to go get the bull and then come back and work in his greenhouse."

But the farmhand, Michael Beasley, had misgivings. "I didn't want to go," Beasley testified later. "But I didn't try to talk him out of it, because it wasn't any use."

Ames's wife may have been more vocal. The weekend before the shooting, when Matthew Coleman phoned Holly Hill Farm to arrange the bull's pickup, Jeanne Ames said, "Don't let [Brooks] come up here with you," according to Ames attorney Benjamin Dick.

Brooks waited for Orlett under the old farm bell that once belonged to his father. At Holly Hill Farm, meanwhile, Jeanne Ames left for Richmond, but John Ames waited. He went to retrieve his mail, Dick said. And he waited some more. Dick said Ames, seeing an unfamiliar vehicle, went down to the barn area to investigate, and that Brooks, when told to put the bull back, "shook his stick" at Ames.

Frances Hurt was sitting in her small ranch house a few fields over at the time. It was spring; the forsythia bushes were blooming, and the air was so sweet that she'd flung open all the windows and doors. She was puzzled when she heard the shots. Hunting season had been over for months. She counted six shots in all, in a distinct pattern: one shot—*pop*—followed by a pause, and then five more, in quick succession—*pop-pop-pop-pop-pop.*

"I thought: What in the *world*? Who is shooting a gun at 10:15 in the morning?"

Beasley testified later that Ames's first shot had knocked Brooks to the ground. Ames fired five more times.

Orlett was sitting at the wheel of Brooks's truck, his grandson beside him. At the shots, he looked in the rearview mirror and saw Brooks curled in a fetal position on the gravel. "I could tell by the way Perry was laying that he was dead," Orlett said later. "Two tours in the infantry in Vietnam, I've seen a lot of dead people."

When Orlett looked back again, he saw Ames with his gun up beside his ear. "It looked like he was reloading," Orlett testified. Then he saw Ames using a cell phone.

Beasley was walking slowly back toward the truck, his head in his hands, "moaning and groaning something awful," Orlett said. Beasley climbed in and asked, "What are we going to do?" Orlett said.

"We're going to get the hell out of here," Orlett replied.

Beasley later told police that Ames had shot Brooks once in the face, and then, after Brooks was on the ground, stood, firing down "four or five" more times into Brooks's right side.

Within minutes, the Rev. Kevin James, minister at Brooks's church and a volunteer firefighter, got a call from the firehouse about the shooting. He heard the address—Holly Hill Farm, Route 207—and felt only dread. "I just knew. I said, 'One of those two guys is dead.' "

Kim Brooks, who lives in Oakland, California, would get a call from her sister, Jacqueline. Kim had stayed home from work that day, feeling ill and unsettled. "My sister told me John Ames had shot my father and he hadn't made it back," she said.

At Brooks's wake, the crowd of mourners was larger than expected, and the service, scheduled to end at 9:00 P.M., stretched on until well after ten.

Ames was charged with first-degree murder, which carries a maximum life sentence, and a second felony count of using a firearm in commission of a felony. He hired Cooley, whose recent accomplishments include delivering Lee Boyd Malvo, the younger defendant in the Washington sniper case, from the death penalty.

Ames's lawyers have called the shooting a case of simple self-defense. Ames, said co-counsel Dick, was in mortal fear for his life. After all, Brooks was trespassing in violation of a court order and had once fired a shotgun in Ames's direction.

The trial date is set for September 12, in Bowling Green. But Cooley has asked the court for a change of venue, saying he believes it will be hard to find an impartial jury in Caroline County, where most people "have taken sides on this one." The court has put off a decision until after jury selection begins.

Dick said his client has not had an easy time of it since the shooting. "John is not going around gloating. He has nightmares and sleepless nights," Dick said, adding that Ames fired reflexively at Brooks when he saw the farmer raise his stick. "All John saw was the anger in [Brooks's] eyes. John was in the Army for four years, you know, and the Army trains you to shoot if you're being attacked."

Evelyn Brooks has been selling off her husband's farm equipment and remaining livestock, in part to help stave off legal action from one of the lawyers who represented Brooks in the fence law-suits. Ames has a cattle sale scheduled for next month, and he recently told one associate that he is shopping for a calf for his young granddaughter, to get her started in the cattle business.

Matthew and Wick Coleman retrieved the bull a few days after the shooting. A rumor flew around Bowling Green that the bull had been found with a broken penis, that someone at Holly Hill Farm had swung a hammer at it. With its elements of cruelty and violence, the grisly report seemed to resonate in a community stunned that a disagreement over a fence had ended in death. But Wick Coleman said there was no evidence of any such assault. Rather, the bull's penis sheath, which runs under more than half of its belly, was badly bruised, consistent, perhaps, with a leap over a partially downed fence. In any case, the bull was taken directly from Holly Hill Farm to the slaughterhouse in Fredericksburg, where it was sold for meat.

MARY BATTIATA *is a staff writer for the* Washington Post Maga-zine. *She was a Pulitzer finalist for her coverage of ethnic cleansing in the former Yugoslavia, and also has reported from Poland, Romania, and East Africa for the* Post. *She lives in Arlington, Virginia.*

Coda

I did not cover the criminal trial of John Ames. I had moved on to another assignment by then, and in any case still felt too close to the story and too drained by it to attend as a spectator. For reasons I still can't quite understand, this story was as grinding, emotionally and physically, as any I've written in my twenty-four years as a reporter at the *Washington Post*, including years as a war correspon-dent in East Africa and the former Yugoslavia.

Part of it was simply the usual reporter's lament: none of the parties wanted to have anything to do with me for months on end, well past my first and then second deadline. Part of it was simple sadness at the sorry details of the feud and the pain it had caused all parties. And another giant stressor was my interviews with a long line of John Ames's former business associates, who told me they'd been sued by him and warned that he was likely to do the same to me. That never happened, as it turned out. But the case continues to reverberate in my head, and I still get calls about it from all over the country, from people who've read the story and want to know how it all turned out. Not surprising, really. Nearly everyone has had problems with a neighbor at one time or another, and this story of tragedy in a corner of rural paradise, a landscape where we like to think an older, more courteous way of life survives, seemed to strike a particular chord.

The trial lasted a week, and at the outset, the judge turned down Ames's lawyer's request to move the proceedings to another county. On Friday, September 16, 2005, almost a year and a half to the day after the feud's bloody conclusion, a jury in Caroline County, Virginia, found John Ames not guilty in the shooting death of his neighbor, Perry Brooks. After the verdict was read, according to the *Richmond Times-Dispatch,* Ames closed his eyes, then hugged his wife and cried. Some in the courtroom and in the surrounding town of Bowling Green expressed surprise at the verdict, not least Brooks's oldest daughter, Kim, who said it was as if her father had been unable to see the danger that continuing the feud posed to him, despite warnings from family and friends.

One juror said the jury had been evenly divided between acquittal and a charge of involuntary manslaughter at the start of the trial. But over the next three days, they were persuaded by evidence that undercut the eyewitness account of the Brooks's family farmhand. The scattered pattern of bullet casings found around Brooks's body after the shooting seemed to show that Brooks had been moving forward, toward Ames, with his stick raised, when

Ames fired. "I started backing away," Ames said. "He took a swing at me with the stick . . . I ducked, and as I ducked, I cocked the 9mm [pistol], and I fired and kept firing—there were no conscious thoughts."

Ames testified that Brooks dropped his stick after being struck by the second or third bullet, but continued to lurch forward in a tackling position. "I wanted to be left in peace," Ames told the prosecutor on the stand. "I wanted this to stop . . . I think I saved my own life. He left me with no options." Ames's wife, Jeanne, testified that she had been so frightened by Perry Brooks's occasional verbal threats against her family during the fifteen-year feud that she kept a pistol on her nightstand, and the window blinds drawn. Other farm employees told of being threatened by Brooks as well. The jury evidently was less moved by the prosecutor's argument that Perry Brooks had not threatened the Ames family directly in many years.

Ames defense attorney, Craig Cooley, argued that Ames's reaction, when confronted with a three-foot stick about the thickness of a shovel handle, had not been excessive. "People have been killed with billy clubs," he said. The first sheriff's deputy to reach Holly Hill Farm on the morning of the shooting testified that Ames declined to make a statement, then pointed to Brooks's body and said: "He's over there if you want to try to help him."

Three months after the verdict, in December 2005, Perry Brooks's widow, Evelyn, accepted a settlement in her $10 million wrongful death suit against John Ames. The settlement was sealed by the court and the amount was not disclosed. Kim Brooks said afterward that her mother had struggled with the decision of whether to settle or let the case go to trial, where the family had hoped additional facts, more favorable to their father, might emerge.

At the time of the settlement, the $45,001.12 lien that Ames had placed on Brooks's farm back in 1989, in an attempt to force

Brooks to pay for his fence, remained unpaid. With interest, it was estimated to have grown to about $150,000.

I have not been back to Caroline County since the story. But one memory of the reporting has stuck with me. It is from my second visit to Holly Hill Farm, in the fall of 2004. I turned up on the day when a visiting vet was on hand to suction multiple embryos from four cows that had been super-fertilized with hormone treatments and then artificially inseminated. The removal of embryos is an exacting task in the best of circumstances. But this day, nothing seemed to go right—one cow was difficult to suction, another seemed to have no embryos, and a third became restless in the holding chute, jumped, and knocked loose the hypodermic needle that had been planted in her back. "John, it's been a long time since I've had a morning like this," the vet said.

As they worked, I scanned the fields outside the barn. In the distance, just beyond a row of trees, lay Brooks's farm, and the dirt track that Perry Brooks had traveled on the morning of his death. Then I turned back to Ames, the vet, and the cows. That's when I noticed a pure white cat sitting like a sentry on top of a stall post. It was watching us coolly, in the way cats do. And for just a moment, it looked to me like the ghost of Perry Brooks, prowling among us, and watching the difficulties in the barn that day with a certain bleak satisfaction.

HIT MEN IN BLUE?

FROM *Vanity Fair*

IF BETTY HYDELL HAD NOT turned on the television that afternoon in 1992, she might never have learned the stranger's name. But there on the *Sally Jessy Raphael* show was the bruiser who had knocked on her door six years earlier looking for her son. He had come asking for twenty-eight-year-old Jimmy on the day he disappeared—and, she had no doubt, was murdered. Only, now that she knew the man's name, justice, she was convinced, was impossible. He was beyond the law.

Six years later, she lost another son. Frank, thirty-one, the younger brother, was found lying between two parked cars in front of a Staten Island strip club with three bullets pumped into his head and chest. Now she needed to talk; and slowly, despite her anxieties, she was growing ready.

Finally, in the fall of 2003, say those who participated in the case, Betty Hydell, then sixty-five, shared her long-held secret. It was a secret that would have momentous consequences. This single name resurrected old suspicions and set in motion a covert eighteen-month investigation that led a team of retired New York

cops and Drug Enforcement Administration agents back to the
bloody gangland wars of previous decades, and had them hunting
through seemingly ice-cold cases and unsolved murders. And at the
end of their long investigative journey they uncovered what law-
enforcement officials are calling "the worst case of police corruption in the history of New York."

In March, two retired New York City Police Department detectives, Louis Eppolito, fifty-six, and Stephen Caracappa, sixty-three,
were charged with working for the Mob. Even as detailed in the
careful sentences of the twenty-seven-page federal indictment, the
alleged betrayal, which began in the mid-1980s, was both riveting
and complete. On the surface, as many of their astonished fellow
cops were quick to point out, the pair had been exemplary police
officers. Eppolito, big, beefy, and loud, had been a tough street cop,
a head-banger who bragged that he had been in eight shoot-outs
and had survived to become the NYPD's eleventh-most-decorated
officer. Caracappa was more cerebral, quiet and ruminative, a cool
dandy in the trim black suits he had made in Hong Kong. He, too,
had put together an impressive two-decade career, serving on
the elite Major Case Squad and winning a promotion to detective
first grade.

Yet, according to the indictment, while they had been building
their careers and passing themselves off as gung-ho cops, they had
been taking orders from the Mob. In dozens of cases, they allegedly
gave the Mafia the edge, allowing wiseguys to get away with murder—literally. They revealed the names of individuals who were
cooperating with the government, and as a result three informants
were killed and one was severely wounded. They shared information about ongoing investigations and pending indictments with
the Lucchese crime family, one of New York's five major Mafia
clans. But most shocking of all, and unprecedented in the history of
the NYPD, they had acted as paid killers. The two detectives were
charged with taking part in at least eight Mob hits—including one

where they were the shooters. (The body of a ninth suspected victim was discovered after the indictment.)

Incredibly, allegations about the two detectives were first made more than a decade ago. But officials were never able to get the evidence they needed for an indictment.

"We were only able to make this case," says one of the key investigators on the task force, "because after years of stonewalling we succeeded in getting the man who paid Eppolito and Caracappa to talk."

However, unknown to the task force, their star witness had long been an informant for the FBI. And according to dismayed law-enforcement officials, if the FBI had shared this information with the NYPD, the two rogue detectives could have been prosecuted years ago.

Instead, the case of the two "Mafia cops" remained little more than a swirl of suspicions until a mournful and angry Betty Hydell decided to speak.

AFTER TWENTY HECTIC YEARS on the job, Detective Tommy Dades was counting the days until his retirement. He had worked narcotics and then gone up against the Colombo crime family as a hard-charging detective in Brooklyn's Sixty-eighth Precinct. Now, in September 2003, the detective was finishing his career in a Brooklyn organized-crime intelligence unit. His plan was to draw his pension at age forty-two and move on to what he'd been contemplating for years—running a boxing gym on Staten Island while he was still able to go a couple of rounds himself. He'd nurture some tough kid from the projects who had the heart and skill to be a contender. But before he could begin his new life, Dades, always the dutiful cop, hoped to wrap up some of the unresolved cases in his files.

The April 1998 murder of Frank Hydell, a Mob hanger-on, was

a case that, despite several arrests, still gnawed at him. With only small justification, Dades felt responsible: Frankie had been working for him—and the FBI—as an informant. The burst of bullets that knocked Frankie down and left him stretched out flat on the street was, Dades believed, the Mob's retribution.

Over the years, Dades had made a point of keeping in touch with Frankie's family. He would visit Frankie's mother, Betty, at her Staten Island home. Flashing his wide smile, Tommy would chat her up in his easy, affable way, hoping their meandering conversations might unearth some buried clue.

But when Dades stopped by that day at the tail end of September 2003, Betty Hydell didn't want to talk about Frankie. Instead, she focused on his older brother. As people close to the case describe the moment, she began slowly, tentatively; and then, as if suddenly liberated from years of indecision and misgivings, she let the whole story tumble out.

Two men had come looking for Jimmy the day he disappeared. One was fat, the other thin. And, she gravely announced to the detective, she knew the fat one's name. She even had his picture.

She had seen him on television, talking about his book. Watching him banter with Sally Jessy, believing he had played a part in the murder of her son, had left her, she said, "with a sinking feeling in my stomach." That same day, Betty bought the book. She couldn't bear to read it, but she wanted to study the photographs just to be sure. One look and she was certain: *He was the man.*

Later, Dades got a paperback copy of *Mafia Cop,* written by Lou Eppolito (along with journalist Bob Drury). He felt mounting rage as he scanned the cover, with its photograph of retired second-grade detective Eppolito's gold shield and its subtitle, *The Story of an Honest Cop Whose Family Was the Mob.*

Dades, like most officers in the city who worked organized crime, knew a bit about the accusations surrounding Eppolito and Caracappa, which had surfaced with great fanfare a decade earlier. Lucchese-crime-family underboss Anthony "Gaspipe" Casso, a stone-cold killer turned government witness, had boasted to his FBI debriefers that he had placed the two detectives on his payroll and, even more disconcerting, had used them for hits. In 1994 the *Daily News* trumpeted the allegations against Eppolito and Caracappa on its front page with the headline HERO COPS OR HIT-MEN? When nothing further happened, Dades, who knew firsthand about the unreliability of wiseguys, figured it was all smoke and no fire. But now, staring at Eppolito's smug photograph in the paperback, he thought, as he later confided to investigators in the Brooklyn district attorney's office, Gotcha!

Very quickly, a plan took shape in his mind. He'd go to his friends Mark Feldman, the organized-crime chief in the Brooklyn U.S. Attorney's Office, and Michael Vecchione, who had a similar job in the Brooklyn D.A.'s office, and argue that Betty Hydell's eyewitness testimony was enough to get the case reopened. Since he was retiring from his NYPD job, he could even come on board as an investigator. It shouldn't take much to build a case against the two retired detectives for their roles in Jimmy Hydell's murder.

But Dadés was mistaken. Betty Hydell's tip was just the beginning. By the time the investigation concluded, one and a half years later, seven other murder cases would be documented. By then, Dades would be long gone, finally retired to his gym.

THE YEAR WAS 1986, and on the sidewalks of New York the Mafia was busy settling grudges. Every day, or so it seemed, bold yellow police tape stretched across another crime scene where a wiseguy had been brought down.

Gaspipe Casso, forty-six at the time, was one of the lucky victims. On September 6, 1986, he was at the wheel of his black Cadillac, pulling into the parking lot of the Golden Ox Chinese restaurant, in the Flatlands section of Brooklyn, when a hit team opened fire. Two slugs smashed into his left shoulder, but Casso, bleeding and seething with anger, raced out of the car and into the restaurant. He was leaning against a refrigerator in the kitchen, crouched like a wounded, dangerous animal, when the cops found him.

The police on the scene also found something else. In the car was a confidential printout listing the license-plate numbers of the department's unmarked surveillance cars. Casso, they realized with sudden alarm, had a hook deep inside the NYPD.

Further evidence that Casso had an infuriatingly reliable inside source surfaced four years later. Just before the unsealing of an indictment charging Casso along with fourteen other Mafia heavies in a federal bid-rigging case that could have brought him, if convicted, a sentence of up to one hundred years, he disappeared.

It took authorities more than thirty months to zero in on his hideout. Shacked up in suburban New Jersey with an old girl-friend, Casso readily surrendered when an FBI SWAT team crashed through his bedroom door.

After sulking through a long year in federal prison, Casso, with a wiseguy's easy relativism, agreed to a deal. He would tell all he knew, and in return the feds, no less pragmatic, would forget about his complicity in thirty-six murders, enroll him in the witness-protection program, and then set the volatile sociopath loose in some unsuspecting corner of America.

With their first questions, the earnest debriefers focused on Casso's sources in the New York City Police Department. "My crystal ball," he acknowledged. Then Casso quickly gave up Eppolito and Caracappa. He detailed how, starting around 1986, he had placed the two cops, as the government put it, on "retainer." Employing one of his associates, Burton Kaplan, as the middle-man, he claimed he paid his moles four thousand dollars a month. In exchange, the two detectives, wired into the world of organized-crime investigations, let him know whatever the police and federal organized-crime units were secretly up to.

But there was more. Casso matter-of-factly went on that, after the attempt on his life, he was determined to get even. (Or, as one of the alleged hit men was heard wailing on an intercepted phone call that was leaked to the *Daily News,* Casso wanted to "put me on a table, cut my heart out, and show it to me.") So, using Kaplan once again as negotiator and paymaster, he said he gave the two detectives "additional work."

Jimmy Hydell had been one of the hapless shooters in the botched assassination, and, as Casso told the story, the two detectives were sent out to bring him in. They tracked him down in Bensonhurst, Brooklyn, and, with a flash of their gold badges, arrested him. Only, Hydell wasn't taken to the precinct. They drove him to a nearby body shop, where they shoved him, kicking and screaming, into the trunk of a car. As Casso told the FBI, the detectives drove the car to a Toys "R" Us parking lot in Flatbush. Gleeful and triumphant by his own account, Casso was waiting. He got behind the wheel and, with Hydell curled up in the trunk, headed to an associate's home in Brooklyn.

Hydell was carried into the basement. It became a torture chamber. After Hydell shared the names of his two accomplices, Casso was satisfied but not finished. "I shot him fifteen times," he boasted.

In subsequent sessions, Casso told his interrogators that he had employed the two detectives in connection with seven other murders. In one, according to Casso's unapologetic account, they somehow made a mistake and gave him the address for the wrong Nicholas Guido. As a result, a twenty-six-year-old who had the same name as one of the men who had allegedly ambushed Casso was gunned down on a Brooklyn street on Christmas Day 1986. On another occasion, in November 1990, according to Casso, the two detectives pulled Eddie Lino, a captain in the Gambino crime family, over to the side of the road. When Lino lowered the window of his Mercedes, Caracappa allegedly pulled out his revolver and fired into his head and chest. The detectives, Casso said, were paid $65,000 for the hit.

To the FBI, Casso seemed like the perfect witness. His stories flowed easily and without apparent embellishment. The details were convincing. There was only one problem—Casso had never actually talked to the two cops or handed them any money. He claimed he had left it to Kaplan to handle those chores. In fact, he conceded to his suddenly disconcerted debriefers, Kaplan never even shared their names.

But, he explained, he had seen them once: when he retrieved Hydell in the parking lot. And the way things worked out, it was enough.

On the lam, looking for ways to fill the long days in his suburban hideout, Casso had picked up a book. The author's photo came as a shock. He later said it was the same stolid tough guy who had stood guard while Jimmy Hydell lay in the trunk. He'd never have trouble identifying Lou Eppolito or his grim, wraithlike partner, Stephen Caracappa, to any jury.

Only, despite Casso's willingness to get on the stand and point a condemning finger at the two detectives, he would never get his chance. He screwed up. Repeatedly. Housed in a prison section with other cooperating prisoners, he hatched a bug-eyed plot to kill a federal judge. He persuaded a prison employee to provide him with food, drugs, and fellatio. To avenge a jailhouse fight he had lost, Casso attacked Salvatore "Big Sal" Miciotta in the shower room after discovering that the three-hundred-pound wiseguy had been left handcuffed. And he offered the feds a loopy story about Sammy "the Bull" Gravano's role in the 1991 stabbing of the Reverend Al Sharpton, a tale quickly proved false, since Gravano had been in prison at the time of the attack. In the end, the feds had to concede that Casso was pathologically savage, reckless, and ultimately unreliable. And, more significant, any defense attorney worth his six-figure retainer would shoot their star witness's credibility full of holes.

In the summer of 1998, after determining that Casso had

breached the terms of his agreement, the government sentenced him to life without parole. Without his testimony, police and federal authorities quickly decided, there was no hope of ever making a case against the two Mafia cops.

THAT, IN BRIEF STROKES, was the story that was told in the mountain of FBI criminal-investigation summaries, police reports, and crime-scene accounts that the U.S. Attorney's Office delivered on four overloaded handcarts to the "war room" on the fourteenth floor of the Brooklyn district attorney's building, on Jay Street. It was the fall of 2003, and in the weeks after Tommy Dades shared his new discovery, there was a flurry of activity.

Mark Feldman of the Brooklyn U.S. Attorney's Office, a man whom Eppolito had admiringly described in his fateful book as "a tough Jew," issued the marching orders. The D.A.'s investigative unit, a team of retired detectives whose long careers had been measured out in Mob cases, would lead the charge. They were assisted by William Oldham, an ex-cop and federal investigator in Feldman's office. Their mandate was to dig up the past and scrutinize the present. To go back, and to go forward. To do whatever was necessary to make the cases against two cops who had allegedly betrayed the city's trust. The men whose crimes they were investigating were of their generation, detectives who had been their colleagues. It was their own legacy they would be working to redeem.

To a man, they looked forward to the task with a special zeal. "I know what happened back then. I know all the names, all the players. This isn't history to me," says Robert Intartaglio. A fabled detective known throughout the department as Bobby I., he had retired after twenty-eight years on the job and had spent the last nine working in the D.A.'s office.

"All the years on the job," he explains with a forlorn shake of his head, "you couldn't help feeling that the wiseguys were onto us.

You don't talk on the phone. You don't call some people. Leaks are the worst thing that can happen. And yet they kept happening. Now it was payback time."

Retired detective Doug LeVien embraced the case as his unexpected summons to the front lines. Back in the seventies he had posed as a corrupt cop to infiltrate the Lucchese crime family. Now, after twenty-five years on the streets, he was strapped to a desk as a detective investigator in the D.A.'s office. This was, he realized, a chance to head back into battle. Maybe his last one. And if it were, it would be a fitting last hurrah. "We would clean our own house," he says. "Cops would get other cops."

Yet as the team members prepared to set off on their quest, they were also given a warning. Keep this secret, they were instructed. We don't know whom we can trust. Wiseguys, feds, cops—there's no guarantee which side they're playing on. No telling who will try to stop this investigation if word gets out of what we're up to.

Joe Ponzi, chief investigator in the Brooklyn D.A.'s office, set the team's direction. The son of a detective sergeant who had worked with Eppolito in the Brooklyn South Robbery Squad, Ponzi needed to find a path through the complex evidence. He looked at the daunting pile of old reports and files reaching toward the ceiling of the war room and realized he had no choice but to plunge in.

For long, intense days, he locked himself in his eighteenth-floor office, file after file open on his desk, and relived a time when wiseguys routinely delivered their own unforgiving justice on the streets of New York. His concentration was so complete that, he would tell people, he "could almost hear the bullets zipping by as I turned the pages."

When he emerged from his self-imposed isolation, it was with a smile of triumph. There was, he realized, "one small thread we could pull."

Burton Kaplan was known as "the old man." The nickname seemed appropriate. Heading into his seventies, wizened and
liver-spotted, he squinted out at the world through thick, dark-
framed glasses. But one had only to listen to the deference in a
wiseguy's voice as he spoke of Kaplan to understand that the short-
hand was a term of respect, a tribute to Kaplan's sagacity more than
his age. For Burton Kaplan had accomplished the one goal every
Mob guy, from soldier to capo, admired without qualification: he
made money.

The old man had done well in the Garment District, importing
knockoffs of designer jeans from Hong Kong. And he had schemed
his way to even bigger profits trafficking in heroin, cocaine, and, his
biggest seller, marijuana. In the early 1990s, according to the government's estimate, he began smuggling about four thousand
pounds of marijuana per month from Texas to New York.

With all that money coming in, with all those drugs going out,
not to mention the old man's penchant for gambling hundreds of
thousands of dollars in a single night, it was only a matter of time
before he crossed paths with another Brooklyn player out to make
it big any way he could—Gaspipe Casso. And the two hit it off. In
fact, Casso, eager to hide his assets from prying government eyes,
reportedly thought enough of Kaplan to put the deed to his family's home in the old man's name.

According to investigators, they cemented their friendship and
business relationship when, in the early 1980s, after Kaplan finished
a three-year stint in Allenwood for manufacturing and distributing
quaaludes, he suggested a new and promising deal. In prison, the
old man had met a wiseguy named Frank Santora, who confided
that his cousin Lou Eppolito was a hotshot Brooklyn detective. But
despite his badge, Santora reportedly told him, Lou was one of us:
he was always looking to make a little extra money, and he was not
too judgmental about what he had to do to earn it. Shortly after
Santora was released, around 1985, the way Casso told it to the
FBI, the two greedy detectives, with an accommodating Kaplan

acting as the go-between, went into business with the Lucchese family.

To bolster his short-lived deal with the government, Casso had unhesitatingly ratted out Kaplan. Then, concerned that his close friend might feel upset about having been betrayed, Casso, in prison but not out of touch, decided there was one way to ensure that the old man wouldn't have any hard feelings: he reportedly ordered a hit on Kaplan.

The government got to Kaplan first. The feds pounded him with a massive indictment. In 1998, after reportedly posting bail of twenty million dollars and retaining a team of expensive lawyers to plead his case during a three-week trial, Kaplan was convicted of marijuana trafficking and tax fraud. They threw the book at him. He got twenty-seven years.

Nevertheless, according to the frustrated accounts in the case memos Ponzi had read, the old man was determined to hang tough. He would not share what he knew about the two detectives.

But the way Ponzi figured it, nearly seven years in jail might have softened Kaplan's resolve. And looking at things with as much objectivity as he could muster, Ponzi felt confident that "if there's anything I can do, it's speak to people." After all, he had spent most of his years in the D.A.'s office as a polygraph interrogator and had managed to secure 125 murder confessions. (HE GETS SLAYERS TO SING, marveled the headline of a laudatory 1988 newspaper profile.) He'd sit down with Kaplan and give it his best shot.

Ponzi couldn't simply rap on Kaplan's cell door and ask to talk, however. The old man was a federal prisoner in a federal jail. The team would need federal muscle to get ongoing access. They decided to ask the Drug Enforcement Administration to come on board.

The pitch was made to John Peluso, the assistant special agent in charge of the New York office. A hulk of a man with a bushy mustache and a Kentucky drawl, Peluso was a veteran who had spent twenty-two years fighting the drug wars in the United States and South America. Along the way, he had perfected the undercover operative's knack for affecting a disinterested calm. So as Intartaglio and Oldham laid out the case one morning in November 2003, Peluso sat mute, his eyes fixed on some imaginary point on the horizon. "My thousand-yard stare," he calls it. But when they were done, he spoke up without hesitation: "I see the challenge. But I also see the promise. We're in."

Peluso and Ponzi now went off to see Kaplan, to try to pull the thread. They spoke to him as a team. And they confronted him individually: Ponzi in his laid-back, persuasive way, one kid from the neighborhood talking to another; Peluso more commanding and direct, an authoritative voice hoping to instill confidence that a promise made by the government would be a promise kept.

In the weeks of conversations, they made sure, as Peluso puts it, "to touch all the buttons." Kaplan, old and growing older, could face death alone in prison without the companionship of his wife, his daughter, Deborah (a recently appointed criminal-court judge in Manhattan who had taken the stand at her father's trial and impugned the testimony of a government witness), and his baby grandson. Or Kaplan could tell all he knew, and live to cash in the get-out-of-jail-free card they kept waving in front of him.

Kaplan listened attentively, but it was difficult for either of the men to read his mood. Was he weighing their offer? Or was he simply playing them, glad to fill his empty days with a diversion?

The answer came shortly after New Year's Day of 2004. Kaplan's lawyers notified the U.S. Attorney's Office that their client wanted to negotiate a deal.

When Ponzi announced the news, the men in the war room broke out in a cheer.

FOR THE NEXT THREE MONTHS, Intartaglio met several times a week with the old man. With a squad of federal marshals stationed outside, they sequestered themselves behind closed doors, not too far from the Brooklyn prison where Kaplan returned each night. The talk, fueled by food and drink, flowed freely. With Kaplan as his guide, Intartaglio went back over the gangland wars he had lived through in a previous life. Missing pieces were filled in and mysteries explained. Yet of all the ancient episodes that these rambling sessions brought back to life, two shootings held him like a magnet.

In his mind's eye, Intartaglio could once again see the thick fog rolling in. He was on the roof of New Dorp High School, on Staten Island, peering across the street as best he could on a night in October 1987. He and a team from the NYPD's Major Case Squad were staking out a garden store called Frank's. Informants had told them that the Bypass Gang, a mobbed-up group of thieves who had found a way to defeat sophisticated alarm systems using electronic devices, were going to strike. The gang, the police believed, was raking in tens of millions of dollars, and the word had come down from One Police Plaza: *Get those crooks!*

Suddenly, the microphone the techies had planted in a flowerpot on top of the store's safe started broadcasting: *tap, tap, tap!* It was the sound of the gang coming through the roof—and the signal the police had been waiting to hear. A police helicopter swooped toward the roof. Squad cars rushed from their hiding places.

But no one had counted on the fog. It had sheathed the island in a dense black veil. In the darkness, the Bypass Gang escaped.

That same month, John "Otto" Heidel, a safecracker who was cooperating with the police on the Bypass case, was gunned down. He bent down to examine the flat tire on his car and a fusillade of bullets riddled his back. A year later, another informant, Dominick Costa, got shot five times as he pulled into his driveway. Somehow, he survived.

After those two shootings, Intartaglio knew "without a doubt" that there was a leak. Something was rotten in the department. Now, fifteen years later, he felt able to confirm his suspicions: Stephen Caracappa had been a detective in the Major Case Squad.

HIT MEN IN BLUE?   *237*

FOR DOUG LEVIEN, the hit on Eddie Lino back in November 1990 gave a definitive shape to his wary thoughts about the department. He had gone over the crime-scene reports at the time and seen right away how it must have gone down. The black Mercedes pulling obediently to the side of the road on the Belt Parkway. Lino lowering his window. And the shooter squeezing off nine bullets at close range. Mortally wounded, with his foot on the accelerator, Lino had crashed into a schoolyard fence. At the scene was a wristwatch the shooter presumably had lost as he fled. Lino, it seemed, would have never stopped his car and rolled down his window to speak to another wiseguy. But he would have for someone flashing a badge.

At the time, LeVien had called up a buddy who was advising the NYPD's Organized Crime Control Bureau. LeVien listened carefully as his friend shared a similar fear. Then the friend spoke the unspeakable: "You're right. I think a cop whacked Eddie Lino."

TO THIS DAY, Joe Ponzi wears a gold ring with his eighty-year-old father's shield number. In fact, he had first met Lou Eppolito when the detective worked under his father in a Brooklyn precinct. Now his thoughts focused on the two accused cops. Why did they do it? he kept asking.

Back in 1984, when Internal Affairs had suspended Eppolito for several months for passing intelligence files to Rosario Gambino, a major Mob heroin trafficker, Ponzi felt the detective was getting a bad deal. Sure, Lou was full of himself, a slow-witted, self-aggrandizing onetime muscleman going quickly to seed, a "parade cop" who seemed more intent on collecting headlines and medals than collars.

Still, the way Ponzi looked at it, the department was coming down on him not because of anything Lou had done but because of who he was: the son of Ralph "Fat the Gangster" Eppolito, a Gambino-family killer, and the nephew of James "Jimmy the Clam" Eppolito, a genuine power in the family. When Lou threw himself a fund-raiser—a "racket," as cops call their shindigs—to help him make ends meet during the suspension, Ponzi was one of the several hundred people who bought a ticket. And when a departmental trial cleared Lou and he went on to be promoted to detective second grade, Ponzi thought justice had been done.

Now he had other thoughts. Perhaps Eppolito had been rotten all along. Perhaps he had been leading a double life since the day he joined the department, in 1969. He was his father's son. Or maybe the Internal Affairs investigation and the suspension had pushed him over the edge. Made him a killer for the Mob. Ponzi was not sure he would ever know.

Steve Caracappa was even more perplexing. He seemed in every way an unlikely friend to the ebullient Eppolito. Caracappa was dour, reserved, a rail-thin presence who looked as if he'd had all the life squeezed out of him. "The Undertaker," fellow detectives called him. Sure, he had been arrested on a burglary charge in his youth. But he had served in Vietnam, and, by all accounts, he was a good cop and a skillful, conscientious detective. Was it really his watch that had been left at the Lino hit, as the precinct scuttlebutt had it at the time? Was he the leader of the two? Perhaps, Ponzi speculated, the old adage was true: Still waters run deep.

But after eighteen months of his team digging up the past— "We're archaeologists," Intartaglio jokingly said—Ponzi had worked his way to several certainties. The two retired detectives, he felt, were traitors—and killers. And the time had come to bring them to justice.

IN RETIREMENT, the two former detectives, bound by friendship and their secrets, stayed close. In 1994, Eppolito moved to Las Vegas, settling into a big bright house with a five-foot fountain on the lawn and baronial columns flanking the entrance. The Cadillac in the pink cobblestone driveway completed his idealized picture of gaudy success. Caracappa and his second wife followed a year later, moving into a more modest home across the street.

Starting in the fall of 2004, the task force, assisted by local DEA agents, began keeping a close watch on the two men. And they also began looking for a way to gather evidence about what the pair were up to in good-time Vegas. An inspired plan was hatched. Eppolito's book had set the investigation in motion, providing both Casso and Betty Hydell with a name to match the husky face. And now, John Peluso hoped, Eppolito's book would bring him down for good.

Posing as a high-flying Hollywood producer named Steve Corso, a DEA agent phoned Eppolito and announced that he was interested in making a movie based on *Mafia Cop*. He'd be coming to town and would like to meet.

That was all the starstruck would-be actor and screenwriter needed to hear. Eppolito had hovered, fierce, bloated, and largely mute, in the crowd scenes of a handful of Mob movies, starting with Martin Scorsese's *GoodFellas* (1990), and had written a predictable and sentimental tough-guy feature called *Turn of Faith,* which had gone straight to DVD. But Eppolito had even larger ambitions. He just needed his break. Over the next few months the "producer" spent many days and evenings with both of the retired detectives and their families. And all the time he had a Kel transmitter about the size of a pack of cigarettes taped to his chest. Nearly every word they spoke—close to seventy-two hours' worth—was recorded.

A convivial Eppolito bragged about all the wiseguys who were still his pals. He also reminisced about cops looking up license-plate numbers as favors. And when Corso, one swinger to another, asked Eppolito if he could score him some crystal meth—a bunch of his Hollywood friends were coming to town and wanted to party, he explained—Lou said, No problem. With the help of his twenty-four-year-old son, Anthony, the deal was done, according to authorities.

Several days later, the task force moved in for the arrests. Corso invited both Eppolito and Caracappa to dinner on March 9, 2005, at Piero's, a flashy Italian place not far from the Strip. As the two men walked in, Peluso followed, talking into his cell phone, seemingly arguing with a coldhearted girlfriend. Not far behind him was Intartaglio.

Just as Eppolito and Caracappa were about to give their names to the maître d', Peluso, gun drawn, announced, "You're under arrest." DEA agents seated at the bar rushed over and slammed the former detectives against the wall. Eppolito and Caracappa stared at each other as if in shock. Then they surrendered without a word.

As they were led handcuffed to the waiting unmarked cars, the maître d' rushed after them. "You've got to give me their names," he insisted to the agents. "I need to cancel the reservation. This is a busy place."

"Pick up the papers tomorrow," a gleeful Intartaglio shot back. "You want their names, read the front page."

AS THE CASE MOVES TO TRIAL, the task force is still fighting. Only, now they're battling among themselves—for the spoils.

"True crime," as the genre is called by eager publishers and producers, is truly big business. Once the story broke—cops accused of murder! cold-blooded mafiosi! intrepid investigators!—phones started ringing.

In fact, news of the case leaked even before the indictment was announced. CBS's *60 Minutes,* according to people close to the investigation, planned to be in Las Vegas to witness the arrests. It didn't take a furious Mark Feldman, of the U.S. Attorney's Office, long to react. First, he made it clear that any reporters and cameramen on the scene could be prosecuted for impeding a federal investigation. Then, convinced that someone in the Brooklyn D.A.'s office had begun whispering to a CBS producer in an attempt to grab the glory and the rich deal that would inevitably follow, he called up Joe Ponzi. Your men are off the case, Feldman announced.

But it was too late. The gold rush was on. Tommy Dades, having retired from the D.A.'s office, scored first. After a busy week of meetings, Dades wound up cutting a lucrative deal with Warner Bros. for a potential movie. He talked to various publishers and is presently firming up a book deal. At least one member of the Brooklyn D.A.'s office has been, through his agent, talking to publishers and movie people but will not sign anything until given permission to do so. "How can Joe Hynes, the Brooklyn D.A., allow this?" demanded Arnold Kriss, one of the candidates running against Hynes in this year's primary. "The case hasn't gone to trial and his man is out selling the story." Through a spokesperson, Joe Hynes declined to comment.

William Oldham, of the U.S. Attorney's Office, signed a book deal with Scribner, and as a result is said to have been asked to retire. ("Call my editor, and if he says it's okay, I'll speak with you," he told *Vanity Fair* when reached at his federal office shortly before being forced out. In the end, neither Oldham nor his editor would comment.)

The talented veteran Mob author and screenwriter Nick Pileggi is doing a script "inspired" by the case for Columbia Pictures. Jimmy Breslin, the grand old man of tough-guy prose, is writing a treatise on the modern Mafia which focuses on the alleged killer cops for HarperCollins's literary imprint Ecco. Even Eppolito, although behind bars, was finally getting interest in the screen rights to his book. Universal played with the idea of optioning *Mafia Cop,* but then dropped it as other studio deals fell into place. And the deal-making is not done. Studios and publishers continue to "take meetings" with investigators who worked on the case. (In the interest of full disclosure, it should be noted that the writers of this article have also been approached and done a bit of zealous approaching.)

Big cases also attract big lawyers. Both of the defendants are represented by attorneys who know how to put on a show and clearly enjoy doing it. Bruce Cutler, who came to fame with his bombastic, in-the-government's-face defense work for John Gotti, is representing Eppolito. Caracappa's case will be argued by Ed Hayes, a self-invented package of street smarts, mercurial temper, and flash tailoring. Cutler and Hayes are the sort of canny, insider lawyers who play not simply to the judge and jury but also to the press gallery.

Yet, as a result of the wads of movie and book money some of the investigators have stuffed into their pockets, Cutler and Hayes will have more to work with than they had previously anticipated. "All of a sudden these cops and prosecutors get Kaplan to talk and now they're making money off of it," Hayes gripes. "It sure seems to me like they had a real vested interest in getting him to say exactly what they want him to—so they can run off to Hollywood. Sure, cops and prosecutors sell their books. But never *before* the trial. These guys are potential witnesses. Now what's a jury going to think of them and their so-called objectivity?"

And that is not the only problem facing the government. In all his months of debriefing, Kaplan, *Vanity Fair* has learned, never disclosed that during the 1980s he had been a confidential informant (C.I.) for the FBI.

According to a retired Major Case Squad detective who worked hijacking cases, "There's no doubt that Kaplan was working [for the FBI] as an informant." Another retired organized-crime police supervisor agreed that the FBI "was using Kaplan as an informant. If they say otherwise, they're lying." And the FBI agent identified by three sources as Kaplan's handler confirmed his role: "He worked as a C.I. not just for me but also for an agent in New York." A week later, however, the FBI agent changed his story and denied that he had ever used Kaplan as an informant.

Nevertheless, Kaplan's alleged lack of candor raises disturbing questions for the prosecution about his credentials as a witness. "His [Kaplan's] failure to disclose his status as a C.I. to his current interrogators is a clear indication of his desire to keep something

secret," says an indignant Hayes. "The question is what. The crux of
this case will be to answer that question." The defense attorney
adds, "If he lied to the government in order to keep secret criminal
activity to his profit or to whomever is holding his money, then his
current testimony is worthless."

No less significant, Kaplan's previously undisclosed history of
cooperation with the government focuses attention on another lin-
gering mystery: Why was the initial investigation in 1994 into the
two detectives' crimes—the most stunning allegations ever made in
the history of the NYPD—shut down? Why were such incendiary
charges not pursued for a decade?

The answer routinely dished out by police and federal agents is
that there were no witnesses: Casso had proved unreliable, and
Kaplan was a hard case from the old school, a man who would
never betray anyone. The law-enforcement party line on Kaplan
was succinctly articulated in March by a source quoted in a *Daily
News* report: "The tough Jew who could never be accepted as a
member of the Mafia held to his own principles and honor."

However, according to what two retired New York police officials and an active federal agent have told *Vanity Fair*, Kaplan had a
history of compromising his "principles and honor" in return for
government deals. Did either the FBI or the police, agencies with
direct knowledge of Kaplan's role as a government informant, truly
pressure him to testify against Eppolito and Caracappa?

"I can't believe that he was offered a deal in 1998 and refused
it," says Robert DeBellis, who as the former head of the FBI cargo-
theft unit in West Paterson, New Jersey, knew Kaplan well. "If it
was either [Kaplan] or someone else going to prison for twenty-
seven years, he wouldn't have hesitated for a second."

One of the principal lawyers who defended Kaplan in his
marijuana-trafficking case agrees that there was never a concerted
effort to get his client's cooperation. "To my knowledge," he says,
"there was never a formal deal on the table for Kaplan to roll over
on the cops. It never got that far. The U.S. attorney said that they

would like to sit down with him and talk. Kaplan said he wasn't interested and that was the end of it." Through his lawyers, Kaplan declined to comment.

But why did the police and FBI not actively attempt to get his testimony? Why did they, in effect, allow the case to die?

One theory being whispered in law-enforcement circles is that these agencies wanted the case to disappear. Casso, according to sources familiar with his debriefing sessions, had not merely incriminated the two city detectives but also made allegations about a corrupt FBI agent. And, police officials concede, Eppolito and Caracappa must have had "rabbis" in the department, officials who in the 1980s continued to give them promotions despite the flurry of suspicions. There were, some say, many reasons for powerful people to want the past to remain firmly past.

I WANT TO BURY MY SON," Betty Hydell has said, according to a report by Mob authority Jerry Capeci. "For nine years, whenever there is a body found or dug up, I always call the morgue. They have my son's dental records on file. I just want to bury my son."

The trial of the two detectives, both of whom face life sentences, is scheduled to begin this September. And perhaps, with a verdict, a mother's grief will finally be assuaged.

HOWARD BLUM, *a former reporter for the* New York Times, *is the author of eight bestselling books and a contributing editor at* Vanity Fair. *His new book,* American Lightning, *will be published next year.*

JOHN CONNOLLY, *a former NYPD detective, is a contributing editor at* Vanity Fair. *His book,* The Sin Eater, *the story of Hollywood's P.I. to the stars, Anthony Pelicano, will be published by Atria early next year.*

Coda

Not much more than a year after the indictments, Louis Eppolito and Stephen Caracappa went on trial in a Brooklyn courtroom. The trial stretched on for nearly four weeks, and the scene was reminiscent of the big-time New York mob trials of the late eighties and early nineties when John Gotti strutted his way into notoriety: a gaggle of attentive journalists, photographers, and television crews crowding the courthouse steps, and a parade of morally flawed yet pragmatically born-again government witnesses taking the stand.

But it was the "Old Man" who stole the show—and sealed the case for the prosecution. During his four days on the stand, Burton Kaplan was a perfect witness: a model of careful, well-reasoned recollection. In his soft, lulling voice he told his tale with authority and detail. The courtroom was hushed, riveted, as he described, for example, how Eppolito came to visit him when he was in the hospital for eye surgery in 1990 and the detective rather matter-of-factly detailed the Lino murder. Caracappa was the shooter, the Old Man recalled Eppolito's confessing to him, because "Steve's a much better shot."

Eddie Hayes and Bruce Cutler, the tag team of celebrity lawyers who took on the burden of defending the two dirty cops, seemed overwhelmed by the government's case. They shouted, hurled innuendos against the witnesses, and, raging and furious, pontificated with bombastic indignation in their well-cut suits to the jury. But they never refuted the facts, or seemed really to try. In the end, after only a cursory deliberation, the jury convicted the two former detectives of all the charges.

Caracappa and Eppolito will spend the rest of their lives in jail. And also locked away with them is the big secret that went unmentioned at their trial: Why the New York Police Department allowed the most notorious scandal in its history—two of its own acting as Mafia hit men—to remain ignored for a decade. Until, as fate would have it, this very, very cold case was accidentally resurrected.

Richard Rubin

THE GHOSTS OF
EMMETT TILL

FROM THE *New York Times Magazine*

WE'VE KNOWN HIS STORY FOREVER, it seems. Maybe that's because it's a tale so stark and powerful that it has assumed an air of timelessness, something almost mythical: Emmett Till, a fourteen-year-old black kid born and raised in Chicago, went down in August 1955 to visit some relatives in the hamlet of Money, Mississippi. One day, he walked into a country store there, Bryant's Grocery and Meat Market, and, on a dare, said something fresh to the white woman behind the counter—twenty-one-year-old Carolyn Bryant, the owner's wife—or asked her for a date, or maybe wolf-whistled at her. A few nights later, her husband, Roy Bryant, and his half brother, J. W. Milam, yanked young Till out of bed and off into the dark Delta, where they beat, tortured, and, ultimately, shot him in the head and pushed him into the Tallahatchie River. His body, though tied to a heavy cotton-gin fan with barbed wire, surfaced a few days later, whereupon Bryant and Milam were arrested and charged with murder.

Reporters from all over the country—and even from abroad—converged upon the little courthouse in Sumner, Mississippi, to

witness the trial. The prosecution mounted an excellent case and
went after the defendants with surprising vigor; the judge was eminently fair, refusing to allow race to become an issue in the proceedings, at least overtly. Nevertheless, the jury, twelve white men,
acquitted the defendants after deliberating for just sixty-seven
minutes—and only that long, one of them said afterward, because
they stopped to have a soda pop in order to stretch things out and
"make it look good." Shortly thereafter, the killers, immune from
further prosecution, met with and proudly confessed everything to
William Bradford Huie, a journalist who published their story in
Look magazine.

Yes, we know this story very well—perhaps even too well. It has
been like a burr in our national consciousness for fifty years now.
From time to time it has flared up, inspiring commemorative out-
bursts of sorrow, anger, and outrage, all of which ran their course
quickly and then died down. But the latest flare-up, sparked by a
pair of recent documentaries, *The Murder of Emmett Till* and *The
Untold Story of Emmett Louis Till,* has spread to the federal government: last year, the Department of Justice announced that it was
opening a new investigation into the case. This spring, Till's body
was exhumed and autopsied for the first time. It has been reported
that officials may be ready to submit a summary of their findings—
an "exhaustive report," as one described it—to the local district
attorney in Mississippi by the end of this year. The only person in
the Department of Justice who would comment on any aspect of
the investigation was Jim Greenlee, U.S. Attorney for the Northern
District of Mississippi, who would say only that its objective was
"to get the facts about what exactly happened that day and who
might be culpable."

I have spent a good bit of time trying to do the same thing, even
though it's hard to see how I might have any kind of connection
with the story of Emmett Till. I am a white man from the
Northeast who is not a lawyer or an investigator or an activist;
what's more, the whole thing happened a dozen years before I was

born. But as is the case with so many other people, the story took fierce hold of me the first time I heard it, as a junior in college in 1987, and it has never let go. It drove me, after graduation, to take a job at the *Greenwood Commonwealth*, a daily newspaper in Greenwood, Mississippi, just nine miles from Money. There, I found myself surrounded by people who really were connected, in one way or another, with the case: jurors, defense lawyers, witnesses, the man who owned the gin fan. My boss, a decent man who was relatively progressive when it came to matters of race, nevertheless forbade me to interview any of them—even to ask any of them about it casually—during the year I worked for him.

In 1995, when I found myself back in the Delta to conduct interviews and cover a trial for what would eventually become a book about Mississippi, I took the opportunity to try to talk with the people I couldn't back when I lived there. Unfortunately, many of them had died in the interim, including Roy Bryant. (J. W. Milam died in 1980.) After a good bit of detective work, I managed to track down Carolyn Bryant, only to be told by a man who identified himself as her son that he would kill me if I ever tried to contact his mother. I laughed loudly into the phone, more out of surprise than amusement. "I'm not joking," he said, sounding a bit surprised himself. "Really, I'm not!"

There were others, though, who were willing to talk, were even quite obliging about it, which surprised me, because these were men who had rarely, if ever, been interviewed on the subject. You see, I wasn't interested in talking to Till's cousins and other members of the local black community, the people who had been there with him at the store, who had witnessed or heard tell of his abduction and had worried that they might be next. Those people had been interviewed many times already; I knew what they had to say, empathized with them, understood them. The people I wanted to interview were those with whom I couldn't empathize, those I didn't understand. I wanted to sit down with the men who were complicit in what I considered to be a second crime committed against Emmett Till—the lawyers who defended his killers in court and the jurors who set them free. I wanted to ask: How could they do it? How did they feel about it now? And how had they lived with it for forty years?

I talked to four of them. They're all dead now.

THE KID

Ray Tribble is easy to spot in the photographs and newsreel footage of the trial: whereas eleven of the jurors appear to be staid middle-aged or elderly men, Tribble is wiry and young, in his twenties. Later he became an affluent man, a large landowner, president of the Leflore County Board of Supervisors. Whenever his name came up—which it did fairly often, at least when I lived in Greenwood—it was uttered with great respect. I was in town for six months before I learned that he had been on the Emmett Till jury.

Six years later, I called Tribble to see if he would talk to me about the trial. He didn't really want to, he said, but I was welcome to come over to his house and visit for a while. He might discuss it a bit, and he might not, but in any event, he didn't feel comfortable with my bringing a tape recorder, or even a note pad.

Tribble lived way out in the country, about five miles north of the crumbling building that had once been Bryant's Grocery. He met me on the front lawn and ushered me inside, where we talked a good while about everything, it seemed, but what I had gone there to discuss. Then, I recall, he suddenly offered, "You want to know about that thing, do you?" I did.

He had first suspected it might not be just another trial, he said, when reporters started showing up; then the camera trucks clogged the square, and the jury was sequestered, lodged in the upper floor of a local hotel. He recalled one member managed to bring a radio in so the men could listen to a prizefight. And then, without any emphasis at all, he added, "There was one of 'em there liked to have hung that jury." One juror, he explained—not him, but another man—had voted twice to convict, before giving up and joining the majority.

I was stunned. I had always heard, and believed, that the jury's brief deliberation had been a mere formality. This news forced upon me a belated yet elementary epiphany: the Emmett Till jury was not a machine, an instrument of racism and segregation, a force of history. It was just like any other jury—a body composed of twelve individuals. One of whom, apparently, was somewhat reluctant to commit an act that history has since ruled inevitable.

Tribble told me he couldn't recall which juror, but said it in a way that made me wonder if he truly couldn't remember or if he could but didn't care to say. I ran some names by him, but he would neither confirm nor deny any of them, and fearing that the conversation might soon be coming to an end, I changed the subject and posed the question I had wanted to ask him for six years: Why did he vote to acquit?

He explained, quite simply, that he had concurred with the defense team's core argument: that the body fished out of the Tallahatchie River was not that of Emmett Till—who was, they claimed, still very much alive and hiding out in Chicago or Detroit or somewhere else up North—but someone else's, a corpse planted there by the NAACP for the express purpose of stirring up a racial tornado that would tear through Sumner, and through all of Mississippi, and through the rest of the South, for that matter.

Ray Tribble wasn't stupid. He was a sharp, measured man who had worked hard and done well for himself and his community. How, I asked him, could he buy such an argument? Hadn't Emmett Till's own mother identified the body of her son? Hadn't that body been found wearing a ring bearing the initials LT, for Louis Till, the boy's dead father?

Tribble looked at me earnestly. That body, he told me, his voice assuming a didactic tone, "had hair on its chest." And everybody knows, he continued, that "blacks don't grow hair on their chest until they get to be about thirty."

THE BOOTSTRAPPER

In 1955 Joseph Wilson Kellum was a lawyer in Sumner, Mississippi. In 1995 he was still a lawyer in Sumner, and still practicing out of the same office, across the street from the courtroom where Bryant and Milam were tried and acquitted. J. W. Kellum was their defense attorney.

He was actually one of five; it is said that the defendants hired every lawyer in Sumner so that the state would not be able to appoint any of them a special prosecutor on the case. Kellum gave one of two closing statements for the defense, during which he told the jurors that they were "absolutely the custodians of American civilization" and implored them, "I want you to tell me where under God's shining sun is the land of the free and the home of the brave if you don't turn these boys loose—your forefathers will absolutely turn over in their graves!"

Kellum was a twenty-eight-year-old grocery clerk who had never attended college when, in 1939, he took the state bar exam, passed it, and immediately started a solo law practice. For more than fifty years his office was a plain, squat concrete structure bulging with messy piles of books and files and papers, unremarkable but for its proximity to the courthouse. We talked there for ninety minutes, and he never once grew defensive or refused to answer a question. At the start, he told me, he had regarded the defense of Bryant and Milam as "just another case over the desk." Had he ever asked them if they killed Emmett Till?

"Yeah," he said, "they denied that they had did it."

I asked if he had believed them. "Yeah, I believed them," he replied, "just like I would if I was interrogating a client now. I would have no reason to think he's lying to me."

I quoted his statement about the jurors' forefathers turning over in their graves if the defendants were convicted. What had he meant by that? "Their forefathers, possibly, would not have ever convicted any white man for killing a black man," he explained. I asked Kellum if he'd had any misgivings about appealing to the jury's racial attitudes that way. "No, not at the time," he replied.

"Did you feel the same way at the time?" I asked.

"Not now," he said. He told me about a Vietnamese boy he sponsored in 1975, after the fall of Saigon. I restated the question. "Put it this way," he said. "I didn't feel that it was justifiable in killing an individual, regardless of what his color might be. I didn't think any white man had a right to kill an individual—black individual—like he was a dog."

How, then, could he have so passionately implored the jury, in his closing argument, to rule in a way that would nullify those very values? "I was trying to say something that would meet with— where they would agree with me, you see. Because I was employed to defend those fellas. And I was going to defend them as much as I could and stay within the law. Those statements were not—I received no admonition during the argument from the judge at all."

"So you just looked at it as part of your job?"

"Part of the day's work," he said.

Did he now believe that Bryant and Milam had, in fact, murdered Till?

"I would have to see something," he said. "But they told me they did not. They told the other lawyers that they did not. I have not seen anything where it was supposed to have been an admission of guilt on their part."

If that statement were true, it would make him quite possibly the only man alive at the time who had not read or at least heard about Huie's *Look* article. But I didn't press him on it, didn't call him a liar. The strange thing is that, in my memory, I had always pressed J. W. Kellum hard, maybe even a bit too hard; for ten years,

I felt a bit guilty about how pointedly I had posed difficult questions to a rather genial octogenarian who had graciously invited me into his office and offered me as much of his time as I wanted. Today, though, when I read through the transcript of that conversation, I can't help feeling that I was too easy on the man. I guess we all make accommodations with the past.

THE ARISTOCRAT

It is not widely known, but shortly after they were acquitted, Roy Bryant and J. W. Milam suffered a series of reversals. The family owned a string of small stores in the Delta; almost all of their customers were black, and most of them boycotted the stores, which soon closed. Local banks, with one exception, refused to lend money to Milam, who was also a farmer, to help him plant and harvest his crop. The one exception was the little Bank of Webb; Huie speculated that the bank came to Milam's rescue because John Wallace Whitten Jr., another member of the defense team, sat on its loan committee. According to Huie (who later paid the brothers for the film rights to their story), it was Whitten who brokered the *Look* interview, which took place in Whitten's small law office. Forty years later, Whitten sat down in that same office to discuss the trial with me.

Whitten was a most unlikely savior for two such men. A scion of one of the area's oldest and most prominent families, he went to college and law school at Ole Miss. After graduation, he shipped off to the war in Europe, where he rose to the rank of captain and was awarded a Bronze Star. When he returned home, J. J. Breland, the senior lawyer in town, asked Whitten to join his law firm. Such was the stature of the Whitten name that Breland, who was more than three decades older than Whitten, immediately renamed his firm Breland & Whitten.

Whitten was seventy-six and suffering from Parkinson's disease when we met in 1995, and though he was still practicing law, he often had difficulty speaking. Despite that—and the fact that, as he told me later, his wife had "fussed" at him for agreeing to speak with me—he was a gracious and open host, and like Kellum, never grew defensive or refused to answer a question.

One of his responsibilities before the trial, he told me, was to go down to Greenwood and meet with Dr. L. B. Otken, who examined the body after it was pulled from the Tallahatchie River. Otken, he recalled, had told him, "This is a dead body, but it doesn't belong to that young man that they're looking for." Did he really believe that? "I'm sure I did at one time," Whitten said. "I'm sure he convinced me of it." Had his thinking since changed? "Oh, yes," he said. "I believe that it was the body of Till."

I appreciated his candor, even as I suspected it was a bit incomplete. Or perhaps Whitten was merely choosing his words very carefully; when he said, "I'm sure I did at one time," the natural interpretation is, "I must have, or I never would have done what I did." But I doubt very much that a man like John Whitten could have actually believed such a dubious thing at any time; I imagine that he and the rest of the defense weren't really trying to sell that argument to the jurors so much as they were offering it to them as an instrument of plausible deniability should anyone question their judgment in the future. And now, like J. W. Kellum, he seemed to be engaging in a bit of historical revisionism.

And he clung to it, even when I read to him from an account of his closing argument that had been published in the *Greenwood Commonwealth* on September 23, 1955:

There are people in the United States who want to destroy the way of life of Southern people. . . . There are people . . . who will go as far as necessary to commit any crime known to man to widen the gap between the white and colored people of the

United States. They would not be above putting a rotting, stinking body in the river in the hope it would be identified as Emmett Till.

I asked him if he had really believed those things as he was saying them. He said yes, then surprised me by adding: "And I suppose I would probably say I still believe it. I believe there were certain people who would profit by it."

Whitten then revealed something else about himself: clients may have hired him for his old Delta name, but what they got in the bargain was a savvy lawyer who wanted to win and knew how to do it. "That's one of the benefits of arguing where the prosecutor just has a circumstantial case," he said. "If it's just circumstantial, you can go argue your own circumstances over his, and if they believe you, you win."

I asked him if he thought the jury had reached the correct verdict. "Under the circumstances, I don't know if correct would be the right word," he told me. "But I think it was sustainable." Had he since come to believe the defendants guilty? "I expect, yes," he said. "If you had to put me down as—if I had to say one way or the other what my belief was, it would be that the body was that of Till and he had been put in the river. These people either did it or knew of it."

I raised the subject of his having helped get a loan for Milam—who, like Whitten, was a veteran of World War II, and a highly decorated one at that—after the trial. Huie had quoted Whitten as saying: "Yes, I helped him. He was a good soldier. In a minefield at night, when other men were running and leaving you to do the killing, J. W. Milam stood with you. When a man like that comes to you and his kids are hungry, you don't turn him down."

"Did you really feel that he was a good man?" I asked.

"Yes, I did. Now, I don't say I felt like he was a man I wanted to know and be with every day. But I felt like he was honest. I felt like he was—could be counted on to do things and look after his family. I never changed my mind about that."

"Well, how is it possible that he did this, then?"

He was silent for a moment. "I don't know," he said.

I asked him if he didn't see a conflict there: how could he believe both that Milam was a good man and that he was a murderer? "Well, if that's what you're to judge by," he said. "I don't know whether doing this means he's bad or not. I can't—I'm sure I would have done differently, but I don't dismiss him in every respect because he made one mistake—bad mistake, but his children are still—he's still entitled to work and feed his children."

He was clearly feeling uneasy now, and I could see that it was not merely with this line of questioning; his discomfort, I suspected, mirrored the way he had felt forty years earlier when he had been called upon to defend men of a type he did not associate with, men who had committed a crime he no doubt considered distasteful, to say the least. People of John Whitten's background, his station, did not do such things, or embrace those who did. And yet, in killing Emmett Till, Milam and Bryant had drawn fire from the outside world, not just upon themselves and their crime, but upon their state and their region and nothing less than the entire Southern way of life. And John Whitten, as one of the chief beneficiaries of that way of life, had been called upon to defend it by defending them.

Adding to that burden must have been the knowledge that, in the process, he had become something of a spokesman for white resistance: his final entreaty to the jury was the most notorious utterance of the whole affair. "I'm sure," Whitten told the jurors, that "every last Anglo-Saxon one of you men in this jury has the courage to set these men free."

"Why 'Anglo-Saxon'?" I asked him.

At first he offered something about Anglo-Saxons having "a reputation for being a little harder against people who get out of line than do others," but he quickly set that aside and explained: "You said 'Anglo-Saxon,' the jury would understand what you were talking about. You're talking about a white man." He added, making a pointed reference to another trial that at that very moment was also polarizing the country, "I guess you could say I was playing the race card."

And it occurred to me, right then, just how much the defense of O. J. Simpson owed to the defense of Roy Bryant and J. W. Milam, and how little, in some ways, the country had changed in the past forty years. The issue of race was still so potent that it could overwhelm evidence and hijack a jury, even when the case at hand was a brutal, savage murder. I found it interesting that Whitten made the connection; I wondered if anyone in that courtroom in Los Angeles had.

THE PREACHER

Sometimes, when you set out to find answers to what you believe are simple questions, what you actually end up with are more questions, the kind that are anything but simple. That's what happened to me during those four conversations. Especially the last one.

Howard Armstrong. In 1995, he was, aside from Ray Tribble, the only living juror. In 1955, he was a thirty-six-year-old veteran of World War II, just like John Whitten, and was living in Enid, up in the northern stem of Tallahatchie County. Most of the other jurors, he said, were from other parts of the county, and he didn't know them. They might have known him by reputation: he was a lay minister, leader of the deacons at the Mount Pisgah Baptist Church. A few years later he would be ordained, and would serve as pastor to a number of congregations for the next thirty-five years, finally retiring at the age of seventy-five, just a year before we met.

As with the others, I spoke to Armstrong on the phone first, and he invited me to come by and visit—although, like Ray Tribble, he wasn't sure he wanted to talk about the trial. No one, he told me, had ever tried to interview him on the subject. "Ain't a lot of people even know I served on that jury," he said.

He was living with his wife of fifty-three years, Janie, in a small, neat house that sat up on a rise off a dirt road. In 1955, he was a farmer who made ends meet by working nights at a heating and air-conditioning factory in Grenada, Mississippi, about thirty miles away. The first he had heard of the murder of Emmett Till, he told me, was when he received his jury summons. "I didn't have time for much news," he explained, "working night shift and farming during the day."

I asked him how he had felt about serving. "Really and truly," he told me, "I can't remember how I felt about that. I reckon I felt the way I did about serving on any other jury. I wasn't crazy about serving on none of them. . . . I needed to be on my job and on the farm." When I pressed him to tell me what else he remembered, he responded: "I don't want to pull it up. I want to leave it out there— it's just best to leave things alone."

"He just never did talk about that much," his wife, who was sitting next to him, explained.

I asked about the verdict. "I didn't think that they presented the case to prove it," he said of the prosecutors. "I understand that them folks was pretty much outlaws, but I didn't know that. I heard it years later." He was quiet for a moment. "I still don't know."

That truly surprised me. But he stood by it, insisting that the prosecution had not proven its case—otherwise, he said, "I'd never have voted the way I did." When I asked him what the jury deliberations had been like, he said, "I'm sure there was a good bit of discussion. I do remember that there were at least three votes on that thing." He must have anticipated my next question, because he quickly added, "And I voted to acquit all three times."

I was disappointed; somehow, I had hoped he might have been that lone dissenter. I asked if he still believed they had reached the right verdict.

"I still think they were innocent," he said. "I have no reason and no proof, and I don't judge people. I went and done my duty, left my duty where it was at and went on to other things." And no misgivings at all? "I served to the best of my ability, under my prayer to God for guidance and wisdom. And I stand by my decision. . . . I still stand by it. I think I was right."

"I guess you know that an awful lot of people disagreed."

"I was surprised at all the fuss," he said. "I thought we deliberated that thing, came back with a decision and that should be it." I asked him if racial tensions were sharpened there afterward. "There wasn't as much tensions as there are now," he said.

"We've always had some good black friends," his wife added. "Very good."

"Go to Charleston," he told me, "talk to any of the blacks that was raised with me, and they'll tell you I was anything but a racist."

And I found that statement more disturbing than anything that Ray Tribble, or J. W. Kellum, or John Whitten had said to me. Because I believed him. I believed that Howard Armstrong was not a racist. I felt I had gotten to the point where I could spot a racist of almost any type in almost any circumstance, and he was not one. And yet he had voted—at least three times, by his own account—to acquit two men who were clearly guilty of a horrific, racist crime.

I have spent a lot of time contemplating that conundrum over the past ten years, and I have come to the conclusion that at least part of the problem is ours. We tend to think of racism, and racists, the way we think of most things—in binary terms. Someone is either a racist or he isn't. If he is a racist, he does racist things; if he isn't, he doesn't. But of course it's much more complicated than that, and in the Mississippi of 1955 it was more complicated still. Today, we can look back and say that Howard Armstrong should have voted to convict Roy Bryant and J. W. Milam of murdering Emmett Till; but for him to buck the established order like that would have actually required him to make at least four courageous decisions. First, he would have had to decide that the established order, the system in which he had lived his entire life, was wrong. Second, he would have had to decide that it should change. Third, he would have had to decide that it could change. And finally, he would have had to decide that he himself should do something to change it.

Howard Armstrong never made it to that final step. Another juror apparently did, and managed to stay there through two votes before backing down. It is frustrating to me that I will probably never know who that other juror was, where he found the courage that got him that far, and why, ultimately, he changed his mind. But it is even more frustrating to me to imagine that Howard Armstrong made it past Step 1 but got tripped up on 2 or 3.

I only wonder if it was frustrating for him too. In 1995, sitting with him in his living room, I took his answers, his unwavering declarations that he had no regrets, at face value; today, I'm not so sure. Rereading my notes after ten years, I can perceive a certain defensiveness in his words, an urge to keep the conversation short and narrow, perhaps cut off the next question before it could be asked. His insistence, like J. W. Kellum's, that this was just another trial feels flat now. And then there's his vacillation on the matter of whether or not the defendants were "outlaws." Did he really believe, in both 1955 and 1995, that Bryant and Milam were innocent, and that he himself had done the right thing in voting to set them free? Or was this merely something he repeatedly told himself—and others—to get by? I do believe he was not a racist in 1995. But had he been one in 1955 and then grew, in subsequent decades, so ashamed of that fact that he did everything he could to defeat it in his own mind?

I don't know if Howard Armstrong could have answered those questions then, but I imagine he didn't want to try. It was easier on him, I'm sure, to believe that he had just forgotten all about it. "I'm glad I can't remember those old days," he told me near the end of our visit. "You hear so much about 'the good old days.' The good old days weren't so good."

RICHARD RUBIN *has been a regular contributor to the* Atlantic Monthly, *and has written for the* New York Times Magazine, The New Yorker, New York *magazine, and* The Oxford American, *among others. His most recent book,* Confederacy of Silence: A True Tale of the New Old South *(Atria, 2002), is in part a memoir of his experiences reporting for a daily newspaper in Greenwood, Mississippi, in 1988–1989. He lives in New York, and is at work on a book about World War I.*

Coda

I first heard the story of Emmett Till in 1987, as a junior at the University of Pennsylvania, while watching the documentary *Eyes on the Prize* as part of a seminar on the subject of Race in America. I was shocked, of course, by Till's story—most of *Eyes on the Prize* is shocking, really—and when the narrator recounted how an attorney for the killers said, at their trial, "I'm sure every last Anglo-Saxon one of you men in this jury has the courage to set these men free," I remember, clearly, thinking: Why would anyone say such a thing? What could he have been thinking? In a general sense, my desire to find the answers to questions like those is what led me to take a job as a newspaper reporter in the small Delta town of Greenwood, Mississippi, after graduation, and to spend nearly five years living in the Deep South. I never imagined, though, that I would someday have the chance to pose those questions to the man who had inspired them in the first place.

The Emmett Till case seems so straightforward, and has become so iconic, that people often mistakenly believe they know the whole story. One thing you won't hear in *Eyes on the Prize*, or just about anywhere else, is that it was extremely unusual that Roy Bryant and J. W. Milam were even tried for murder in the first place. In fact, no one I've asked in Mississippi can recall another

such trial happening before then. There were a great many lynch-
ings before then, of course, most of them now long-forgotten, but
despite the fact that many of them were public events—and there
are plenty of pictures to document them—no white man had ever
been tried in Mississippi for lynching a black man before
September 1955. What's more, the trial of Milam and Bryant was
widely regarded, at the time, to have been eminently fair (unlike
the verdict). This was a universal conclusion—even the black press,
outraged though they were over the verdict, devoted a lot of ink to
how hard the prosecutors worked for a conviction, and how fair
the judge was in presiding over the trial, the latter going so far as to
exclude the testimony of Carolyn Bryant, which, he determined,
served no purpose other than to inflame the jurors' racial prejudices. James L. Hicks, the legendary pioneer black journalist, was
there in Sumner and wrote:

> I had come here almost with a preconceived idea that I would
> jeer a mockery of justice from the first day of the trial. But, as the
> state spun its web around the two men in five days, I stayed up late
> and long each night, waiting and getting ready to cheer a state
> which I felt was coming over to the side of decency and fair play
> when the rest of the world was saying that it couldn't be done.
>
> And up to the very moment that the jury of white sharecrop-
> pers came out of the jury room to announce their verdict, I was
> inwardly cheering and rooting for the people of Mississippi as
> loud and long as I root for the Brooklyn Dodgers.
>
> For in the five days' conduct of the trial, Mississippi just didn't
> follow the script written for her by the rest of the world.

After my article was published, I was contacted by the son of
one of those prosecutors; he later shared with me a large cache of
letters his late father had received during and after the trial. There
were two basic types: the first from a black or white correspondent

thanking him for his courageous stand in the name of justice; the seond from a white correspondent condemning him, often obscenely, for betraying his race.

As I said, I never imagined, in 1987, that I would someday have the opportunity to confront some of the men involved in the Emmett Till case, if for no other reason than that the whole affair seemed so bizarre and archaic and otherworldly that I just assumed everyone involved in it was long dead. They were not, though most are now. J. W. Kellum died at eighty-four, less than a year after I met him. Ray Tribble died of cancer in 1998, at the age of seventy-one; a senior center in Greenwood is now named for him. John W. Whitten, Jr., succumbed to Parkinson's in 2003, a week shy of his eighty-fourth birthday. Three years earlier, he and his wife gave a million dollars to their alma mater, Ole Miss, to build a new student golf center. Howard Armstrong died of heart failure on August 25, 2003; he was eighty-four years old. The road that leads to the cemetery where he is buried is named for him.

Roy Bryant died of cancer in 1994 at the age of sixty-three. So did his half brother, J. W. Milam, at the age of sixty in 1981. I am told that Milam's cancer was spinal, and particularly painful. The hotel in Sumner where the jurors were sequestered has long since closed, and now looks as if it is being devoured by trees; parts of it appear to have been swatted to the ground by some giant hand. Bryant's Grocery and Meat Market continues to deteriorate; when I last saw it, in the fall of 2004, the roof, windows, interior walls, and floors were entirely gone, and trees were growing inside it. The second-story porch had been reduced to some dangling weather-beaten timbers, and the front doors had vanished; someone had already put them up for sale on eBay, with an opening bid price of five hundred dollars. There were no takers.

For much more on the subject, including an account of my 1989 encounter with Roy Bryant, see *Confederacy of Silence*.

Chuck Hustmyre

BLUE ON BLUE

Murder, Madness, and Betrayal in the NOPD

FROM *New Orleans* MAGAZINE

SATURDAY, MARCH 4, 1995. 1:55 A.M. EASTERN NEW ORLEANS

Antoinette Frank stood in the cramped kitchen of the Kim Anh restaurant, a 9mm pistol clutched in her hand. Kneeling on the dirty floor at Frank's feet were seventeen-year-old Cuong Vu and his twenty-four-year-old sister, Ha.

Cuong was an altar boy at St. Brigid Catholic Church. He played high school football and wanted to be a priest. Ha was considering becoming a nun. Both worked long hours at their parents' restaurant.

Frank fired nine bullets into them.

Ha Vu died instantly. When detectives found her, she was still on her knees, her forehead resting on the floor.

Cuong took longer to die. Frank shot him repeatedly in the chest and back, but his young athlete's heart continued to beat. Frank heard him trying to talk, so she shot him again, this time firing two bullets into Cuong's head.

Frank and her partner in crime, an eighteen-year-old named Rogers LaCaze, ransacked the Bullard Avenue restaurant until they found what they were looking for—money.

Frank and LaCaze bolted through the dining room. On their way to the front door they passed Ronnie Williams. Williams was a twenty-five-year-old New Orleans police officer assigned to the Seventh District. He had gotten off work at 11:00 P.M. and had gone straight to the restaurant to work a security detail. Williams needed the extra money the detail paid. Ten days earlier, his wife had given birth to the couple's second son, Patrick.

Still in his police uniform, Williams would be found face down behind the bar in a pool of blood. He had been shot twice in the head and once in the back.

LaCaze took Ronnie Williams's gun and wallet.

Outside, Frank and LaCaze piled into a battered 1977 Ford Torino. As the car screeched out of the parking lot, a sun-yellowed cardboard sign fluttered on the dashboard in front of the steering wheel. Printed on either end of the foot-wide rectangular placard was the star-and-crescent symbol of the New Orleans Police Department. In the center of the sign, between the symbols, were the words NEW ORLEANS POLICE OFFICER ON DUTY.

The sign and the car belonged to officer Antoinette Frank, a New Orleans cop who worked out of the Seventh District. She, too, had just gotten off at 11 o'clock. Frank was on the same platoon and worked the same shift as Ronnie Williams. The two officers had worked together every day for more than a year.

A POLICE DEPARTMENT IN DESPAIR

Few would argue that by the time 1995 rolled around, the New Orleans Police Department was in sad shape. The department was losing about one hundred officers per year—many of them fired or arrested—and hiring only half that many. In 1994, two officers had been arrested for murder, one for killing a man the officer suspected of having broken into his apartment; the other for ordering the execution of a woman who had filed a brutality complaint against him. Then in December 1994, the FBI arrested ten New Orleans cops on federal drug-trafficking charges.

CBS' Mike Wallace branded New Orleans "The No. 1 city in the nation for police brutality and corruption." Newly elected Mayor Marc Morial told *Time* magazine, "I inherited a police department that was a shambles." By the start of 1995, things were bad, but they were about to get a whole lot worse.

Officer Antoinette Frank—the woman who would become the poster child for police misconduct and the living symbol of a department gone bad—had just met Rogers LaCaze. Just past his eighteenth birthday, LaCaze already had a history of violence and drug peddling. His mother, Alice Chaney, kicked him out of her house when he was seventeen. "Rogers had become a dope dealer," she says.

At the end of 1994, LaCaze managed to get himself shot. He told police that he and a friend named Nemiah Miller were just hanging out when another friend, a nineteen-year-old who went by the name "Freaky D," whipped out a gun and started blasting at them.

Alice Chaney has her own opinion on the reason for the shooting. "It was behind a dope deal," Chaney says. "Rogers and Nemiah had just scored." Miller died. LaCaze went to the hospital. One of the investigating officers was Antoinette Frank.

WARNING SIGNS

Frank said she always wanted to be a police officer. Born in Opelousas, she was a member of the Opelousas Junior Police and the New Orleans Police Explorers. When she turned twenty, Frank applied to the New Orleans Police Department. Almost immediately, Frank's application ran into problems. The applicant investigation unit discovered Frank had been fired from Wal-Mart and had lied about it on her application. Frank also scored poorly on two standardized psychological evaluations. The psychologist who reviewed Frank's tests recommended a psychiatric interview.

Dr. Philip Scurria, a board-certified psychiatrist, evaluated Frank on fourteen characteristics relevant to the job of a police officer. He rated Frank as unacceptable or below average in most categories. In his report, Scurria wrote that Frank "seemed shallow and superficial." He concluded by saying, "I do not feel . . . that the applicant is suitable for the job of police officer." Apparently depressed over her faltering job prospects, Frank disappeared. She left a halfhearted suicide note addressed to her father. Her father filed a missing-person report with the police department, but Frank turned up the next day. Less than three weeks later, the police department hired her anyway.

A Twisted Duo

After Rogers LaCaze got out of the hospital he started getting regular visits from Antoinette Frank. She eventually took him shopping for new clothes. She bought him a pager and a cell phone. She rented him a Cadillac. Frank became obsessed with him, LaCaze says. She started driving him around in her police car. She even answered calls with LaCaze and introduced him as her trainee. Two officers from the Seventh District once saw LaCaze driving Frank's patrol car. Then Frank and LaCaze started hatching a plan to rob the Kim Anh restaurant.

Frank had been splitting the security detail at the family-owned Vietnamese restaurant with Ronnie Williams for months. During that time, the Vu family, who owned the restaurant, grew close to

Frank and Williams. They treated Frank almost like a member of the family. "The Vus took a real liking to her," Frank's former Seventh District partner says. "I mean, they were in love with this girl. They bought her presents for this, presents for that. Anything she wanted, anything she needed, they gave her." Frank knew the Vus distrusted banks. She also knew they kept all their money in cash.

During the weeks leading up to the robbery, Frank acquired a 9mm pistol from the NOPD evidence room. Two weeks before the murders, she reported the gun stolen. LaCaze was with Frank when a police officer arrived at her house to take the report about the stolen gun. LaCaze later told detectives that the report was bogus. The pistol hadn't been stolen. Just hours before they robbed the Kim Anh and murdered three people, Frank and LaCaze stopped at a Wal-Mart to buy a box of 9mm bullets. Frank was on the clock, wearing her police uniform and driving a patrol car.

CRIME SCENE CHAOS

As soon as they heard the explosion of gunshots from the dining room, twenty-three-year-old Chau Vu and her eighteen-year-old brother, Quoc, ran into the restaurant's walk-in cooler. Chau slammed the door shut as Quoc killed the lights. The two huddled in the cold darkness. Through the glass doors at the front of the cooler and a window overlooking the kitchen, they caught glimpses of Frank and LaCaze as they rummaged for cash. They heard shouting, crying, more gunshots. Then silence.

After she was sure Frank and LaCaze had left, Chau crawled into the dining room. Her cell phone was in her purse on a shelf beneath the bar. She saw Ronnie Williams's body on the floor.

"I saw Ronnie was lying with all the blood around him. That's when all my confidence was gone because the person that protects us was lying right there," Chau later said. Chau grabbed her cell phone and scrambled back into the cooler. She dialed 9-1-1 but couldn't get through. She called a friend and begged him to call the police for her. The friend asked what had happened, but the battery in Chau's phone died. Quoc slipped out the back door and ran to a friend's house to call the police. On the way out, he passed the blood-soaked bodies of his brother and sister. Several blocks away, Antoinette Frank was fuming. "One of the bitches got away," she told LaCaze. Frank had seen Chau and Quoc inside the restaurant when she and LaCaze went in, but she'd lost sight of them and couldn't find them again.

After dropping LaCaze off at his apartment on Cindy Place, Frank drove to the Seventh District. There, she hopped into a patrol car and raced back to the restaurant. She had a second gun— a .38-caliber revolver—tucked into her waistband. Sgt. Eddie Rantz, who supervised the homicide investigation, says, "There's no doubt in my mind; she went back there to kill the rest of them." Whether that was Frank's intent or not, she never got the chance.

Chau hid in the cooler until she saw police officers in the parking lot; then she bolted out the front door and dove into the arms of Det. Yvonne Farve. Frank stayed at the restaurant. She caught a break because Chau was so scared she would only speak Vietnamese at first. In the initial confusion at the crime scene, lead investigators Rantz and Det. Marco Demma had no idea that the young Seventh District officer was one of the shooters. They thought they had caught a break because one of their witnesses was a trained police officer.

When the detectives questioned her, Frank told them she had been in the kitchen getting something to drink when she heard gunshots in the dining room. She said she tried to push all the employees out through the back door.

Ha and Cuong wouldn't leave, Frank said. They stayed in the kitchen. Frank told Rantz she drove to the Seventh District station to report the shooting. But Frank had a cell phone and a police radio with her. Why didn't she call it in instead of wasting time driving to the station? Rantz asked. Why did she leave everybody, including a wounded police officer, behind?

"That's when she started talking about Rogers LaCaze," Rantz says. Frank wasn't a witness, the veteran detective realized. She was a suspect. "I wanted to vomit," Rantz recalls. A little while later, Chau calmed down enough to tell her story in English. Quoc returned to the restaurant and also told the detectives what had happened.

Rantz and Demma had heard enough. Rantz approached Supt. Richard Pennington, who had just started, in the parking lot. Pennington, a veteran detective himself, had been on the scene for a while. "I told the chief, 'We're about to book this motherfucker with three counts of first-degree murder,' " Rantz says. Later, at police headquarters, with a tape recorder in front of her, Antoinette Frank confessed to shooting Ha and Cuong Vu in the kitchen of Kim Anh Restaurant. Her justification was simple: Rogers LaCaze made her do it.

The robbery, Frank said, was all LaCaze's idea. He'd been talking about it for a couple of weeks. She just went along with it because she didn't know what else to do. Although ballistic evidence later proved the same 9mm pistol was used to kill all three victims, Frank refused to admit to shooting Williams. She blamed that murder on LaCaze.

Detectives found LaCaze at his brother's apartment in Gretna just a few hours after the murders. It turned out that about forty-five minutes after LaCaze left Kim Anh, he used Williams's credit card to buy fifteen dollars worth of gas at a station three blocks from his brother's apartment. After his arrest, LaCaze admitted that he went into the restaurant with a gun but denied that he shot anyone. Frank, he said, committed all three murders. He just happened to be there.

AFTERMATH

Rogers LaCaze went on trial in July 1995. He decided to take the stand in his own defense. It was a bad move. Against his attorney's advice, LaCaze, a high school dropout with an IQ later measured in the low seventies, pitted himself against lead prosecutor Glen Woods. Woods is a soft-spoken, contemplative man, but he has a mind like a scalpel, a tool he has used to slice people apart on the witness stand. In the battle of wits with Glen Woods, Rogers LaCaze was unarmed.

In the end, LaCaze was reduced to blubbering on the stand and begged the jury to spare his life. "I did not pull no trigger and kill them people," he pleaded. "I don't even know them people."

Seeking justice for "them people" was one of the defining moments of Woods's career. "They were people, they had a life, they had aspirations, they had dreams," he says. The jury convicted LaCaze of murder and recommended he be put to death.

Antoinette Frank went on trial two months later. After prosecutors Glen Woods and Elizabeth Teel rested the state's case against Frank, her lawyers essentially gave up. Although they'd subpoenaed nearly forty witnesses, they didn't call a single one.

The jury took forty minutes to convict Frank on three counts of first-degree murder. They too recommended the death penalty. Woods said, "It would have been a mockery of justice if Antoinette Frank was to walk away without getting the death penalty."

In October 1995, Judge Frank Marullo sentenced Antoinette Frank to death by lethal injection. LaCaze received the same sentence.

A month later, a dog found the remains of a human skeleton buried under Frank's house. It was the same house she shared for a while with her father. Frank had reported her father missing a year and a half before the murders at the Kim Anh restaurant. There was a bullet hole in the unearthed skull.

LOOKING BACK

A decade after the case that rocked the New Orleans Police Department to its foundation and outraged the city and the nation, much has changed.

Under Pennington, the police department completely revamped its hiring practices. It weeded out bad officers and hired good ones. Under Supt. Eddie Compass, the healing process continues.

Still, as bad as the old hiring system was, in the case of Antoinette Frank, it worked—at least initially. The police department had at least four obvious indicators of Frank's unsuitability for the job before they hired her: lying on her application and during her pre-employment interview, two failed psychological evaluations, her disastrous interview with the department psychiatrist, her strange disappearance and suicide note—all were well-known to the NOPD before they offered Frank a job. So why did they hire her?

In the early 1990s, the department was severely shorthanded. They needed anybody who could fit into a police uniform. Crime was ripping the city apart. In 1994, the year before the Kim Anh murders, New Orleans was the murder capital of the United States. The residency requirement restricted the department to hiring only those applicants who lived within Orleans Parish. (That policy still prevents NOPD from hiring well-qualified officers who live in surrounding parishes.)

And in a city that often simmers with racial tensions, Antoinette Frank, a black woman, fit the profile they were looking for. Hiring her allowed the police department to chalk up one more hash mark for its nonexistent, never-talked-about quota system.

As to why she committed the crime, Frank now says it's her father's fault. She claims to have suffered through years of emotional, physical, and sexual abuse at his hands; it's a claim she only recently started making. But a psychiatrist who examined Frank in

1995 and 1999 said she showed symptoms of "narcissistic personal-ity disorder with antisocial features." According to the psychiatrist, Frank exhibits a lack of empathy toward others as well as a feeling of entitlement, flies into rages, and is manipulative in relationships.

Rogers LaCaze has a simpler diagnosis. In a letter from prison, he wrote, "Antoinette is crazy. Hell, she killed her own dad and buried him under her house."

After twenty-seven years on the job, Eddie Rantz retired. He went to law school. Sometimes he still thinks about the case and about Antoinette Frank. "She is, without a doubt, the most cold-hearted person I've ever met," Rantz says.

Prosecutors Glen Woods and Elizabeth Teel are both in private practice. Teel says the LaCaze and Frank trials were the most trau-matic of her career. "I'd be lying if I said it wasn't personal," she says. In his office, Glen Woods keeps a picture of Ha and Cuong Vu. "It's shocking the way they died," he says. The picture reminds him of the evil that exists in the world.

Mary Williams, wife of Officer Ronnie Williams, is busy raising their two sons, Christopher and Patrick. She has grown very close to the Vu family. They see each other often.

The Vus still own the Kim Anh restaurant.

Antoinette Frank and Rogers LaCaze are on death row, still blaming everyone else, including each other, for what happened.

As for those human bones unearthed beneath Frank's house, so far, authorities have made no serious effort to identify them. The ten-year-old case, they say, remains under investigation.

CHUCK HUSTMYRE *is a freelance journalist in Baton Rouge, Louisiana. Before embarking upon a career as a writer, he spent twenty-two years in law enforcement and retired as a special agent with the Bureau of Alcohol, Tobacco, Firearms, and Explosives (ATF). This story is based on his book* Killer with a Badge *(Penguin, 2004). His articles have appeared in a variety of publications, including the* Washington

Post, *the* Baton Rouge Advocate, Law & Order *magazine,* Homeland Security Today, *and* Court TV's CrimeLibrary.com. *He is at work on another true crime book for Penguin.*

Coda

Despite being jaded by more than twenty years in law enforcement, I'm still shocked by this crime. Cops are human. I know it all too well. They sometimes do stupid things. They sometimes get in trouble. They sometimes end up in jail. But a police officer planning the execution-style murder of a fellow officer is something I never would have thought possible. In the two years I researched this story, I think I uncovered everything that could be uncovered about *how* Antoinette Frank became a police officer and about *how* she and Rogers LaCaze committed a crime so brutal, so senseless, and so shocking. But what I did not uncover, at least not to my own satisfaction, was *why* Antoinette Frank did what she did. I can—and do in the article and in the book—speculate about her motivation. Greed and anger, I suspect, played a major role. Greed is certainly why Rogers LaCaze got involved. But nothing in Antoinette Frank's past indicated excessive amounts of either. So why did she plan and participate in the murder of a fellow police officer, an officer she worked with every day, an officer she knew she could rely on to risk his life to save hers? Looking back, I think maybe I was searching too hard for an answer. Maybe it was right in front of me the whole time. Maybe Sgt. Eddie Rantz and Rogers LaCaze are right about the one thing they agree on. Maybe Antoinette Frank is just crazy as hell. Just ask her dad.

Devin Friedman

OPERATION STEALING SADDAM'S MONEY

FROM GQ

BY AUGUST, EVERYONE AT Fort Stewart knew we were headed
to war. It's one thing to go to the UN and pretend that it's all up to
the weapons inspectors. But you can't play semantics with the people who order the bombs. Because preparing for war means buying
stuff. And not just Javelin missiles, Bradley Fighting Vehicles, and
the rest of the photogenic, lethal combat matériel. To shock to life
the plodding, war-making golem of the U.S. Army's Third Infantry
Division, you need toothpaste and shoelaces and sunscreen. As a
supply sergeant, Matt Novak's mission was to procure enough toilet paper for five hundred soldiers to wipe their asses for a month.
He bought video cameras, flight suits, reams of paper, heaters, computers, crates of a luminescent liquid soldiers paint on vehicles so
other soldiers wearing nightscopes don't mistakenly aerate them
with .50-caliber cannons. *It's a free-for-all spending spree when it's time
to go to war.* He rang up about $200,000 on his government credit
cards at OfficeMax and Home Depot and army-surplus stores, and
that's not including the supplies he procured through normal government supply channels. Often, the hard part wasn't buying the

stuff but making sure you got it. He'd fill out a form for six desk chairs, and by the time the shipment got to the dock there were four; when they got to Matt there'd be two. *That's how crooked the system is; that's the nature of the beast.* So he learned to use unofficial channels to get what he needed. To be a good supply sergeant, it paid to be resourceful, flexible, acquainted with people who had somewhat pliant morals. He bartered, appropriated, and occasionally helped certain items fall off the truck before they were delivered to their rightful owner. *There's a joke in the military: There's only one thief in the army; the rest of us are just trying to get our shit back.*

[While this story is told from Matt Novak's perspective, italics indicate actual words spoken by Matt during a series of interviews last November while we drove around northern Wisconsin in his ex-wife's white Dodge Durango. There's constant background noise on the Novak tapes that gives them a wandering feeling. You can hear stuff rattling around in the backseat—his nine-millimeter, his medical records and written confession, a bottle of Celexa, an antidepressant he's just started taking again. At night he rolls the Durango down into the woods behind his parents' house because he doesn't want it to get repossessed, though he knows it's only a matter of time.]

The system only got more perverted once they got to Kuwait. Matt's unit was stationed at an assembly area—Camp New York or Camp Pennsylvania or whatever they named the colonies of tents they'd thrown up in the middle of the desert. The unit didn't have a lot of the equipment it needed: bullets, M-16 magazines, fluorescent lights, VCRs (the tactical purpose of a VCR was unclear to Matt, but his was not to reason why). They needed a generator and light sets, so Matt and some other guys drove into another unit's compound at two in the morning, backed up to a generator unit with light sets, fastened them to their trailer, and *just drove right by the guards and out into the middle of the desert.*

The Third Infantry Division was the first to blow the gates at the Kuwait-Iraq border; the front prong of the longest, fastest combat maneuver ever attempted; the heroic conquerors of Baghdad. There's a book, *Thunder Run,* about their daring assault. Matt wasn't part of that, though. He was attached to a battalion of combat engineers who drove into Baghdad a few days after the initial assault in a convoy of historic proportions that stretched backward to Kuwait, *a huge snake in the desert stretching as far as the eye could see.* Matt's unit reported directly to the palace complex, what would later become known as the Green Zone. They were sent to an outbuilding near Uday Hussein's house that had been gutted by American ordnance and were told to stay put for the night because the area was not yet secure. Get some rest. *Do you really think we were going to sleep? Come on. Let's get realistic.*

Matt's job was to find useful stuff, and that night alone he broke into fifty, maybe a hundred buildings in the palace complex. It was his first foray into the place that over the ensuing weeks would come to be his domain: from the bulrushes on the Tigris to the four-headed palace, from the zoo to the recreation center, from Uday's love shack to the lavish bungalows of the former Baath courtesans. *I had no restrictions; just hopped in a gun truck, grabbed some guys, and went and took the stuff the army needed.*

[This is as good a time as any to introduce you to Specialist Jamal Mann, a twenty-two-year-old black kid from the projects of Newark, New Jersey, with too many teeth and a crooked smile and a permeating innocence that would somehow cling to him even if he murdered someone. He was Matt's subordinate in Kuwait and Iraq. The first time they met, Matt said, "What's your name?" and he said, "My name is Specialist Mann, Sergeant." Matt said, "No. What's your name?" "Jamal." "I'm Matt, and you can call me Matt." He wanted to create a tiny, two-man culture outside the system. Matt's pretty sensitive to feeling crushed by the system, and he likes to find ways to pull power off the grid, unbeknownst. Slipping the command structure was one of the ways Matt could create some self-worth in a culture that he believes institutionally denied him that. That's what drew him out into the postapocalyptic playground that first night in Baghdad, what made being a supply sergeant such a natural fit, and it's likely this instinct played a part in the decision he made a few weeks later, which is what this story is about. But more on that later.]

In the month or two they were in Baghdad, Jamal and Matt acquainted themselves with hundreds of buildings in the city's tonier districts. They used crowbars, C4 explosive, and a big set of bolt cutters referred to as *the master key* to gain entry into the palace storehouses and the former homes of Saddam's inner circle. They obtained what was needed—water, mattresses, mops, hedge clippers, air conditioners, light switches, wiring, lamps. The commander wanted computers; Matt found computers. Not crap computers, either. Sony flatscreen monitors, Intel Pentium 4 processors, and DVD drives. The rule was: *Whatever you can use, you can take.* And that is a rule that can be applied liberally.

The palace complex was a monument to excess, a repository for the glut of stuff Saddam and his minions had stolen from the Kuwaitis, his own people, what he'd hoarded under the auspices of the oil-for-food program. Cash, cellophane bags filled with heroin and hashish, Kuwaiti royal china. Matt drove around in Saddam's armored Mercedes. Climbed aboard Uday's yacht. He requisitioned gold toilet seats. Bidets. Gilt mirrors. *Johnnie Walker Red, Black, Blue, Gold, every label they make. There were crates of it.* Matt and Jamal dried off with monogrammed towels and slept on Uday's satin sheets. Matt carried a sweet chrome nine-millimeter in the small of his back; Jamal was partial to a long-nosed .357 that looked like something Dirty Harry might consider too ostentatious. There was so much stuff to be had that people didn't really get greedy. First come, first served. [Given what happens later, it's likely Matt is playing up the moral vacuum that existed then. Most of the stuff he acquired in Baghdad and in the months leading up to the war had legitimate purposes and was procured through proper channels. But he's not lying about this shadier stuff. "Yes, that kind of thing was being done," says Major Kent Rideout, the man who would investigate Matt Novak. "It was considered war booty, and there were no regulations put forth on what could and could not be taken home." Officially, the Pentagon has since produced a document that dictates the rules and procedures for the procurement of acceptable war trophies—uniforms, insignia, patches, rucksacks, load-bearing equipment, flags, photos. But the lines get pretty blurry on the ground. Soldiers helping themselves to spoils is a phenomenon roughly as old as people fighting each other. There was a time commanders didn't pay their armies except with the promise of fruitful pillaging. See *Conan the Barbarian* for reference. Or, in effect, the Civil War. Isn't the basic rule of military action that once you beat someone, their shit is your shit? Isn't that how we got, say, Montana? Isn't part of the reason colonialism is considered impolite is that it's an extension of the war-trophy rule to the nation-state level? Isn't that a large part of what pisses some people off, rightly or wrongly, about our Iraqi adventure? Isn't there a serious debate about whether we're after democracy or cheap oil—or, more likely, don't we believe in the convenient truth that we get both for the same low, though seriously rising, price?]

Jamal had an acronym for their mission in Iraq: STAR—steal, trade, acquisition, requisition. One of the medics told Matt, "Man, when you get back to the States, they're going to have to send you to stealers anonymous or something. You're gonna need help, dude!" In Baghdad, Matt earned a reputation as the best supply sergeant in the battalion, possibly in the entire Third ID. He was the go-to guy.

The Iraqis called us Ali Baba. We protected the oil ministry while the city was looted. We took what we wanted.

ON APRIL 18, Matt's platoon sergeant, Kenneth Buff, is out with another sergeant, rooting around the Green Zone for saws to trim some trees when he comes across a small building with bricked-over windows and doors. Inside he finds ninety galvanized-steel boxes, and in each box there is four million dollars in American currency. *Then one day he was shootin' at some food, and up from the ground came a-bubbling crude.* They notify command and, as far as anyone knows, they turn in every dollar they found. [Which physically hurts almost every enlisted man who hears about it. *Are you fucking kidding me? You dumb-ass!*] Buff doesn't get any money, but he was interviewed by Fox News that very afternoon. It is, to say the least, an unexpected event. Saddam was not supposed to have American currency. The Third ID was expecting to find mobile chemical-weapons labs, not buildings stuffed to the rafters with $100 bills.

After chow that day, Matt and Jamal go find Sergeant Buff at headquarters and pump him for information. They feel a certain proprietorship for the contraband of the Green Zone. It was Jamal's idea to seek out Buff, and he just conceded to get him to shut up about it. Jamal wasn't looking to steal money; *he just wanted to find some so he could get on TV.* [Jamal was given an honorable discharge and now works installing cable for Cablevision. "I didn't give a shit about being on the news," he says. "That was a story we worked out. We should have just took the money and left." Jamal and Matt like each other immensely and speak highly of each other, but they still don't have their stories straight.] Buff gets in their truck, and the three of them drive over to see where he found the money. The building looks like a maintenance shack for the municipal water company—squat, cinder block, just a few feet off the road, windows bricked over. While they are driving through the area, they see several other buildings that look the same and that appear to be untouched.

It's hard to pinpoint the first stupid move the Novak Eight made, because it's hard to pinpoint a single not-stupid move they made. Maybe it's after Matt and Jamal had gone to look at the buildings with Buff and decided to ditch their truck and ask a specialist named Emanuel to drive them in his Humvee. Because then Lieutenant Greenley and Private Moyer walk over, asking if they could come along, too *(sure, pile in)*. That initial widening of the cast: not good. ["Shoulda just been me and Sergeant Matt, late at night," Jamal says. "Stupid, stupid, stupid."] Or maybe it's a beat later, as they're driving out of the parking lot and someone asks where they're going and someone says, "To look for some money." The first rule of stealing twelve million dollars is not: Tell everyone what you're doing.

When the five of them get to the building, Matt takes a tanker's bar (like a crowbar, only bigger), climbs on the roof, and starts working on the bricked-over door, only to lose his grip, fall off the building, and land on his back. Jamal and Moyer finish the job, and the whole wall comes down in one piece onto the roadway, sounding like C4 charges going off. Which doesn't attract a whole lot of attention, since you hear stuff like that every twenty minutes in Baghdad. Behind the brick is a door, sealed with a lock and dated in Arabic, just like the door on Buff's building. Matt breaks the glass, starts pulling out shards, and slices his hand open. It is like his body is forcibly trying to keep him out of that building and keeps sabotaging itself, throwing itself off roofs and trying to cut off appendages.

Matt had been a medic, and he knows by looking: *This was a bleeder.* Maybe *this* was the first mistake. A liter of DNA: not recommended for crime scenes. He wraps his hand in a mop head he finds under a sink, and they break through another door. Lieutenant Greenley is outside shouting orders, behaving as if being outside the building gives him plausible deniability. Like you go to jail only if you're in the same room as the crime. He is the ranking officer, after all, and he is in charge simply by being present. [This is how Greenley would play things, with only one foot in. He never decided whether he was a disapproving observer or a conspirator. So for the thirty-six hours before the entire thing unraveled, he tried to be both.]

They find another door, and Jamal, Matt, and Moyer work on it. *As soon as it opened, it was stale air, like a closet you hadn't been in for a long time. There were two sheets coming down at real weird angles, covering the windows. And it looked like the floor was tiled with metal boxes.* There is a total of $200 million in $100 bills in fifty galvanized-steel crates, riveted shut, with blue nylon bands around them. *And then it just, one box began to—we had to know what it was—one box began to be opened.* [This is how Matt says it. You can tell on the Novak tapes when he's getting close to the money—his vocal cords tighten, he searches for words. The actions become disembodied. *The box is opened.* Like there is a ghost in the room, a spirit brought to life by the Novak Eight, made up of the shadowy parts of themselves none of them want to own, and this spook does the dirty work.] The top comes off awkwardly, and money spills to the floor in a great avalanche. Jamal can hear his heart beating in his ears. *Is surreal the word? Just fantasy, you know what I mean? When the first box was opened I was like, There's no way this shit is real. I think I said, "Holy fuck."*

At almost the same time, a vehicle pulls up, and in walks First Sergeant Wilson and, depending on whom you ask, First Sergeant Burns. [While first sergeant is a pretty high rank, it's not higher than lieutenant, which means that Greenley still has de facto responsibility. But Wilson has about twenty years' experience on Greenley, which leads to a bit of confusion about who, exactly, is in charge. Right here, you see the notion of rank and the circumstances at that moment in Baghdad, undoing the normal sense of right and wrong. This is a common occurrence in war. Because what war does is turn what we accept as the unimpeachable rules of morality on their head: We can say that incinerating people is right, that exploding skulls with .50-cals can be an average event after which one eats an MRE and watches *Happy Gilmore*. And what we use as synthetic filler for that internal, hardwired moral structure is military discipline. It's right because your superior officer tells you it's right. And Matt's crime was rejecting the synthetic filler, choosing himself over the system, being an individual. Saying, if it's okay for you to blow people up, it's okay for me to take a few million bucks that doesn't really belong to anyone. War invites nihilism, after all, and Matt Novak simply opened the door when it came knocking.]

Matt throws a stack of hundreds to First Sergeant Wilson. *Say, First Sergeant, aren't you getting ready to retire?* Everyone's passing money around the room now. *Don't you have kids going to college? Maybe you need this for a new vehicle.* Some gets shoved at Greenley. *Hey, Lieutenant, this isn't right. You're senior here!* They're just testing it out. They don't know themselves if they're serious about it yet.

"If you're going to do this," First Sergeant Wilson says, "do it smartly." [Keep in mind, this is the way Matt tells the story. But his version of events is almost exactly the same as the lead investigator's.] "Take only the used bills. The new ones are traceable."

But there aren't enough used bills in that first box. Most of them are crisp, untouched, wrapped in plastic. So, and here comes the ghost again, *the second box gets opened. At that point, the whole room got fucking evil. Everything just going through my head. I won't have to live like a dirt-poor soldier. Saw my wife with a new wedding ring on.* Lieutenant Greenley leaves with Jamal to hide one of the boxes *a hundred feet from where they slept* and alert headquarters to the find, faking to the chain of command that all is right and honorable under the watch of First Lieutenant Greenley. Wilson disappears into the night with an unknown quantity of cash. [Wilson has never admitted to stealing money.] This chaos is all the result, as Matt sees it, of the vital error in the plan: opening the second box. Listening to dumb-ass First Sergeant Wilson when he said the old bills weren't traceable. Like he knew what he was talking about.

[But really, the fundamental failure wasn't one of strategy; it was a failure of imagination. The money was like a blinding light to these guys—drawing them toward it, but way too powerful to actually look at and contemplate. *It's not even going to be there,* they thought as they drove over to the building earlier that night, not wanting to jinx it. *It's not really going to be in those boxes,* they thought when they saw the boxes. And once it was there, spilling out onto the floor and soaking up the blood from Matt's hand wound, Matt thought, *There's no way that's real, it's impossible, it looks like Monopoly money,* though logically he knew perfectly well that it was real. And so they found themselves in a situation they hadn't planned for, hadn't even allowed themselves to think about. And this, essentially, was the downfall of the Novak Eight. They lacked both the restraint to be unmoved by $200 million and the ability to imagine, and plan for, coming to possess it.]

Without even speaking to each other, Matt and Moyer take a box and drop it into a canal across the street. The plan is to report to command that they found forty-eight boxes instead of fifty, come back later with scuba equipment Matt had taken from Uday's house, and retrieve the money. Then Jamal comes back in the Humvee and drops another box in the canal, bringing the grand total of reappropriated money to $12 million. Before the curtain falls on the second act, there is about ten minutes of real happiness in the hot Baghdad night. This moment is as close as they would ever come to possessing that money, as close as they would ever come to free and clear. Jamal is drunk with the idea. He literally swoons and falls in the street. *Does like the Nestea plunge.* And Matt jumps on top of him. Who even remembers what they said to each other.

Lieutenant Greenley calls in the money and at that minute Lieutenant Colonel deCamp and Major Rideout are already in their vehicles and headed for the scene. There is still loose money flying around, and Matt finds a nice pocket in the top of a short palm tree and stashes $200,000 in it. Moyer and Jamal have $400,000 they don't know what to do with. It goes up into the tree, too; only now the stack is too high. You can see it from the road. *This is so fucking stupid.* They're walking back toward the building, and Moyer keeps pulling out more money—a handful of hundreds stuffed in his boots, a stack stuffed in his underwear. *What the fuck?* He's stashing money under rocks, in bushes, the Easter Bunny of $100 bills. *This is totally fucking gay.* And then Jamal decides there's no way he is leaving this place without at least a hundred bucks. So Moyer produces three $100 bills, and they each take one as a souvenir. *Oh, this is so fucking fucked—we're fucked fucked fucked.*

[When he gets to this part, you can sense the wheels in Matt's head spinning a little too fast, creating airy spaces in his monologue, and all you can hear is him smoking. Matt smokes almost constantly—Marlboro Menthols—and this moment is permeated by smoking. You can hear it on the tape, the articulated exhale like an audible symptom of self-loathing.]

When Lieutenant Colonel deCamp exits the building after checking out the scene, he says: "There's three hundred thousand dollars missing." *What is he, fucking Rain Man?* [DeCamp was wrong; there was way more than that missing. But still, the man knew all was not right.] *Fucking Lieutenant Colonel deCamp; he was born with a silver spoon in his fucking ass.* And he starts reading Matt Novak his rights as the rest of the guys load the truck with the $188 million, while the rest of the money is . . . everywhere. Because, let's face it, enough people have had their hands on the $12 million, the process of dispersion is so far along, we'll never really know where it all went. (By the next day, Jamal Mann had already sent an envelope of cash to his mother in New Jersey.) The $188 million goes into the bed of the truck, is driven to the airport, and is flown directly out of the country. Because that much money should simply not be around people. That much money has a mind of its own.

IT TOOK FORTY-FIVE MINUTES for deCamp to find the $600,000 in the tree.

In the next couple of days, Matt, Jamal, and Moyer were isolated, pressed by the Criminal Investigation Command. When Matt would see guys from his unit, they'd say, "What's up, Clooney?" [See the movie *Three Kings* for reference.] Matt didn't see the humor in it. In the interim, there was close to $12 million missing and the rest of Matt's conspirators still moving about freely, unsur- veilled. And maybe another person. *I heard someone outside the door that night, and he's never been identified.* [The Novak tapes devolve often into wild conspiracy. *There are men who took money home. . . . I saw pictures of one guy who lives a block away on a bed with thousands of dollars. . . . Captain Ahearn left the country with money.* Most of the conspiracies have to do with what he sees as the wrongdoings of other people, as if there were a finite amount of guilt to go around and by giving some away it makes Matt less guilty. But he's proba- bly right that there's a lot we don't know. Major Rideout believes that another $220 million could still be out there somewhere.]

Eventually, it was Matt who came forward and gave the fullest account of the events of April 18. Of the Eight, only Matt was kicked out of the army with a less-than-honorable discharge. Further evidence that the army exists on a parallel moral plane. Matt thinks it was because Captain Ahearn, his commander, didn't like him. [The way I heard it was that very few people liked Captain Ahearn, but Matt didn't keep his mouth shut about it.] Lieutenant Colonel deCamp says everyone got treated pretty equally, and if you look, several of the other Novak Eight are no longer in the army. [Still, only Matt was forced out.] Blanket immunity was granted, and no one got jail time. Major Rideout says, "My commanding general, General Blount, said, 'This is going to be quieted; we're not going to let this get out. We're going to do a good investigation, but the last thing we need is a big black eye after what we just did, attacking into Baghdad and doing good stuff.' "

Over the next six months, during the protracted process that ended with Matt's removal from the military, he wasn't allowed to work. He would show up at his unit in Georgia and sit out front in his car, smoking cigarettes. Meanwhile, the rest of his life came unstitched. He discovered that his wife, Michell, had been seeing someone else. And now he's separated, on his way to being divorced, without access to his children, living in the Northwoods of Wisconsin with his parents, who believe that yoga is Satan worship.

I had everything when I left for the desert. I did. I left a beautiful wife and two beautiful children, had a beautiful husky puppy and two cats. I had two vehicles, a Camaro and a Mercury Tracer, 1995 vehicles. Not like a couple of beaters. I had a 1997 brick home, corner lot, quarter of an acre. Privacy fence. Now what do I have? The money was the downfall of my entire life.

[THE LAST OF OUR INTERVIEWS takes place late at night in a bar called the Thirsty Whale, located on Lake Minocqua, now abandoned for the season. Outside, the wind is howling through the bleachers, where summer people watch waterskiing shows. On one portion of the tapes, Matt is trying to enlist some help in destroying his ex-wife's Durango. *Come on! Let's push it in the lake! Or set it on fire in the woods out by my folks' house!*

He keeps talking about how he got more resolutely fucked than anyone else who was involved. He confesses that part of the reason he wants to talk about this episode in his life is that he hopes that a letter-writing campaign will ensue. He wants his day in front of the Senate Armed Services Committee. I asked Sergeant Kenneth Buff, Matt's platoon sergeant and the first guy to find money that day, if victimhood was simply Matt's default identity. Buff said that Matt Novak was the kind of guy you wanted to hang out with. He was universally liked. Funny. Clever. It was only after all this that Matt had changed. "Matt sunk into a real depression," Buff said. "And I don't think he ever recovered."

Matt doesn't deny that he tried to steal money, but he is more interested in knowing: In the movie, is he the good guy or the bad guy? Maybe his guilt depends on the precise moment he made that crucial decision that his desires came before the greater good. As Rideout says: "A good supply sergeant, very few of them are probably legally correct. This guy was right on the edge of right and wrong." Was it the hypnotic power of seeing $200 million in cash, *the golden ring in front of you?* Or before that, when he kicked down that first door to take a sweet Sony television so his unit could watch porno movies in more dramatic fashion? Or earlier, when he got to Kuwait and was told he had to steal shit to do right? Or even earlier, when he was an infant, a fetus, a zygote that mutated imperceptibly? Or was it pre-Matt, in the primordial ooze, and it just so happens that anyone in Matthew Novak's position would take that money?

At the Thirsty Whale, Matt picks out a girl from across the room and takes a seat next to her at the bar. Her name is M. She works in customer service, and she recently had a nervous breakdown. She's medicated now. She and Matt hit it off almost immediately. She looks a little stiff, with her primly crossed legs and glossy new handbag. But Matt could smell the emotional injury on her, the fragility, the liability of having had a nervous breakdown.

M says, "Don't I recognize you? Are you from here?" What kind of line is that?

Well, you know the war in Iraq, right? The flush of false modesty rises.

"Yeah," M says.

Anything special you remember about it?

Everyone's silent, staring at him with vague smiles. They desperately want to go there with him, wherever it is he might be taking them, but they don't know what he's talking about. Earlier that night he said: *Hopefully, this chapter in my life is almost over, or this novel in my life, because that's what it is.* But it's not going to be over if it continues to be a more attractive identity for Matt than the one he's currently living.

You remember any stories?

"Like?" says M. "Stories?"

"Jennifer Lynch or whatever?" the bartender says.

You remember anything about money? Something about GIs finding two hundred million dollars and trying to steal twelve million of it? They all smile now and nod, though whether or not they know the story is anyone's guess. *Yep,* Matt says, *that was me, no shit.*]

Devin Friedman *is thirty-four years old, works as a senior writer for* GQ *magazine, where this story was published, and has never been in the army. He believes he would have been tempted by finding two hundred million dollars in American currency in the middle of a war zone, but believes even more strongly that no one really knows what he or she would do unless they've been in those circumstances. He has been a finalist for the National Magazine Award for essay writing, and his work has appeared in the* New York Times Magazine, The New Yorker, *and* The Best American Travel Writing. *He edited a book of photographs taken by soldiers who've served in Iraq called* This is Our War, *and believes that if he didn't mention Fred Woodward, GQ's very talented art director, and the photograph editor Greg Pond, he'd be screwing those two over for their work on the book.*

Coda

If you've ever watched a trial you know the first rule of trying to re-create a crime: events start to break down upon scrutiny. Unless you have a videotape, and sometimes even when you do (Rodney King et al.), you're never really going to know what happened. And in my limited experience reporting crime stories, the more interviews you do the more it starts to feel like reality is coming unstitched. Even in this case, the case of (as they're referred to in this story) *The Novak 8,* when events were widely witnessed and the conspiracy lasted only a matter of hours, facts begin to lose their purchase. Did the lieutenant make off with a bunch of money as charged? Did the first sergeant? Was Matt Novak really the ring-leader, as the army contends, or the fall guy? In any case, pretty much everyone involved in this incident feels they were singularly screwed. Matt Novak especially so.

The last time I saw Matt was via satellite when we were both being interviewed by Geraldo Rivera. Geraldo was being kind of a dick, insinuating that Matt was a quasi-criminal scumbag. It didn't really help Matt's worldview, which, as far as I could tell when I spent those wintry days up in the Northwoods of Wisconsin doing the reporting for this piece, wasn't too rosy to begin with. After we went off the air on *Geraldo*, I tried to talk to Matt, but the connection was dead. My little flesh-colored earpiece was silent. Later, when *60 Minutes II* called me to do a story about Matt (they barely credited my story in theirs, by the way; more on this later) I found out that Matt felt a little screwed over by me, too. And having tried to call him minutes before composing this coda, and being greeted with silence, I cannot report back about what exactly Matt objected to in this piece. Maybe it's that the story didn't completely alleviate his sense of being persecuted, which is what I think he'd hoped it would do.

Finally, a mea culpa: I got the idea to do this piece from seeing an interview with Matt in a documentary called *Soldiers Pay* that the director David O. Russell was working on when I was doing a profile of him for *GQ*. I promised Tricia Regan, the co-director of the film, that I would mention it in the article, since they'd been generous enough to give me contact information for Matt. And, in the final version of the story that got printed, the name of that film did not appear. And for that crime: I am guilty. Add both the direc-tor of *Soldiers Pay* and me (hey, *60 Minutes II!*) to the long list of people who believe the world kind of screws people over.

Denise Grollmus

SEX THIEF

FROM *Cleveland Scene*

RENEE CLUTCHES A CREASED black-and-white mug shot in the dim light of a suburban diner. The forty-three-year-old strokes her strawberry-blond ponytail as she surveys the scrawny Vietnamese man in the photo.

She nods recognition at his deer-in-the-headlights eyes, flared nostrils, and pursed lips. "He looks just the same," she says. "But I look pretty much the same too. I guess not much has changed in twenty-five years."

Now a wife and mother, Renee still remembers the smallest details of the night they first met, though she hasn't spoken of it in two decades.

It was August 29, 1980. Renee—who talked to *Scene* on the condition that her last name not be used—was a petite but tomboyish eighteen-year-old working at a McDonald's in Akron. At 2:00 A.M., she was closing up the restaurant alone.

As she turned off the parking-lot floodlights and walked toward her '69 Pontiac, a man sneaked up behind her. He held a kitchen knife to her throat. "Get in and drive," he said in a thick Asian accent.

The man guided Renee into a sparsely furnished studio apartment in a house on a hidden alley. "I'm not going to hurt you; I just want to talk," he said.

Keeping the knife at her back, he politely introduced himself as Hy Doan. He told her he was from Vietnam and that he was a math student at the University of Akron. "He just kept talking off-the-wall, like we were friends or something," Renee says.

They spoke for several hours, before Doan asked Renee about her sexual history. She didn't have one. "I'm a virgin," she said.

Doan didn't believe her. His small talk became aggressive. At five foot five and 120 pounds, he was almost as tiny as his victim. Renee figured she could take him.

Suddenly, she jumped on his back and wrestled him to the floor. She got her hands around his slender neck and choked him until he appeared to pass out.

Renee jumped up and ran for the door. As she fiddled with the lock, Doan got up. Just before Renee could open the door, he grabbed her long ponytail and yanked her to his bedroom, ordering her to undress.

Afraid for her life, she sacrificed her virginity.

As Doan raped her, Renee stared through the doorway at the kitchen cupboards, which were filled with shiny packs of ramen noodles. "To this day, I can't eat the stuff," she says. "I can't even look at it."

When he was finished, Doan made her lie in bed and cuddle. He asked if she enjoyed herself. "He was talking to me like I was his girlfriend," she says. "I think he really believed it was consensual."

The sun was already peeking through the blinds when he allowed her to get dressed. He said he'd let her go home if she promised to keep seeing him. She gave him a fake phone number and left.

Renee went to a friend's house. The girl talked Renee into

going to Akron City Hospital. Police were notified. Doan was charged with rape and kidnapping.

Two months later, the case went before a grand jury. But Doan, who maintained the sex was consensual, wasn't indicted. The jury didn't buy Renee's story. She knew too much about Doan's home to have been there only once, jurors believed. They assumed the two were friends. "I was there for seven hours, memorizing everything in that house, to make sure I could prove to police that I was there and that this happened to me," Renee says. "The legal system did nothing more for me, other than rub salt in my wound."

It wouldn't be the last time Doan wriggled his way out of a rape case because of a discredited victim. In the past twenty-five years, he has beaten at least six.

Detectives, prosecutors, and judges say Doan has developed the perfect M.O. for stealing sex. "It's not rape," says his lawyer, Jonathan Sinn. "It's theft."

SINN DESCRIBES HIS CLIENT as a "walking stereotype."

"In court, he bows, talks about honor and family, and comes off as a naive immigrant," Sinn says. "In reality, he's very intelligent and understands everything."

Doan's victims all describe him as a petite, polite man, with rotting teeth and foul breath. Though his accent is heavy, making him hard to understand, he has no problem with English.

He was born in Saigon in 1959. It's unclear when he immigrated to the United States. Doan did not respond to *Scene*'s numerous interview requests, though an anonymous man claiming to be a relative called on his behalf. "Hy does not want to talk to you, because he feels he paid for his mistake and has forgotten the past," the man said.

A 1998 incident report states that he has a sister, Nicole, living in Fairlawn, Ohio. But when *Scene* contacted Nicole, she had trouble deciding whether she knew Doan or not. She also denied being related to him.

"Doan is like the last name Smith," she says. "Just because we have the same last name don't mean we are related. Maybe I helped him once. I help a lot of Vietnamese people. I've lived in Akron for a long time, and we are a small community."

Still, amid her denials, Nicole was able to confirm that Doan graduated from the University of Akron in the early 1980s. He then moved to DeKalb, Illinois, where he earned a Ph.D. in math at Northern Illinois University. "He's not a stupid guy," Nicole says. "He has tutored many Vietnamese in math. There's just a lot of stupid people who say stupid things about him."

Despite his academic achievements, Doan returned to Akron only to work a string of low-wage restaurant jobs while tutoring math on the side. Though he refers to himself as a full-time University of Akron tutor, the school has no record of his employment. But former employees of various Akron restaurants remember him.

In the late nineties, Greg Madonia worked at Papa Joe's, an Italian place popular with the elderly. Doan worked the salad-and-dessert line. He told Madonia he had a Ph.D. in math, but couldn't find work in the United States, which was why he was dressing lettuce for six bucks an hour. His much younger coworkers referred to him as "Mr. Hy." Madonia never noticed anything unusual about him.

Tom Feltner, who washed dishes with Doan at the Mustard Seed, an upscale health-food market and restaurant in Montrose, recalls a slightly more offbeat Mr. Hy.

"He was a weird guy," Feltner says. "He didn't say much, but he'd fly off the handle a lot."

Feltner, sixteen at the time, was under the impression that Doan didn't speak much English. He also remembers Doan boasting of his math credentials and marveled at Doan's dishwashing skills. "He could do the work of two people," Feltner says.

"He was like the kung fu master of dishwashing," says the restaurant's owner, Philip Neighbors.

Coworkers pegged Doan for a harmless oddball. Little did they know they were in the presence of Akron's best sex thief.

AFTER THE JURY LET DOAN off the hook in 1980, Renee would see him around town.

He'd show up at McDonald's, stand in a corner, and watch her for hours. She told a security guard, who warned Doan to get lost.

But Akron isn't a big town. Once, while waiting at a red light, Doan crossed in front of her car. "If I knew what I know now, I would have run him over," Renee says.

After all, less than a year after her case, Doan was standing trial for attempted rape.

Nineteen-year-old Lauren Crouser said that she went to a college house party with several friends, according to the police report. She claimed Doan dragged her into a bedroom, choked her, and told her he'd kill her if she didn't do what he wanted. He tried to take her pants off, but she broke away and ran to a nearby Holiday Inn.

Once again, however, the jury apparently didn't buy the victim's story, though records from that time are too sparse to explain why. Common Pleas Judge Patricia Cosgrove, then a notoriously tough prosecutor, handled both cases. She doesn't remember either.

Yet Cosgrove understands how a man could escape two seemingly straightforward rape cases in less than a year, especially in such he-said, she-said situations, in which victims can be easily discredited. "Sometimes people are good at picking their victims," she says.

Shortly after the trial, Doan disappeared. Renee thought he'd finally been deported, but he'd actually gone to DeKalb, Illinois. It would be fifteen years before police encountered him again.

In 1996, Doan was back in Akron and up to his old tricks. This time, he'd added a new twist to his hunt for women.

Though records are scarce, Fairlawn Sergeant Richard Moneypenny has little trouble remembering July 31 of that year. He was called to the front desk to deal with a trio of oddballs—Doan and two exotic dancers. "We'd already gotten a call earlier that morning from a hotel clerk who said an unusual Oriental man checked into a room with two girls," Moneypenny says.

But this time, Doan was the one demanding to file a report.

He said he met the two women at the downtown Akron Hilton. They asked him for a ride to a less expensive hotel. He took them to the Days Inn in Fairlawn, according to the police report.

Somehow, Doan ended up in their room, where the women tried to blackmail him: Hand over four thousand dollars, or they'd claim they were raped. He said he'd take them to an ATM. Instead, he delivered them to police.

Yet Moneypenny soon uncovered the fiction in Doan's tale. Earlier that day, Doan phoned an escort service, requesting two dates. He met Taryn Chojnowski and Teresa Richard at the Days Inn bar.

He told the women he was a doctor and offered them four thousand dollars for a private dance. The women agreed. Doan got a room.

Afterward, Doan said he had to go to the ATM at Akron General Hospital—where he claimed to work—to get their money. He drove toward Market Street, passing numerous cash machines on the way. Chojnowski and Richard never seemed suspicious.

When they got to the hospital, the women waited in the car as Doan disappeared into the building.

When he returned, he claimed the ATM wasn't working; he'd pay them later. Then he drove the women back to the Days Inn.

At the front desk, the three argued over payment. Chojnowski and Richard threatened to say that Doan had raped them if they didn't get their money. The hotel clerk told them to settle it with Fairlawn police.

Doan's claims of extortion and the dancers' accusations of rape were dismissed as nothing more than a failure-to-pay case. "The girls he preys on aren't exactly in a legal line of work," Moneypenny says. "I'd say he's safe." .

That was the end of it, as far as Fairlawn police were concerned. For Doan, however, it was the beginning of something big. He seemed to realize that his rich-doctor shtick worked on women— and that his claims of extortion got him off with cops.

All Doan had to do was con women in shady occupations into having sex with him, then skip out on the bill. Even if they cried rape, their backgrounds would discredit their allegations. And he was right.

IN 2000, DOAN WENT FOR a late-night snack at the Eat 'n Park on Cuyahoga Falls Avenue. There he noticed eighteen-year-old Colleen Imes.

"By the state's standards, she was an adult, but really, she was still a kid," says Summit County Detective Patrick Hunt. "She was so petite, she couldn't have weighed more than ninety pounds wet."

Imes was just Doan's type—tiny and troubled. He approached her with a polite bow and offered to buy her food. Imes agreed.

Doan claimed to be a Dr. Chang. He said he worked at Akron City Hospital.

She told him that she was a dancer at Lisa's Cabaret, a strip joint on Exchange Street. She'd had a troubled childhood, she revealed, and recently moved out of her mom's place.

Doan made her an offer she couldn't refuse, she later told police: He'd pay her six thousand dollars to be his date to various professional dinners and events. No sex, just companionship, he promised. Imes accepted.

Maybe it was his rotten teeth or his too-good-to-be-true offer, but something told Imes to be leery. She had three friends follow her on their first date.

Imes met Doan for drinks before he drove her to Steve's Motel, a by-the-hour roadhouse in Green.

As Imes sat on the bed watching TV, Doan excused himself to go to the restroom. When he returned, his pants were down to his ankles, his penis erect. Imes told him to pull his pants up.

At first, Doan complied, saying it was just a joke. But within minutes, he pushed her onto the bed and raped her, she said.

Imes would've done better to flee at first chance. Instead, she stayed by Doan's side, pressing him for payment.

He drove her to the Fifth Third Bank on Tallmadge Road. But when he couldn't get cash from the ATM, Imes's friends surrounded him. Doan called 911 and claimed he was being robbed.

When police arrived, Imes cried rape. Detective Hunt investigated, but prosecutors ultimately told him to drop the case. Imes died in a car crash less than a year later.

"It was the saddest sight," he said. "She was a cute girl with the lowest self-esteem. She was just desperate. He picked a perfect victim."

It's the same way Summit County Detective Mike Coghenour speaks of Amanda Stamps. She was twenty-one, "ninety pounds soaking wet," he says, a troubled single mother into drugs and dangerous men.

In 2002, Stamps said, a friend set her up with Doan on a blind date. He was a doctor, she was told, willing to pay as much as six thousand dollars for a nonsexual escort.

Stamps met Doan for dinner. After a few drinks, Stamps claims she slipped into unconsciousness. She believed Doan slipped her a roofie.

She briefly awoke to find herself in a motel room with Doan on top of her. When she finally regained consciousness, Stamps was in Doan's car in the parking lot of Akron General, waiting for her money.

Once again, Doan said the ATM wasn't working. Stamps headed to St. Thomas Hospital for a rape exam.

By the time Coghenour got the case, the Summit County Sheriff's Department was becoming all too familiar with Doan— "aka Dr. Chang, aka Dr. Kitano." But once again, there were problems. "Like the rest of the cases, she waited around for her money, which looked bad," Coghenour says. "It looked like she was trying to turn a trick. It threw a wrench right in her story."

No charges were filed. Shortly after the case was closed, Stamps died of a heroin overdose.

ANGELA SMITH CURLS UP on a loveseat in her Tallmadge condo. Surrounded by photos of her husband and children, Smith clutches the same black-and-white mug shot of Doan that Renee held weeks earlier. She's thirty years old, but her light brown ponytail and button nose make her appear barely legal.

She lets out an ironic chuckle. "He told me I was unique," Smith says.

She met Doan in March at Club 1245, a strip joint just blocks from her home. Smith sat at the bar with her ex-boyfriend, Maurice. They were waiting for their friend, a dancer, to get off work.

As she smoked and sipped beer, Doan approached Maurice and asked if he was with Smith. When he said no, Doan gave Maurice his phone number to pass along.

As Doan left the bar, he bowed in Smith's direction. Later that day, Smith called Doan to ask what he wanted. "He laid it on thick," she says.

He said he was a Japanese neurosurgeon at Akron General. He gave her a name, not Doan, but something Smith couldn't pronounce. She decided to call him "Wu."

Smith had had hip-replacement surgery a few years earlier at Akron General. She asked Doan if he knew her surgeon,

Dr. Weiner. "Dr. Weiner! I just bought a house next door to Dr. Weiner!" he said.

Doan finally asked Smith if she'd accept six thousand dollars to be his date. "You've got the wrong idea," she said. "I'm not a stripper, and I don't have sex for money."

"No, no! I don't pay for sex," he said. "Only for companionship."

He explained that eighteen-hour days at the hospital made it hard for him to meet women. He was worried that his colleagues thought he was gay, because he always came to hospital functions alone. He'd pay her six thousand dollars to accompany him. "He knew I had two kids and I could use the money," she says. "He said I could use the six thousand dollars to buy a computer for my son."

Smith accepted. The next morning, Doan called. "Can you meet me?" he asked.

Smith met Doan at a gas station. He said he'd just been paged and had to go to work, and asked Smith to follow him to the hospital. He went into the building, while Smith waited in her car.

When he came out, he said he found someone to cover for him. "Would you like to go to dinner?" he asked. "We take my car."

Smith got into Doan's blue Honda. In the back seat were medical books and a lab coat. He began talking about medicine, using terminology Smith had never heard. "I totally believed he was a doctor. I had no reason not to," she says. "He like studies this shit, just so he can go out and do this."

They didn't go to a restaurant. Instead, Doan drove them to the Office Motel in Springfield Township. Smith had no idea where she was. "I don't make a habit out of going to hotels that charge by the hour," she says. "And I never leave my side of town."

Doan told her he wanted to take a look at the scars from her hip replacement and caesarean section, which she'd mentioned on the phone. He could fix them with advanced laser surgery, he said.

Inside the room, Doan covered the bed with crisp white sheets and asked Smith to take off her pants so he could see her scars. "He sensed I thought it was weird," Smith says. "He said he had to do it there, because if the hospital found out he was helping me for free, he'd get in trouble. He was so nice and soft-spoken. I wasn't worried. He looked like if you pushed him, you'd break him."

As he pretended to examine Smith, Doan asked her if she'd dance for him. Smith said no. "He started his smooth-talking shit again, claiming it was just a joke."

Then, Smith says, Doan went down on her. Smith said she tried to wriggle away, but she was afraid that if she didn't cooperate, he wouldn't pay her.

Doan slowly pulled a dildo from underneath his clothes and began inserting it into her. She kicked him away, but he slapped her in the face with the latex phallus, pinned her down, and raped her.

When it was over, he insisted that she shower. Then he drove her back to the hospital to get her car. On the way there, he suggested that they pick up her kids and get a bite to eat. Smith said no; she just wanted her money. He said he'd pay her later.

Smith never told her husband about the arrangement. In a panic, she called her ex-boyfriend, Maurice. Doan had promised him an extra two hundred dollars for setting them up. Maurice said he'd get her money.

Then Smith called a friend, who encouraged her to go to St. Thomas for a rape exam. She also contacted the police.

Doan was charged with rape. For the first time, he was placed in the Summit County Jail.

As THE GRAND-JURY HEARING approached, Smith's story posed serious problems.

She admitted to sticking around after the rape, to allowing Doan to drive her back to her car. She confessed that Maurice had contacted Doan to seek payment. When the six thousand dollars never appeared, she went to police.

None of this would help prosecutors. But it left plenty of ammo for Doan's lawyer, Jonathan Sinn. "All along, I said this wasn't a rape case; it was a theft of services," he says.

Doan claimed that he offered Smith money for sex and that she consented; it was only when he didn't pay that she cried rape. He denied pretending to be a doctor. "But even if he does lie, if we locked up everyone who claimed to be a doctor to get laid, the jails would be overcrowded," Sinn says.

The grand jury reduced the indictment from rape to gross sexual imposition. "A grand jury will indict a ham sandwich," says Sinn. "They indict any case that shows probable cause. If they aren't buying that this is rape, you know the victim has serious credibility issues."

Throughout numerous hearings, Sinn attacked Smith's character, pointing out that she met Doan in a strip club rumored to house a prostitution ring. He even accused her of being a dancer, though she isn't.

"It was like, oh, look at this poor little Vietnamese guy, and then look at this slut who'll grind on anyone for a buck," Smith says.

Sinn also exposed problems with Smith's story. "A guy tricking women into having sex by promising them pie-in-the-sky money—it's a theft case, not a rape case," he says.

Knowing that they couldn't get a conviction on Smith's story alone, the prosecution asked to submit additional evidence, hoping to unfold Doan's twenty-five-year history.

As he sat in jail, prosecutors and detectives scoured Doan's favorite pickup joints and strip clubs. They called women from old cases. But each story turned out to be as wobbly as Smith's, and two victims were already dead. Strippers and drug addicts don't make good witnesses.

But detectives never contacted their sturdiest witness, Renee. "If they'd have called, I would have been more than happy to testify," she says.

Finally, in July, prosecutors agreed to a deal. Doan pleaded guilty to assault and soliciting, both misdemeanors. He earned credit for time served and was released in August.

Within a week, Doan was back in the clubs, approaching dancers with his doctor routine, say detectives. "I'd have thought he'd move—or at least start pretending to be a lawyer or something," Smith says.

Though Doan doesn't frequent downtown joints anymore, he hasn't been forgotten. Jim West, operations manager for Flashdance, remembers once kicking Doan out. "I never liked the look of him," West says. "He looks like a squirrel, which is what I call the pervs that come in here and mess with the girls."

But West also says that men like Doan aren't uncommon. They hit the clubs, attempting to make dancers offers they can't refuse. West says that only the "stupid" dancers take the bait. "The dancers I've worked with in Akron are the most naive I've ever met," he says. "They don't want to acknowledge that this line of work can be dangerous."

Even Sinn doesn't believe that the women plan to have sex with Doan. "They probably really hope they're going to get thousands of dollars for talking," Sinn says. "But then they end up in the hotel room, clothes come off, and then they just hope they're still going to get paid."

The consensus among lawyers and cops is that Doan has a talent for profiling victims whom juries won't believe. Moreover, his appearance—the meek mathematician with superb Asian etiquette—seems to pose no threat.

Even Renee had credibility problems. She was a poor girl who left home before graduating from high school, so she could get away from her abusive stepfather. Though she worked two jobs to support herself, her background fit the profile of a girl primed for trouble. "I thought they were supposed to protect the victim,"

Renee says. "Instead, they protected him. If my parents had been rich, I would have won my case."

Police share her frustration.

"I think he's already proved that he's a predator," Detective Coghenour says. "And he'll keep doing as he's been doing until we can find a way to put him away."

DENISE GROLLMUS *is a staff writer for* Cleveland Scene. *She is a graduate of Oberlin College and a former fellow of the Academy of Alternative Journalism, Medill. Her work has also appeared in* Wax Poetics *and the* Akron Beacon Journal. *She lives in Akron, Ohio.*

Coda

My boyfriend, Patrick, and I were gorging ourselves on ten-pound burritos a few days after I picked up Hy Doan's mug shot from the Akron Police Department.

I'd been working on the story for two weeks already, and I still couldn't pronounce Doan's first name correctly, always saying "high," instead of "he."

Patrick asked to see the photo, already creased into the back pocket of my jeans. As he smoothed out the picture, he gagged on his carnitas. "Mr. He!" he screamed.

"No, High," I said. "High Doan."

"No. That's Mr. Fucking Hy!"

It turned out that Patrick and all his friends had worked with Doan as dishwashers and busboys in high school. Patrick worked with him not at one, but three different restaurants in a span of four years. He developed an affinity for the short-tempered Vietnamese man who claimed to be a brilliant mathematician. Patrick and his friends knew Doan simply as "Mr. Hy," and, to this day, he remains one of their favorite Akron characters.

Up until that conversation, I'd known Doan only as the formidable sex thief. I'd spent two weeks scouring police reports and interviewing detectives, trying to wrap my mind around a man who'd spent the past twenty-five years cracking the code for raping women without consequence. Now that man was suddenly "Mr. Hy," a goofy old dishwasher who gave my sixteen-year-old friends innocent lunchroom fodder. When I began sharing stories of Doan's sex crimes with Patrick's friends, everyone reacted with total shock. One friend, who'd seen Doan just months earlier at a local bar, actually appeared saddened.

"I can't believe I bought him a drink," he said.

Deanne Stillman

THE GREAT MOJAVE MANHUNT

FROM *Rolling Stone* MAGAZINE

ALONE IN HIS SMALL TRAILER, Donald Charles Kueck had been hearing voices. *Daddy, why did you leave us? . . . Mr. Kueck, put your hands where I can see 'em. . . . okay, shit for brains, it's thirty days in the hole. . . . Don, do you need some help? We're your sisters. . . . Dad, everything's okay now*—and it was this last voice that always got him because it was his son, lying in the gutter with a dirty needle jammed into his arm, and he would try to tell his son he was sorry, but the voices would not be quelled, swirling into some vast and formless thing in the desert around him, conjuring finally the one thing that would shut it down—Death herself, who threw him a spade, and he picked it up and began to dig his own grave.

NORTH OF LOS ANGELES—the studios, the beaches, Rodeo Drive—lies a sparsely populated region that comprises fully one half of Los Angeles County. Sprawling across 2,200 square miles, this shadow side of Los Angeles is called the Antelope Valley. It's in the high Mojave Desert, surrounded by mountain ranges, literally walled off from the city. It is a terrain of savage dignity, a vast amphitheater of startling wonders that put on a show as the megalopolis burrows through the San Gabriel Mountains in its northward march. Packs of coyotes range the sands, their eyes refracting the new four-way stoplight at dusk, green snakes with triangle heads slither past Trader Joe's, vast armies of ravens patrol the latest eruption of tract mansions you can buy for NOTHING DOWN!

Many have taken the Mojave's dare, fleeing the quagmire of Los Angeles and starting over in desert towns like Lake Los Angeles, population 14,000. Nestled against giant rocky buttes studded with Joshua trees and chollas and sage, Lake Los Angeles is a frontier paradise where horses graze in front yards and the neighbors say howdy. For the most part, its many longtime residents—a mix of fighter pilots, ranchers, real-estate developers, winemakers, Hispanics who work the region's onion fields, and blue-collar crews who grease the engine of the Hollywood studio system "down below"—get along just fine. But Lake Los Angeles is also a siphon for fuckups, violent felons, meth chefs, and paroled gangbangers who live in government-subsidized housing. For years, law-abiding locals felt they were under siege as the city and its problems climbed Highway 14 into the desert, an underpatrolled area where if you called a cop, it might take two hours for a black-and-white to arrive. In 2000, the beleaguered town finally got its own resident deputy—Stephen Sorensen, a ten-year veteran of the sheriff's department. "Resident deputy" meant that you lived where you worked, a gig that was undesirable to some because it involved solitary travel to remote locations on calls involving violent people. "Out there, you're a loner," says Sgt. Vince Burton of the area's Palmdale station. "Whatever happens you have to deal with it yourself."

But Sorensen liked the solitude of the desert and was thriving in Lake Los Angeles. He lived in a sprawling, *Bonanza*-style ranch surrounded by pine groves. He built a corral for his horse and animal runs for the stray dogs and other critters that he always brought

THE GREAT MOJAVE MANHUNT *311*

home. With his wife and baby, the forty-six-year-old ex-surfer from Manhattan Beach became a desert Andy of Mayberry, buying groceries for poor people, doing yardwork for seniors, brokering deals between minor scofflaws and offended parties when others might have hauled the small-time crooks off to jail. Some residents thought Sorensen had literally been sent by God to carry the cross of goodness into a parched desert wilderness of evil. "Looking back on the whole thing," one resident recalls, "I see why Steve was in such a rush to do so many things. He didn't have much time."

Nobody knows why Sorensen decided to drive onto Donald Kueck's property on Saturday, August 2, 2003. It was Sorensen's day off, but when a neighbor of Kueck's named Wayne Wirt called him that morning with a request, the deputy said no problem, as he always did if someone on his remote desert beat had a need.

Wirt wanted Sorensen to make sure that a squatter who was living between his property and Kueck's had vacated the premises that day, as required by an eviction notice. The guy had been leaving piles of trash everywhere, taking dumps all over the desert, turning the view from Wirt's forty-acre spread into one big toilet. The area—a far-flung outpost called Llano—wasn't really in Sorensen's jurisdiction, but he lived two miles away, and that meant it was in his back yard. So Sorensen checked the site, saw no sign of the squatter, and told the Wirts. Then he got back in his Ford Expedition and started for home. But something changed his mind—maybe the squatter was hiding nearby?—and he decided to visit Kueck.

THE TWO MEN HAD FACED OFF nine years earlier, when Sorensen pulled Kueck over for reckless driving on a desert road at high noon. Kueck accused him of being a phony cop, and Sorensen radioed for backup. Furious, Kueck spent months trying to get the deputy fired, writing letters to everyone from Internal Affairs to the FBI.

Now, as Sorensen headed onto Kueck's property, it was almost high noon again, 110 degrees in the shade. Sorensen passed a NO TRESPASSING sign and cautiously proceeded down the dirt road toward Kueck's tiny trailer, spotting abandoned cars and mountains of junk everywhere. In a few minutes, his brains would be in a bucket.

Kueck, like all desert creatures in the midday heat, was probably lying low. A hermit who had lived in the Mojave for nearly thirty years, he had a thing about snakes. He kept a Mojave green, one of the most lethal reptiles in North America, at his front door, the rippling embodiment of the great battle cry "Don't Tread on Me."

The Mojave—a desert nearly as large as Pennsylvania—has historically been a haven for people who hate the system, from Charles Manson to Timothy McVeigh, and Kueck was no exception. A psychotic ex-con who fed his anger and self-recrimination on a cocktail of meth and Darvon and Soma, he had moved out here to get away from society's relentless demands for smog checks and food-stamp registration and housing permits. But now that system was closing in on his front door, in the form of a deputy with a gun.

According to the disjointed account that Kueck gave later, he was in bed when Sorensen arrived. "What's up, buddy?" he asked. The deputy told him to step outside, but Kueck, perhaps half-tweaked after a weeklong speed binge, believed Sorensen was there to hurt him, maybe even evict him. Although Kueck wasn't trespassing—he was living on land bought for him by one of his sisters—he knew he was in violation of a myriad of codes, eking out an existence in a ramshackle trailer without the proper permits. Worst of all, he feared going back to jail—"a concentration camp," as he called it. Confronted by Sorensen, he felt like he was down to his last card. "I figured I better dig up the old rifle and shoot him," he admitted later.

What happened next, according to police, is that Kueck kicked open his front door, aimed his Daewoo at Sorensen, and blasted him with .223s. The high-velocity bullets screamed into the deputy's body below his vest, shattering and buckling him like a piece of glass as he spun around and managed to get off three shots before Kueck blasted into Sorensen's right side and arm, tearing the 9mm from his grasp as rivulets of blood quenched the Mojave's hot sand.

But Kueck wasn't finished. We know from witnesses who heard the shots that a second volley of bullets was fired, and we also know from the coroner's report that Kueck put a round directly into Sorensen's face. He kept firing into the deputy's torso, using the rifle like a stiletto to carve up Sorensen's insides. When it was over, Kueck had raked the deputy's body with fourteen shells.

Unbeknownst to Kueck, he was being watched. After hearing the shots from their home a mile away, Wayne Wirt's wife and kids had climbed a tower and now, through a scope, observed Kueck ransacking Sorensen's Ford. They immediately dialed 911. Kueck disappeared from their view; he was on his knees, hidden by the SUV, tying a rope around Sorensen's legs, crisscross, crisscross, trussing him like a bagged deer, right ankle over left. He dragged the body toward the back of his yellow Dodge Dart and tied it to the bumper. Then he picked up the deputy's brains and threw them in a bucket.

As sirens wailed across the Mojave, Donald Charles Kueck vanished. A few minutes later the phone rang at his daughter's house. "I'm sorry," he said in tears. "I won't be coming over on Monday." In a land infamous for its outlaws, Kueck was about to become the target of one of the largest manhunts the desert had ever known.

AT THE REPORT OF GUNFIRE, a Code 3—"Deputy needs assistance"—went out. Within minutes, dozens of patrol cars from nearby towns and counties were screaming across Highway 138 toward Kueck's trailer. In Long Beach, a Sikorsky H-3 helicopter took off carrying five deputies, and a three-man SWAT team scrambled aboard a chopper in East Los Angeles and headed for the scene.

The first to arrive was Sgt. Larry Johnston, followed by Officer Victor Ruiz of the California Highway Patrol. Johnston spotted spent shell casings and human tissue all over the blood-soaked sand in front of the trailer. There was Sorensen's SUV, its passenger door flung open, his two-way radio gone. But the Dodge Dart was missing, and Sorensen himself was not in sight. Was he being held hostage? Was he bleeding to death in a nearby desert wash? Did the assailant have them in his sights just waiting to ambush two more cops? Other deputies arrived and helped Johnston set up the first perimeter. Ruiz got in his Crown Victoria, siren shrieking, and followed a set of deep and freshly made tire grooves leading away from the bloody site.

As the SWAT team landed in the brush, Ruiz saw the body. "I went to listen for his carotid, and there was nothing," he says. "It looked like he took a round to the eye because it was pushed in. Then I saw that his head was flat. When I looked inside, there was no brain." The SWAT guys teared up at the sight of a fellow deputy reduced to a pile of mangled flesh. A commander told them to suck it up and someone said a prayer, and then they put a blanket over Sorensen's body lest the news media, now swarming the skies like vultures, broadcast the scene on the evening news.

"This was the most bizarre murder of a sheriff I have ever seen," recalls Detective Joe Purcell, a thirty-year veteran of the department. A vicious cop-killer with an automatic weapon was on the loose, and the search rapidly expanded beyond the sheriff's department. In 1873, the bandito Tiburcio Vasquez eluded a mounted posse in this very region for a year; two centuries later, Kueck was contending with an arsenal developed for modern warfare. A few miles away, air traffic control at Edwards—one of the world's largest Air Force bases—picked up the news and passed it on to the pilots who fly over the desert every eight minutes on maneuvers. The FBI dispatched a super-high-tech signal-tracking plane to pinpoint

Kueck if he used his cell phone, picking up his signal as it bounced off local radio towers. By the end of the afternoon, as backup poured in from other desert towns, Lake Los Angeles had become the Gaza Strip—no one was getting in or out without showing ID; every parolee in every trailer park and tattoo joint in the Antelope Valley was hauled in and questioned. Officers from all over Southern California combed Kueck's property and the surrounding desert, looking under every rock, behind every Joshua tree, deep into animal lairs and wrecked muscle cars and down ancient gullies and washes. Less than two hours after Kueck shot Sorensen, the SWAT team found his yellow Dodge Dart two and a half miles from the deputy's body. A dog from a K-9 unit picked up a scent at the car and led deputies to an abandoned shed about fifty yards away, through a dilapidated doorway, still on the scent, right to Sorensen's notebook, hat, and empty gun belt.

But if the cops thought all their manpower and technology would flush out the killer, they didn't know who they were up against. Inside Kueck's trailer, a team of criminalists found a pack rat's library of books on electronics, telescopes, aeronautics, the geology of the nearby Los Angeles Aqueduct, and time travel. Kueck's family confirmed what the evidence suggested—he was a self-taught scientist who, as one of his sisters put it, could "hook up a tin can to a cactus and power a city," a desert savant who built model rockets and talked physics with engineers at secret military test sites in his back yard, a wilderness expert who could survive in the mine shafts and buttes of the Mojave for a long time with nothing but his gun if he had to. He knew the desert's secrets and now became one himself—burrowing under a rock like one of his beloved snakes, or vanishing into one of the countless tunnels rumored to honeycomb the desert, underground hide-outs used by survivalists and meth cooks and lunatics. At one point, he told his daughter while on the run, he coiled under a piece of cardboard in a desert wash, watching the boots of his hunters as they tramped past. Kueck had studied the desert's creatures like a shaman, fascinated with the idea of shape-shifting into a coyote or bobcat or raven and then fading into the scenery until the light changed or the pact he had sealed with whatever dark force had come to an end. Even if it was only in his mind, it gave him an advantage, a mental edge. Some people know how to blend into a crowd. Kueck knew how to vanish into empty space.

Within hours, the search began to unravel. At 6:14 that evening, the dogs lost Kueck's scent. A half-hour later, the SWAT team received some disturbing information—Kueck's car was dumped a few hundred yards from Sorensen's home. They raced to the house and kicked down the door and did a room-to-room search, but no one was there. A few minutes later, they got a tip that Kueck was hiding out next to his property, on the site of the recently evicted squatter. The SWAT team tore back across the desert in off-road vehicles. When they turned the squatter's trailer upside down, they found an elaborate tunnel system, a demented leprechaun's world of canned food, a piss-stained mattress, *Hustler* centerfolds taped to the crumbling walls, and a cockatoo at the end of a hallway.

In 1965, after a series of cop killings in Los Angeles, the LAPD developed SWAT, the paramilitary unit quickly adopted by law enforcement everywhere. But now SWAT needed help. It was dark, and as the coroner's office finished examining Sorensen's body and hauled it away in a van, there was still no sign of Kueck. It was time for the FLIRs—forward-looking infrared thermal imaging—used by the military to target the enemy in Operation Desert Storm. Sorensen's commander, Capt. Carl Deeley, called in the U.S. Air Force. A nearby base immediately dispatched a thermal-imaging plane, which flew over the Mojave at 30,000 feet, scanning every inch of the desert floor, looking for the telltale blip of heat that would indicate a human form. A special SWAT team backed up the FLIRs, ripping across the sands on ATVs, joined by deputies on foot and horseback, and by K-9 units from three jurisdictions.

But by midnight, as the refrigeration unit in the county morgue

slammed shut on Deputy Sorensen, the FLIRs had picked up
nothing but coyotes and kit foxes and all manner of desert preda-
tors on the move. The cops were right back where they started—at
Kueck's abandoned car in the middle of the desert. "People are
creatures of habit," says Detective Paul Delhauer, a profiler with the
sheriff's department. "Their personality is their fingerprint." The
cops knew there was only one place Kueck would hide—right in
his own back yard, the Mojave.

WITH EVERY HOUR a criminal is on the loose, the chances of
finding him diminish exponentially. By the next morning, a thousand cops and deputies had joined the manhunt. Some traversed
the desert in quadrants, walking every cubic centimeter of its
lonely stretches. L.A. County was sparing no expense on the
search, which had morphed into exactly the kind of hydra-headed,
Orwellian monster that Kueck feared—an overwhelming display of
manpower, vehicles, food, searchlights, trailers, aircraft, mounted
civilians, dogs, Andy Gumps, weapons, ammo, fuel, surveillance
equipment, and tracking gear. At the Mount Carmel Retreat
Center in Lake Los Angeles, detectives Phil Guzman and Joe
Purcell approached the nuns just as morning Mass ended and asked
if they could use the retreat as a staging area. The sisters readily
agreed—and so followed a surreal marriage of war and peace as the
SWAT team moved in with the nuns, praying with them at dawn
and sharing their meals before fanning out across the desert to
search for a killer.

Guzman and Purcell hoped to catch a break—maybe some
desert rat would live up to the name and drop a dime on Kueck;
maybe as Kueck got more desperate he'd surface somewhere. But
Kueck had another edge. In his possession were his cell phone,
rifle, Sorensen's gun—and the deputy's two-way radio. While on
the run, he was flipping through the frequencies and paying close
attention to all the police chatter. When a call went out for backup

at East 200 and Palmdale Boulevard, he knew to head in the oppo-site direction. On another channel, he learned that Black Butte Basin Road was hot, so he backtracked.

As the heat-seeking tentacles of law enforcement continued to probe every fissure in the Antelope Valley, cops squeezed Kueck the old-fashioned way. An old mug shot had been broadcast and plas-tered everywhere. Kueck looked like Mephistopheles. It shocked people who knew him in the old days, when he used to look like an Eddie Bauer model, but it proved all too familiar to certain locals, who called in to report sightings of the guy with the demented gaze, the defiant Mojave ponytail and Fu Manchu, the collapsed speed-freak face—someone had seen a man running down the Southern Pacific tracks in Llano; there was a strange guy in the aqueduct at 170 Street and Highway 138; someone just stole someone else's rifle. In a furious attempt to bag the killer, cops in black-and-whites and SUVs raced all over the Mojave, only to find the sad truth of the American desert—another ex-con with no place to go, lying facedown in the sand, blasted on Yukon Jack.

At the Saddleback Market in Palmdale, everyone had a theory. "Maybe he flew out of here in one of those ultralight planes," said one local chick, sucking hard on a Marlboro. "I hear he's in Mexico," said a guy in a T-shirt that read SHOW ME YOUR TITS. Someone else ascribed the murder to secret Army experiments up in the buttes, while another theorized that Kueck had floated down the aqueduct to Los Angeles.

Actually, Kueck hadn't gone anywhere. He was hiding in plain sight, down the road a piece, about a mile from where he dumped his car. After avoiding the FLIRs that first night, he made a move. He knew that to escape detection, he could travel only at twilight or dawn, when his body temperature was the same as the ambient heat on the ground. As the sun rose and warmed the sand, he went to visit his buddy Ron Steres.

Kueck had been on the run for twenty-four hours, and his first priority was that of any desert creature: water. But Steres, an ex-con with an extensive arrest record, was known to have possessed controlled substances, and Kueck, jacked from the murder and the target of a massive manhunt, may have been looking for a fix. In the months before he shot Sorensen, Kueck had invested his meager income—a combination of disability checks, cash from selling junk at flea markets, and gifts from his sisters—in gems from the Home Shopping Network. When he showed up at the remote compound of collapsing sheds and trashed cars where Steres lived, the jewels had become his only currency, something he could trade for drugs and supplies.

Kueck didn't stay long before fading back into the desert—he knew he had to keep moving. Although he shunned civilization, he couldn't last indefinitely without it. And for a man who wanted nothing to do with the modern world, he was strangely obsessed with it: In one of the many phone calls he made to his daughter, he worried about how he looked on TV. He even considered cutting his hair for the first time in two decades—with his picture all over the news, maybe it was time for a change.

On Tuesday, after three days on the run, he visited Steres again. This time, Guzman and Purcell caught their break. Steres had been talking to his friends, and one of them called the cops. A SWAT team quickly swarmed the Steres compound. But no one was there. Once again, Kueck had vanished.

AT WHAT POINT do those attracted to the desert yield to its gravitational pull? Donald Charles Kueck was born in 1950 into a Southern family that prided itself on military service and law enforcement. His father's father served in Kaiser Wilhelm's navy, fleeing Germany after World War I as Hitler began to seize power. His father was a rescue-boat pilot at Eglin Air Force Base in Florida. His mother's brother was the top cop in Louisiana, the head of the state troopers. Two of his sisters joined the Army and the Navy. A good-looking, charismatic guy who had no trouble

attracting women, Kueck could have succeeded at anything he set
his mind to. But in 1970, he followed the hippie trail and moved to
Southern California, taking a job at a sheet-metal plant. He married early, at eighteen, and became an instant father to the daughter
his wife already had, and together they had a son. On the face of it,
Kueck was a typical working-class suburban dad.

But within a few years, he lost his job because of a back injury.
Kueck started taking painkillers, got divorced, and moved into an
apartment in North Hollywood. For the next thirteen years he had
no contact with his family. He worked a series of jobs that led
nowhere. When he could no longer pay his rent, he moved into his
van, parking it next door in a friend's driveway. "He would come in
and shower every couple of days," recalls the neighbor, Barb
Oberman. "He was like a brother."

The two delivered telephone books together, but Kueck wasn't
interested in the money. "It was this spiritual thing," says Oberman.
"He could make or fix anything. He made some kind of back
brace out of rubber bands. He made a telescope from a cardboard
tube and lenses that he put into it. He talked a lot about wanting to
live in the desert." After Kueck found a place in the Mojave where
he could park his van, he moved. But he kept in touch, sending
photos of the animals who trusted him and became his friends—
the ground squirrels that danced on his head, the raven that would
alight on his arm, the jackrabbits that gathered every morning for
breakfast at the table Kueck had set for them in the greasewood.

In the late 1980s, Kueck's family tracked him down through a
friend who was a cop. "My brother and I were teenagers, and both
having a lot of problems," says his daughter, Rebecca Welch. "My
mom knew we needed him." At the designated reunion time,
Welch and her mother sat in a Bob's Big Boy in Riverside,
California. "My dad came in, and I was crying," says Welch. "He
said he knew I was the one who would be the most hurt by his
abandonment, and he had stayed away because he didn't want to
deal with my sadness and anger."

From then on, Kueck was back in the lives of his children, trying to make up for lost time. His teenage son, Chuck, who went by the nickname Jello, came to live with him in the desert in what Kueck called his "anarchy van." "My dad was very happy when my brother was out there," Welch recalls. "They were anarchists together, living free, in control, with no government in their lives." But the relationship was volatile. Jello was addicted to heroin, and Kueck would lock him in the van sometimes to get him to sober up. Kueck himself was degenerating, strung out on painkillers and sinking into a deep depression.

Jello finally split for Seattle. In the city, the good-looking teenager defended younger street kids, attended anti-globalization rallies, played in a band called Fuckhole, and spare-changed female tourists with a line so smooth that one, from Romania, took him back home for a month-long affair. Jello managed to kick junk a few times, but in 2001, at the age of twenty-seven, he returned to Southern California. "He was very intelligent, witty, and passionate," says Fritz Aragon, a musician who knew him at the time. "He was an incredible storyteller, like his father. He was also a compulsive liar, the biggest cheat, always in need of attention." Jello fought with skinheads over his anti-KKK tats and did time for assault. Soon after, he died of an overdose in an abandoned Los Angeles warehouse. "He had been trying to kill himself since he was twelve," a friend says. "He identified with Kurt Cobain."

Jello's death sent Kueck into a tailspin. He left the desert and made a pilgrimage to the warehouse where Jello died. Shortly afterward, he was busted for slicing a guy's stomach with a box cutter while waiting for his daughter to complete an errand in the Department of Social Services in Riverside. "It was another speed freak," she says. "He asked my dad for a cigarette, but then my dad thought he was making a move for a weapon, so he cut him."

Kueck went to jail for a year and came out a changed man: more paranoid, scarred for life—burrowing deep like a lot of ex-cons into the desert sands outside L.A., waiting for a trigger to strike. He called his daughter every day; when Welch said she wanted to be a cop, her father tried to talk her out of it, saying he would kill any cop—or at least white ones—who tried to pull him over. On his frequent visits to his daughter's home, he always brought toys for her four toddlers, whom he adored, and gave her at least two guns. Once, he threatened to bury Welch's ex-boyfriend in the desert if he continued to abuse his daughter. Another time, he spun a bizarre tale of going to the site of busted meth labs and extracting chemicals from the dirt.

A month before he killed Sorensen, Kueck visited his daughter for the last time. "He almost ran over some guys who were working on the driveway," she says. "I knew he was doing speed. He slept for a couple of days and then he was all right." Before he left, he took a few hits of speed from his nasal inhaler. "He was like Charlie Chaplin," Welch says, recalling her final image of her father. "He was running around and breaking things."

AS THE FOURTH DAY of the manhunt wore on, the killer was still at large and the media were clamoring for answers. Cops from all over the West poured in by the hour. By now, Kueck could have been anywhere—or nowhere. He could have been nailed by a Mojave green—in the summer they were all around, especially the newborns, which were the most lethal. He could have succumbed to hyperthermia, which sets in when you are overheated and you have no water and your temperature spikes to 106 degrees, at which point your brain literally cooks. He could have fallen into a mine shaft. But without his body, there was no way of knowing if the desert had taken Kueck down.

Lake Los Angeles is close to top-secret aeronautical sites such as Plant 42, where the Stealth bomber was developed, and the mysterious Gray Butte, second only to Area 51 in terms of high-tech weirdness, from which Predator drones are launched by night to drag the skies over the Mojave and test the latest surveillance equipment. "We are used to seeing strange things flying above us out here," says Deputy District Attorney David Berger, who had joined the hunt for Kueck. But now, Berger and others noticed a C-130 Hercules flying low over the Antelope Valley, making repeated sweeps, as if probing the desert for the fugitive.

But there was no sign of Kueck until Tuesday afternoon, when a local cop decided to have another look at his trailer. Snakes always return to their lairs, and there it was—a rattlesnake stuck to Kueck's front door, with a knife through its head. Somehow, it seemed, Kueck had survived both the desert and his human hunters, slithering under the crime-scene tape to leave his calling card.

Two days later, Deputy Sorensen was laid to rest at Lancaster Baptist Church. "Greater love has no one than this, that one lay down his life for his friends," said Capt. Carl Deeley, as he eulogized the deputy before Sorensen's family, Gov. Gray Davis, and thousands of spit-shined deputies and cops from all over the country who filled the pews and spilled out onto the somber streets. The grief-stricken cops were uneasy. What if Kueck were hiding somewhere, looking through a rifle scope at the congregation as they laid their fallen deputy to rest? They prayed for their fellow officers who were still out searching for Kueck, wondering why nothing could flush him out, not the bloodhounds, not the two-bit snitches, not the cell-phone signals, not the thermal-imaging helicopters, not even bad luck. They knew that every outlaw in the desert was suddenly living with a proud defiance—one of their own had outsmarted the system. The world was watching, and if Kueck got away, the cops would be nothing.

Then, shortly after the bagpipes sounded and an honor guard placed the deputy's coffin into the hearse for his last ride, they got their break. On Friday, August 8, a signal from Kueck's cell phone was picked up coming from the dilapidated compound where Ron Steres lived. Maybe it was because Kueck's birthday was in two weeks and he couldn't face the idea of another year, or maybe he was just tired of hiding, tired of the whole thing. According to the

Annals of Emergency Medicine, at least ten percent of the shootings involving the Los Angeles County Sheriff's Department are cases of "suicide by cop." If that was the goal, Kueck was about to get his wish.

It was the third time that week that Kueck had shown up to see Steres; a woman who lived in the house next door saw him appear on a bicycle like a desert mirage. This time, though, Steres was gone when Kueck arrived: fearing for his life, he had moved to a local motel. The SWAT team closed in, setting up a perimeter with snipers. It was time for the heavy artillery. A SWAT commander placed a call to L.A. police, requesting the BEAR: the Ballistic Engineered Armored Response, a tactical vehicle that weighs 28,000 pounds and can rapidly deploy up to fifteen cops against urban combatants armed with assault weapons.

Around noon, Detective Mark Lillienfeld called Kueck's daughter on a special cell phone that he gave her the day after Kueck killed Sorensen. "Mrs. Welch, get off the phone," he told her. "Your father is trying to call you." Detectives had been following every lead, and this one was the strongest—Kueck had been calling her while on the run, strung out and crying and apologizing for never being able to see her again, saying how much he loved her and recounting a bizarre although possible version of the murder in which he had shot the deputy with Sorensen's own gun, suggesting that there was hand-to-hand combat before he opened up on him. "He kept coming," Kueck said, "and I said, 'Stop, man, stop.' " Now, in Kueck's last hours, Welch was walking an emotional tightrope, trying to help the sheriff's department and at the same time calm her father down as he threatened to go out like Scarface.

Meanwhile SWAT was closing in, as the radios went berserk with news that the fugitive was cornered. Deputies from three counties burned down the highway, racing toward the site where they joined other law-enforcement personnel and stood arm to arm at the outer perimeter, a human barrier through which no one could escape. With everybody positioned, an announcement was made—"Donald Kueck, this is the Los Angeles Sheriff's Department. We know you are in there. Come out with your hands up." There was no response, no movement. *Was Kueck really in there?* many of the frazzled deputies wondered. *Or had he escaped the noose once again?*

At 1:20 P.M., Welch got another call. It was her father. He had been trying to contact police on Sorensen's radio. They spoke for a couple of minutes and then Detective Lillienfeld arrived. "Dad, the sheriff's right here," she said. "You talk to him." By now, every satellite van in Southern California was racing toward the scene.

A twenty-five-year veteran of the department, Lillienfeld is a self-effacing guy with a quiet and soothing voice—one that may have provided Kueck with a few moments of grace before he went up in flames. Kueck seemed most concerned about returning to prison. "Once I get in there," he told Lillienfeld, "those Asian doctors are worse than Mengele."

"We got all kinds of doctors in there," Lillienfeld told him. "Why don't we let you see some non-Asian doctors?"

For the next several hours, as Kueck tried to recharge his faltering cell-phone battery with the one in Sorensen's radio, there were dozens of calls made back and forth from Lillienfeld to the staging area at Mount Carmel to SWAT in the field. At one point Kueck told Lillienfeld to wait while he took a leak; at other times he rambled about dirt bikes, his back pain, suicide, taking cops down with him. At another point, in the middle of it all, he choked up and asked Lillienfeld not to tell his mother, in her late seventies and unaware of her son's situation.

At 3:30 P.M., Sheriff Lee Baca stepped out of an Air 5 chopper and was escorted to a bank of microphones to address the news media. He gave an assessment of the situation and the suspect, and ended the press conference with a terse summation: "We're down to what's known in this business as dead or alive."

As SWAT commanders positioned the BEAR and set up a tactical plan, Lillienfeld tried one last time to get Kueck to surrender.

"We'd like to kind of resolve this thing before it gets dark out," he said. Kueck replied that he did not want to get arrested or killed before sundown. "Nobody wants to kill you," Lillienfeld said.

At 5:26, the loudspeaker began blaring—"Donald Kueck, come out with your hands up." A half-hour later, the first round of tear gas was deployed, quickly followed by a second. As the gas billowed through the main compound, Kueck called Lillienfeld and claimed to be in the bushes, daring him to "send in the dogs."

SWAT launched another volley of tear gas and the BEAR moved in for the kill, obliterating sheds as it barreled toward the main compound. Kueck opened up with his automatic, spraying the giant assault vehicle with gunfire. Air 5 and 6 hovered over the sheds as fires broke out in one shed, then two, then a third, as Kueck—perhaps shot himself—darted in and out of the flames, blasting rounds. By 8:45, the entire compound was on fire, and the fire grew and as the moon appeared above the Mojave, it became a conflagration with giant freak-show flames that scorched the heavens, and some wondered if it was the Twilight of the Gods, and the news choppers came to the fire like mechanical moths, relaying the image to millions who watched the flames dance on television, the phony hearth that interrupted regular programming with coverage of the End. Around the perimeter of Kueck's last stand, hundreds of deputies and law-enforcement personnel watched the grisly bonfire burn and wondered if they had finally got him. A few miles away at Mount Carmel, the nuns watched the flames in the distance and prayed.

AT MIDNIGHT—MORE THAN three hours after the fire began raging—SWAT was ordered to search the area. Ten minutes later they found Donald Kueck on his back, nearly cremated, clutching his rifle. When they went to move the body, it crumbled. A few days later, his family scattered his ashes off one of his favorite buttes.

Months after it all went down, the crime-scene tape at Kueck's trailer still fluttered in the wind. There were some old jars of peanut butter and a pair of Nikes (size eleven)—just waiting for the next hermit with a useless dream. The land remained a scavenger's paradise of busted bicycles and generators, engines and furniture, lawn mowers and tables and chairs. There was a broken-down La-Z-Boy facing the buttes—Kueck's chair, according to his family, the one he sat in when he watched the sun rise over the Mojave. From here he could survey his strange desert kingdom. He had come out here to escape civilization, but he knew he could be evicted at any point. The desert was shrinking, and civilization didn't like people who violated its codes.

"Lynne," he said in one of his last letters to his sister, "I'm writing this down because I get choked up when trying to talk about personal issues. . . . I know the next life is waiting for me. . . . I don't want you to blame yourself if the inevitable comes to pass. This feeling has been growing for the last one to two years." Then, in a burst of optimism, he added, "Of course the future *can* be changed and it would be fun trying. Since I was twenty years old, I've had a dream of building a little place in the desert."

To the right of the La-Z-Boy sits a pallet stacked with eighty-pounds sacks of lime—construction material for the house that Kueck never built. One of these days, he was going to make a course correction. But as always happens with fuckups, he never got there—and never would. Instead, he had picked up a spade and dug his own grave at the edge of his property. It's the first thing you see on the way in and the last on the way out, a project he made sure to finish, now filled in by wind and erosion.

DEANNE STILLMAN'S *latest book is* Twentynine Palms: A True Story of Murder, Marines, and Mojave *(William Morrow). It was named as a "Best Book 2001" by the* Los Angeles Times Book Review*, and Hunter Thompson called it "a strange and brilliant story* *by an important American writer." She is writing* Horse Latitudes: Last Stand for the Wild Horse in the American West *(Houghton Mifflin). Thanks to Mark Lamonica for help on this piece.*

Coda

This story was originally much longer, taking me down another strange trail on my desert beat and into one big empty scream. But this time I had a map, an escort, and a pit bull. "Go down V Avenue," said the map. "Just before the pavement ends there is a small fenced in area with some gas lines in it. Take a right-hand turn. Then go 0.9 miles and take a left where a house used to be. Go 2.3 miles, take a right hand turn, then go 0.45 miles and turn left—you might notice some Christmas tinsel in the sage brush. In another 3.5 miles take a right at the intersection. At this point if you look into the mountains, you should be lined up with a road going towards them . . ."

It was as if I had dropped through some freeway sinkhole in Los Angeles and ended up in its sad and lonely heart—an hour from the Warner lot, just beyond the San Gabriel Mountains, where Donald Kueck had watched the stars, studied search-and-seizure law, and talked to animals. This was a berg called Llano, once home to a utopian community where Aldous Huxley lived. Like most utopian communities, Llano vanished. Today, packs of stray dogs are drawn to its crumbling stone ruins and hard-core desert eccentrics eke out a living in its shadows. Llano was part of Steve Sorensen's turf and he knew it well. In fact, in the year prior to his murder, he had driven past Donald Kueck's property at least twenty times, on his way to the squatter's to try to evict him. Considering their violent confrontation nine years earlier, I have often wondered what each man was thinking as they came into each other's orbit. Perhaps Sorensen thought he should finish the job. Or perhaps he was on a personal tactical alert, knowing he was within range of someone who had tried to get him fired. And what about Kueck, increasingly paranoid in his last months? He would have heard the big SUV rumbling across the desert dirt, might have even had the deputy in his rifle sight. Or perhaps it was nothing like that at all; perhaps Kueck was too baked to hear anything but the voices in his head and maybe, when Sorensen turned down Kueck's driveway on that August day, he had no idea that he was about to confront a guy he had subdued at gunpoint a long time ago. When he saw the Dart and ran the plates and the dispatcher identified the owner of the car, did he then recognize the name? If he did, he wasn't saying, and anyway, the dispatcher garbled "Kueck" (it's pronounced "cook"). But the stage was set: two men who loved the desert, one with a future, and one with memories only, were about to finish their dance. Maybe *that's* when it all came back—just before Kueck opened up with the assault rifle—"Oh Christ," Sorensen might have thought as his knees buckled, "it's that lawsuit nut!" Or maybe he said it out loud; his mic was keyed and the dispatcher heard the gunshots—although my sources tell me no words were broadcast.

Three years after it happened, there are some images I can't forget. One is a photo sent to me by Don's sister Lynne. It's a breakfast table for jackrabbits, outside Don's trailer. Long ago and a few miles away, jackrabbits were nearly clubbed to extinction, lest they raid settlers' crops. In this picture, each is eating out of its own dish. I've seen other photos of Don with animals, and although he's not in this one, I'm sure he's smiling. The other image is something a childhood friend of Sorensen's described to me. "I remember how happy he was the day he went off to the army," she said. "He sat on the lawn and polished his boots."

Some say that LASD should have waited Kueck out instead of going in for the kill. As it turned out, the tear gas was blown away by the high winds and what started the fire was road flares, dropped into the hideout as a last-ditch effort to flush Kueck. But it was his script, his ending, and he went up in flames. In an investigation, the D.A. called the tactic unusual, but LASD was cleared. If you kill a sheriff and throw his brains in a bucket, you can't expect much more than that—and I'm sure Kueck didn't. Ironically, the squatter who triggered this sad chain of events survived. Last I heard, he was living on a dry lake bed near Barstow.

Permissions

GRATEFUL ACKNOWLEDGMENT is made to the following for permission to reprint previously published material:

"Blood Feud," by Mary Battiata (*Washington Post Magazine*, May 22, 2005). Copyright © 2005 by Mary Battiata. Reprinted by permission of the author.

"Hit Men in Blue?" by Howard Blum and John Connolly (*Vanity Fair*, August 2005). Copyright © 2005 by *Vanity Fair*. Reprinted by permission of the authors.

"The End of the Mob," by Jimmy Breslin, originally appeared in *Playboy* magazine, August 2005. Copyright © 2005 by Jimmy Breslin. Reprinted by permission of the David Black Literary Agency.

"Operation Stealing Saddam's Money," by Devin Friedman (*GQ*, March 2005). Copyright © 2005 by Devin Friedman. Reprinted by permission of the author.

"Sex Thief," by Denise Grollmus (*Cleveland Scene*, September 14, 2005). Copyright © 2005 by the *Cleveland Scene*. Reprinted by permission of the *Cleveland Scene*.

"Dr. Evil," by S. C. Gwynne (*Texas Monthly*, September 2005). Copyright © 2005 by *Texas Monthly*. Reprinted by permission of *Texas Monthly*.

"The Choirboy," by John Heilemann. First published in (*New York* magazine May 30, 2005). © 2005 by John Heilemann. Reprinted by permission of the Wylie Agency.

"The Last Ride of Cowboy Bob," by Skip Hollandsworth (*Texas Monthly*, November 2005). Copyright © 2005 by *Texas Monthly*. Reprinted by permission of *Texas Monthly*.

"Blue on Blue," by Chuck Hustmyre (*New Orleans* magazine, January 2005). Copyright © 2005 by Chuck Hustmyre. Reprinted by permission of the author.

"The $2,000-an-Hour Woman," by Mark Jacobson (*New York* magazine, July 18, 2005). Copyright © 2005 by Mark Jacobson. Reprinted by permission of *New York* magazine.

"Altar Ego," by Robert Nelson (*Phoenix New Times*, July 7, 2005). Copyright © 2005 by the *Phoenix New Times*. Reprinted by permission of the *Phoenix New Times*.

"The Ghosts of Emmett Till," by Richard Rubin (*New York Times Magazine*, July 31, 2005). Copyright © 2005 by Richard Rubin. Reprinted by permission of International Creative Management, Inc.

"The Great Mojave Manhunt," by Deanne Stillman (*Rolling Stone* magazine, September 22, 2005). Copyright © 2005 by Deanne Stillman. Reprinted by permission of the author.

"Killer Instincts," by Jeffrey Toobin (*The New Yorker*, January 17, 2005). Copyright © 2005 by Jeffrey Toobin. Reprinted by permission of *The New Yorker*.

"How to Lose $100,000,000," by Paige Williams (*GQ*, January 2005). Copyright © 2005 by Paige Williams. Reprinted by permission of the author.